Study Guide

Burk Foster
University of Louisiana--Lafayette

Corrections in America
an introduction

NINTH EDITION

Harry E. Allen, Ph.D.
Professor Emeritus
San Jose State University
San Jose, California

Clifford E. Simonsen
City University
Renton, Washington

Prentice Hall

Upper Saddle River, New Jersey 07458

Production Editor: Barbara A. Cassel
Acquisitions Editor: Marion Gottlieb/Kim Davies
Director of Production and Manufacturing: Bruce Johnson
Managing Editor: Mary Carnis
Manufacturing Manager: Ed O'Dougherty

Prentice-Hall International (UK) Limited, *London*
Prentice-Hall of Australia Pty. Limited, *Sydney*
Prentice-Hall Canada Inc., *Toronto*
Prentice-Hall Hispanoamericana, S.A., *Mexico*
Prentice-Hall of India Private Limited, *New Delhi*
Prentice-Hall of Japan, Inc., *Tokyo*
Prentice-Hall Singapore Pte. Ltd.
Editora Prentice-Hall do Brasil, Ltda., *Rio de Janeiro*

10 9 8 7 6 5 4 3 2 1
ISBN 0-13-089542-3

CONTENTS

PREFACE

This study guide accompanies the ninth edition of Harry E. Allen and Clifford Simonsen's *Corrections in America: An Introduction*, a leading introductory corrections text for more than two decades. The study guide follows the chapter sequence of the text. Within each chapter, the format is the same:

    1. Chapter objectives. These are the important themes or issues that structure the chapter.

    2. Key terms and concepts. These include the terms and concepts that Allen and Simonsen emphasize and others from the text that I believe are important.

    3. Chapter summary. The narrative summary of the chapter follows the authors' outline but does not necessarily include every heading; some material is reorganized and some only briefly discussed in overview form.

    4. Self test. There are objective questions of four types--multiple choice, true/false, matching, and fill in the blanks--and several discussion questions. Answers to the objective questions are in an answer key arranged by chapters at the back of the study guide. Each answer is referenced to a page number in the text.

The usual study guide disclaimer applies: this is my study guide based on their text. In some instances my interpretation of their material may not be exactly as they intended. Although I am in enough agreement with the authors to have used their text for most of the 25 years I have taught introductory corrections courses, the opinions expressed herein are my own and not those of Harry Allen and Clifford Simonsen, except where indicated. Likewise any factual errors are mine and not theirs, unless I am citing them directly, in which case we are all wrong.

ACKNOWLEDGMENTS

Most of what I know about corrections comes from teaching corrections courses at the University of Louisiana at Lafayette for more than 25 years. I am grateful to my present and former colleagues here, especially Dr. Clifford Dorne, for sharing their knowledge with me. I am also grateful to the officials and inmates of the Louisiana State Penitentiary at Angola--in particular Wilbert Rideau, Douglas Dennis, Lane Nelson, and the late Ron Wikberg--for showing me the real world of prisons. Among the folks at Prentice Hall who have worked with me on this project, I would like to thank Christopher Ruel, Marion Gottlieb, Kim Davies, and Barbara Cassell, all good people to work with.

Burk Foster

CHAPTER ONE

Early History (2000 BC to AD 1800)

CHAPTER OBJECTIVES

This chapter looks at the roots of corrections from earliest historical times through the Age of Enlightenment, when the physically punitive practices of earlier times began to yield to more enlightened ideas of reform. This trend of thought would give rise to the penitentiary by the end of the 1700s. After reading the material in this chapter, you should be familiar with:

1. early methods of seeking individual remedies for criminal wrongs.
2. the provisions of the earliest criminal codes.
3. the changing view of crime as an offense against the state.
4. the common forms of capital and corporal punishment.
5. the uses and conditions of early prisons.
6. the European legal reformers who argued for change in punishment practices in the late 1700s.
7. correctional practices and conditions that warranted reform.
8. the institutions that made up the corrections system of eighteenth century England.
9. early leaders and institutions of correctional reform.

KEY TERMS AND CONCEPTS

folkways
mores
laws
personal retaliation
blood feud
vendetta
lex salica (wergeld)
outlaw
lex talionis
civil death
friedensgeld
"get right with God"
Code of Hammurabi
Code of Justinian
the Inquisition
corporal punishment
the stocks
the pillory
the brank
the cat-o'-nine-tails

lex eterna
lex naturalis
lex humana
Mamertine Prison
sanctuary
Bridewell
Age of Enlightenment
Cesare Beccaria
Classical School
Jeremy Bentham
Utilitarianism
hedonistic calculus
John Howard
Penitentiary Act (1779)
jail fever (gaol fever)
house of correction
workhouse
gaol
transportation
banishment

hulks
Maison de Force
Hospice of San Michele
William Penn
the Great Law
Walnut Street Jail
Pennsylvania system
penitentiary
Benjamin Rush

1

CHAPTER SUMMARY

Behavior as a Continuum

Both positive and negative behaviors can be represented on a scale of controls. **Folkways**, or traditional social customs common to a group of people, are the most informal controls. **Mores** are still informal but more important and socially binding. **Laws** are formal rules or sanctions which enforce standards of behavior on social groups.

Redress of Wrongs

The earliest remedy for criminal wrongdoing was retaliation, either **personal retaliation** as an individual right or duty, or through the **blood feud** involving the victim's family or tribe. **Vendettas**, or back-and-forth conflicts in which each side sought to gain advantage, often resulted from this primitive form of justice. As early societies sought ways to limit destructive conflict, they developed the concept of *lex salica*, or **wergeld** in Europe. *Lex salica* meant in practice a payment of money or property to the victim or the victim's family in place of blood vengeance. As this form of resolving disputes became more accepted, those who refused to accept their sentences were declared **outlaws** and exiled from the group.

Early Codes

The retributive concept of *lex talionis*, or equivalent vengeance within a set of laws, is basic to the early historical legal codes--the Sumerian codes, the **Code of Hammurabi**, King of Babylon, and the Hebrew law of Moses. These codes provided for fines or compensation (what we would call restitution today) to be paid to victims' families as part of the punishment. They also provided for extensive use of capital punishment, mutilation, and other corporal punishments, and penal servitude, or **civil death**, in which the offender was sentenced to a life of slavery. Penal servitude was usually applied to people from the lower classes. Over time the idea of money being paid directly to the victim was replaced by the idea of money being paid to the state, or **friedensgeld**, much like our practice of paying fines to the government today.

Early Roman codes, particularly the **Code of Justinian**, the Eastern Roman Emperor in the sixth century AD, served as the basis of legal codes on the continent of Europe over the next thousand years. These developing codes were strongly influenced by the canon law of the Catholic Church, a separate body of religious offenses that existed parallel to the secular or civil law of the developing European nation-states. Secular law incorporated religious doctrine to give civil authorities the power to compel the offender to "**get right with God.**" A good illustration would be **the Inquisition**, an investigative tribunal of the Church, which reached its peak of influence in Spain in the late 1400s. It wielded life-and-death power to suppress heresy and dissent within the Church.

Punishment

Before modern penology developed, criminal offenders were subject to a wide variety of punishments-- capital punishment, corporal punishments, exile or banishment, economic sanctions such as fines and forfeiture of property, and forms of public humiliation. Judges at one time enjoyed practically unlimited discretion in choosing from among these possible penalties.

Capital punishment, progressing from stoning in primitive societies to hanging in the early modern era, but with side-tracks into crucifixion, decapitation, burning, drowning, and other more elaborate forms of execution for ceremonial purposes, was extensively used. **Corporal punishments**, defined as any punishment using physical force to inflict pain on the offender, were also widely employed. The most common corporal punishment was whipping, but branding and mutilation were also common.

Exile or banishment, akin to the earlier practice of outlawry, was used to cast the offender out of society. The practice of transportation to the American colonies or later to Australia, which was founded as a British penal colony at the end of the 1700s, illustrates this method of disposing of offenders.

In many small, closed-in societies, such as small towns in colonial America, public humiliation of offenders was a popular practice. Offenders would be put on display in a public place, such as the town square, for all to see. They might be placed in **stocks** (sitting down) or in the **pillory** (standing up). Gossips and nagging wives might be punished with the ducking stool, tied in a chair to be ducked under water, or they might have their heads placed in a **brank**, a cage that fit over the offender's head with spikes that stuck into the mouth. Public whippings with a **cat-o'-nine-tails** or a leather strap were also common in colonial America.

Legal scholars and philosophers argued about the purposes and usefulness of these punishments. For a long time, the argument was expressed as a need to balance the laws of God, as embodied in Church law, and the laws of man, as embodied in the secular law. St. Thomas Aquinas in the thirteenth century, defined three types of laws: *lex eterna*, or eternal law, *lex naturalis*, or natural law, and *lex humana*, or human law. The secular law gradually displaced and absorbed the Church law.

Early ideas about punishing offenders emphasized the deterrent value of punishment--thus supporting the increased severity of penalties as a way of discouraging other potential offenders. Correcting the offender was entirely incidental to punishment. Imprisonment was used primarily for detention, either pre-trial in the case of ordinary criminals, or long-term and conditional, in the case of debtors, political criminals, and religious heretics. Early prisons were thus more like modern jails, in terms of whom they held in confinement. The **Mamertine Prison**, built under the sewers of Rome before the birth of Christ, is cited as an example of the dungeon-like nature of early jails.

Not many offenders were sentenced to long-term confinement before the late 1700s. Some offenders, following the old church tradition of **sanctuary** or asylum, were allowed to seek refuge from the criminal law within monasteries or other church-operated facilities. The **Bridewell**, a workhouse in London, became the prototype for a kind of involuntary detention and employment center in European cities from the late 1500s into the modern era. Bridewells were looked upon as progressive institutions, at a time when jails and other facilities were seen as places of disease, exploitation, brutality, and despair.

The Age of Enlightenment and Reform

The eighteenth century is called the **Age of Enlightenment** because many of its rational ideas, contrasting with the lingering vestiges of the Middle Ages, gave rise to modern political systems and social institutions. The names of many of the thinkers of this era--Montesquieu, Voltaire, Diderot--are remembered today. The most influential legal reformer of this era was **Cesare Beccaria**, whose book *An Essay on Crimes and Punishments*, published in 1764, is considered the foundation of the **Classical School** of Criminology. This widely read essay set forth several humane principles considered radical for the day:
1. utilitarianism--the greatest happiness for the greatest number.
2. crime as an injury to society.
3. legal education and punishment as crime prevention measures.
4. criminal trials with procedures fair to defendants.
5. certainty and swiftness of punishment.
6. improved physical facilities for prisons.

Many ideas and innovative practices influential in America came from England. **Jeremy Bentham** was an English political philosopher of the late 1700s and early 1800s. His school of thought, called **Utilitarianism**, argued a **hedonistic calculus**, asserting that people seek pleasure while avoiding pain. **John Howard**, a prominent English sheriff from 1773 until his death from **gaol fever** (typhus) in 1790, travelled widely observing European prisons and suggesting reforms at home. At his influence, Parliament in 1779 passed the **Penitentiary Act**, which contained four important reform measures:

3

1. secure and sanitary structures.
2. systematic inspection of confinement facilities.
3. abolition of fees the sheriffs had traditionally charged inmates.
4. a reformatory regime.

Wyndomham, the first English penitentiary, incorporated these principles. John Howard's legacy in corrections is preserved today in the name of one of the most widely respected prison reform groups, the John Howard Society.

Houses of Correction, Workhouses, and Gaols

The main institutions of English corrections were badly in need of reform by John Howard's time. Three basic types of institutions could be identified--houses of correction, workhouses, and gaols (jails). The **house of correction**, modelled after the original Bridewell, was a penal institution requiring hard physical labor. **Workhouses** were intended specifically for the training and care of the poor. **Gaols**, under the control of local sheriffs, housed primarily inmates awaiting trial and sentencing. In practice the functions of these different types of institutions tended to blur together; conditions in all of them were generally deplorable--poor sanitation, rampant disease, sexual exploitation, and brutality among inmates, who were not separated by age or gender; and, finally, to top it all off, sheriffs charged inmates daily fees for room and board. Inmates remained in jail until their fees were paid or worked off.

Transportation Systems

For almost three centuries English law provided a disposition called **transportation**, which was really a direct descendant of the earlier punishment of **banishment**. Debtors and felons were transported first to the American colonies and later to Australia. The practice was useful for three reasons: it saved precious jail and prison space, it removed social nuisances from the streets of English cities, and, because most of those transported were sold as indentured servants for periods of seven or fourteen years, it provided a steady source of labor for the colonies. If they survived the ocean crossing, transported convicts were worked like slaves, but they could earn their freedom in time. Less fortunate were the convicts sentenced to confinement on the **hulks**, old ships at anchor in British waterways. A direct response to prison overcrowding, the use of the hulks to house unfortunate convicts (1776 to 1875) is often called one of the most sordid episodes of modern imprisonment.

Early Cellular Prisons

Reformers of the Enlightenment sought out institutions that seemed to offer the kind of humane, reform-oriented confinement they believed prisons ought to provide. Two institutions much admired during this period were the **Maison de Force** (stronghouse) at Ghent, Belgium, and the **Hospice of San Michele** (hospital) in Rome. Jean-Jacques Vilain's Maison de Force was a workhouse that applied many practices later to become standard in corrections: classification and separation of categories of inmates, the rule of silence, stern discipline and fair treatment of inmates, and individual cells. The Church-sponsored Hospice of San Michele housed boys and young men up to age twenty. It featured strict discipline also, with religious indoctrination, separate sleeping cells, and a common work hall. Its emphasis on penitence and contemplation of past wrongs illustrated the spiritual side of imprisonment, another important aspect of the early penitentiaries.

In the American colonies, the spirit of prison reform was most vital in Pennsylvania, the colony founded by the Quaker **William Penn**. **The Great Law** of the Quakers, in effect from 1682 until Penn's death in 1718, was a model of humane punishment for its day. It provided the death penalty only for premeditated murder. Hard labor in a house of correction became the standard punishment for felons, replacing whipping and the other corporal punishments. Pennsylvania law was changed after Penn's death to more closely resemble the laws of the other colonies, which were modelled on British law, naturally. But the reform spirit lived on in Pennsylvania well into the next century.

In Philadelphia in 1790, reformers opened the institution that is called the first penitentiary in the United States--the **Walnut Street Jail**. The Quakers of Philadelphia, under the leadership of such men as **Dr. Benjamin Rush**, advocated the operation of this penitentiary house for the correction of convicted felons. In what became known as the **Pennsylvania system**, inmates were to be housed in solitary confinement without work, the better to speed the process of penance needed for reformation--the avowed purpose of the "**penitentiary**." Although the Walnut Street Jail soon broke down under the pressure of overcrowding, its ideas about changing human behavior through confinement would serve as a model for corrections in the next century. The age of building real penitentiaries was about to begin.

SELF TEST

Multiple Choice

1. Which of these would be considered the most formal method of controlling behavior?
   a. mores
   b. folkways
   c. laws
   d. they are all equally formal control methods
   e. none of them has anything to do with controlling behavior

2. Personal retaliation or the blood feud was eventually replaced by the idea known in Europe as:
   a. vendetta
   b. *lex eterna*
   c. barter
   d. wergeld
   e. habeas corpus

3. The concept of *lex talionis* most closely related to the modern idea of:
   a. rehabilitation
   b. incapacitation
   c. reformation
   d. treatment
   e. retribution

4. An offender sentenced to penal servitude was in essence being sentenced to a life of:
   a. solitary confinement
   b. banishment
   c. slavery
   d. military service
   e. paying an annual fee to the court to remain free

5. The investigative tribunal established by the Catholic Church to root out heretics in the later Middle Ages was called:
   a. the Star Chamber
   b. the Inquisition
   c. the Citation
   d. the Bishops' Court
   e. the Crusades

6. According to St. Thomas Aquinas, this was the human law which had to avoid conflict with the other principal types of law:
    a. *codex scholastica*
    b. *fiat justitia*
    c. *corpus juris civilis*
    d. *lex humana*
    e. *statutus inferioso*

7. Which of the following would have been least likely to be found locked up in a jail several hundred years ago?
    a. a dangerous inmate awaiting trial
    b. a debtor
    c. a political dissident
    d. a felon serving a sentence of ten years in prison
    e. a religious heretic

8. The basic purpose of the Bridewell was:
    a. a floating jail
    b. an insane asylum
    c. a workhouse
    d. to hold those awaiting hanging
    e. to hold grooms who had run away from their weddings

9. The Italian legal scholar whose work, *An Essay on Crimes and Punishment*, promoted sweeping legal reforms, including the development of the penitentiary, was:
    a. Cesare Beccaria
    b. Guido Sarducci
    c. Vito Corleone
    d. Giuseppe Garibaldi
    e. Enrico Fermi

10. The English practice of transportation was most closely related to the earlier practice of:
    a. mutilation
    b. public humiliation
    c. property forfeiture
    d. banishment
    e. hanging

11. This infectious disease, carried by body lice, was so prevalent in English jails that it was called gaol fever:
    a. malaria
    b. typhus
    c. diphtheria
    d. mumps
    e. rheumatic fever

12. What were "prison hulks" in England?
    a. a type of cell
    b. the guards
    c. old ships
    d. a torture device
    e. inmates who had been locked up a long time

13. Who made up the clientele of the Hospice of San Michele?
    a. terminally ill inmates
    b. women inmates training to be nuns
    c. boys and young men
    d. political criminals
    e. senile elderly inmates

14. The first so-called "penitentiary" in America opened in Philadelphia in 1790; it was named the:
    a. Maison de Force
    b. Newgate Prison
    c. House of Detention
    d. Walnut Street Jail
    e. Sing Sing Prison

15. Why did Pennsylvania become the source of many ideas of prison reform in the colonial and early national eras?
    a. It had the highest crime rate.
    b. The major universities were located there.
    c. Probably because of the Quaker influence.
    d. It had the most primitive prisons and jails.
    e. The colony was founded by ex-convicts.

16. Which of the following was intended to hold pre-trial inmates in England?
    a. the gaol
    b. the penitentiary
    c. the workhouse
    d. the house of correction
    e. the borstal

17. Jeremy Bentham's idea that human beings seek pleasure while avoiding pain is called the:
    a. hedonistic calculus
    b. expiation syndrome
    c. operant conditioning
    d. logical positivism
    e. sybaritic response

18. Four of the following were provisions included in the Penitentiary Act of 1779 in England. Which one was NOT?
    a. secure and sanitary prison facilities
    b. a reformatory regime
    c. regular inspection
    d. abolition of fees charged inmates
    e. early parole of reformed inmates

True or False

_____ 19. The *lex salica* was the blood feud requiring the victim's family to seek vengeance on the offender.

_____ 20. The early legal codes of Sumeria and Babylonia, like most ancient codes, stressed the need for reform of the offender as the first purpose of the law.

_____ 21. Outlawry was an early practice which expelled the offender from the tribe or community.

_____ 22. If you were sentenced to penal servitude in ancient times, you could expect to work like a slave until you died or were set free by your master.

_____ 23. The legal codes of the Middle Ages on the continent of Europe rejected any influence of the Catholic Church, recognizing that the Church should not influence matters of state.

_____ 24. The Inquisition was a Church-sponsored appeals court with the power to overturn criminal convictions from the secular courts.

_____ 25. Although early courts made frequent use of physical punishments, they also applied economic sanctions such as fines and forfeiture of property to many offenders.

_____ 26. Small towns in colonial America rejected the practice of public humiliation of offenders, holding that it was "degrading and barbaric."

_____ 27. The primary purpose of confinement in the pre-modern era was to detain persons awaiting trial or the imposition of sentence.

_____ 28. Historians agree that the jails of the Middle Ages were generally pleasant, comfortable environments for the offenders confined there.

_____ 29. The Great Law of the Quakers was unusual for colonial times in that it provided for the death penalty only in cases of premeditated murder.

_____ 30. The principal feature of the Pennsylvania system was that convicts were sentenced to a term of penal servitude performing labor on state building projects.

_____ 31. The basic purpose of the Maison de Force was to house criminal lunatics.

_____ 32. Most of the rationalist scholars of the Age of Enlightenment agreed that the courts were too soft on crime; they wanted to see more severe punishment of criminals.

_____ 33. The "penitentiary" is named after William Penn, who designed the first model prison in America.

_____ 34. The English Penitentiary Act required sheriffs to charge convicts fees for room and board, as a way of increasing revenues for jail operations.

_____ 35. During the last years of "transportation," British convicts were shipped to Australia.

_____ 36. Most jails of the 1700s were simply large, open rooms where men, women, and children moved freely about without classification or segregation as we would expect today.

Fill In the Blanks

37. Early legal codes were based on the concept of _____, or vengeance within a system of rules and regulations.

38. A wrongdoer who was declared outside the law of the tribe or community was called a(n) _____.

39. If the retaliation was up to the individual victim, it was called personal; when it was expanded to the victim's family or tribe, it was called the _____.

40. According to Allen and Simonsen, the main contribution of the medieval church to corrections was the concept of _____.

41. Two forms of public humiliation frequently used in colonial America involved the offender being locked in wooden frames on public display; these were called _____ and _____.

42. According to the concept of friedensgeld, the wrongdoer owed a financial obligation to _____.

43. The weakest or most informal controls over human behavior are the social customs called _____.

44. The efforts of the Inquisition were directed at this particular class of criminal offenders in the Middle Ages: _____.

45. Torture, mutilation, branding, and whipping are all examples of that class of punishment called _____.

46. The first "penitentiary" in the United States could be found in one wing of the Philadelphia institution called the _____.

47. Beccaria and Bentham are two of the leading thinkers of the _____ of criminology.

48. The most feared "killer" of English jail inmates in the 1700s was _____.

49. Most of the English criminals who were "transported" out of country were sent to either _____ or _____.

50. According to Cesare Beccaria in *An Essay on Crimes and Punishment*, the focus of society should not be on the punishment for crimes; instead the focus should be on _____.

51. The principal piece of prison reform legislation accomplished through the efforts of Sheriff John Howard was the _____.

52. The first institution widely admired for its work in reforming juvenile offenders was the _____.

53. The system of confinement that provided for offenders to be confined in isolation without work, to speed the process of reform and penance, was called the _____ system, after the state in which it first developed.

54. The English philosopher who is associated most closely with the "hedonistic calculus" is _____.

Matching I

_____ 55. Any punishment using physical force to inflict pain on the offender.

_____ 56. Literally the "law of the claw," or law of retaliation.

_____ 57. An early jail found under the sewers of ancient Rome.

_____ 58. The traditional social customs that represent the most informal control over behavior.

_____ 59. An early London workhouse for the poor that served as a model for other European cities.

_____ 60. A form of the blood feud in which one clan or family engaged in a continuing battle with another.

_____ 61. A Roman code of laws that served as the basis of laws on the European continent.

_____ 62. The concept of paying a fine to the state instead of the wronged victim.

_____ 63. The status associated with exile from the tribe.

a. folkways
b. mores
c. laws
d. personal retaliation
e. blood feud
f. vendetta
g. *lex salica* (wergeld)
h. outlaw
i. *lex talionis*
j. civil death
k. friedensgeld
l. "get right with God"
m. Code of Hammurabi
n. Code of Justinian
o. the Inquisition
p. corporal punishment
q. the stocks
r. the pillory
s. the brank
t. the cat-o'-nine-tails

u. *lex eterna*
v. *lex naturalis*
w. *lex humana*
x. Mamertine Prison
y. sanctuary
z. Bridewell
aa. Age of Enlightenment
bb. Cesare Beccaria
cc. Classical School
dd. Jeremy Bentham
ee. Utilitarianism
ff. hedonistic calculus
gg. John Howard
hh. Penitentiary Act (1779)
ii. jail fever (gaol fever)
jj. house of correction
kk. workhouse
ll. gaol
mm. transportation
nn. banishment

oo. hulks
pp. Maison de Force
qq. Hospice of San Michele
rr. William Penn
ss. the Great Law
tt. Walnut Street Jail
uu. Pennsylvania system
vv. penitentiary
ww. Benjamin Rush

Matching II

_____ 64. The Quaker leader whose "Great Law" was a humane high point of the colonial era.

_____ 65. The institution intended to give offenders time and "space" to reflect and do penance for their crimes.

_____ 66. The Belgian "stronghouse" whose regime of work and silence would prove very influential in the development of later prisons.

_____ 67. The English practice of sending criminals to the American colonies and Australia.

_____ 68. The English sheriff who was recognized as the most influential correctional practitioner of his time.

_____ 69. The philosophy, important to the development of the penitentiary, that viewed the aim of society as being to provide the greatest good for the largest number of citizens.

_____ 70. English prisoners in the late 1700s were moved to these floating jails as one response to overcrowding.

_____ 71. This physician/politician was a leading advocate of humane corrections in Philadelphia.

_____ 72. A time of great intellectual and political activity, from which many ideas critical to modern government emerged.

a. folkways
b. mores
c. laws
d. personal retaliation
e. blood feud
f. vendetta
g. *lex salica* (wergeld)
h. outlaw
i. *lex talionis*
j. civil death
k. friedensgeld
l. "get right with God"
m. Code of Hammurabi
n. Code of Justinian
o. the Inquisition
p. corporal punishment
q. the stocks
r. the pillory
s. the brank
t. the cat-o'-nine-tails

u. *lex eterna*
v. *lex naturalis*
w. *lex humana*
x. Mamertine Prison
y. sanctuary
z. Bridewell
aa. Age of Enlightenment
bb. Cesare Beccaria
cc. Classical School
dd. Jeremy Bentham
ee. Utilitarianism
ff. hedonistic calculus
gg. John Howard
hh. Penitentiary Act (1779)
ii. jail fever (gaol fever)
jj. house of correction
kk. workhouse
ll. gaol
mm. transportation
nn. banishment

oo. hulks
pp. Maison de Force
qq. Hospice of San Michele
rr. William Penn
ss. the Great Law
tt. Walnut Street Jail
uu. Pennsylvania system
vv. penitentiary
ww. Benjamin Rush

11

Discussion

73. How is behavior controlled by folkways, mores, and laws?

74. What concepts were important to early legal codes before the time of the **Roman Empire**?

75. What influence did Church law have on the development of the criminal law **during the Middle Ages**?

76. What punishments were most commonly used in pre-modern societies?

77. What kinds of offenders were kept in secure confinement?

78. Why did the state gradually take over the responsibility for retaliation that had earlier belonged to the wronged party?

79. What legal principles are associated with Cesare Beccaria's Classical School of Criminology?

80. What was John Howard's impact on English corrections?

81. What principal institutions made up the basic correctional alternatives of eighteenth century England?

82. Describe the practice of transportation.

83. What features of the Maison de Force and the Hospice of San Michele attracted so much favorable attention among correctional reformers of the 1700s?

84. Why did Pennsylvania become the leader in sentencing and correctional reform in the early United States?

CHAPTER TWO

Prisons and Ideologies (1800 to the Present)

CHAPTER OBJECTIVES

The corrections system of today, emphasizing imprisonment of convicted felons, is the direct descendant of institutions built in the 1800s. Today we expect serious and habitual offenders to enter this system. What happens to them next, while they are being "corrected," is determined by society's wishes as molded by politics and carried out in public policy. After reading the material in this chapter, you should be familiar with:

1. the two contrasting models of American penitentiaries.
2. rules and discipline in early penitentiaries.
3. the development of alternatives to the penitentiary, including parole and the reformatory.
4. the rise and fall of the industrial prison.
5. how prisons changed after the end of the industrial prison.
6. the pressures of the modern era in American prisons.
7. the most important ideologies shaping public policies in corrections today.
8. the reasons behind the punishment ideology.
9. the influence of the treatment model in corrections.
10. the effects of ideological shifts on corrections policies.

KEY TERMS AND CONCEPTS

Pennsylvania system	Irish system	punishment ideology
outside cells	ticket-of-leave	retribution
Eastern Penitentiary	conditional liberty	deterrent effect
separate system	American Prison Congress	stigma of conviction
Auburn system	Zebulon Brockway	theory of disablement
inside cells	Elmira Reformatory	incapacitation
congregate system	industrial prison	selective incapacitation
Elam Lynds	Hawes-Cooper Act	determinate sentencing
silence	Ashurst-Sumners Act	prediction
lockstep	Sanford Bates	brick-and-mortar solution
prison stripes	Alcatraz	treatment model
solitary confinement	lock psychosis	positivism
treadmill	convict bogey	Quakers
Alexander Maconochie	prison riot	reformatory movement
mark system	total institution	medical model
Sir Walter Crofton	ombudsman	indeterminate sentencing
indeterminate sentence	ideology	reintegration model

prevention ideology   "get-tough" laws   intermediate punishments
diversion   restorative justice   War on Drugs
community corrections   President's Crime Commission

CHAPTER SUMMARY

The Pennsylvania System

The penitentiary was originally an idea without a physical form. The men who set out to build penitentiaries in the early 1800s probably had most in mind the basic form of a jail, but with many changes to avoid the evils of the jail and to accomplish the desirable aims of penance and reformation of offenders.

One major American model of the penitentiary, the **Pennsylvania system**, was incorporated into two prisons, the Western Penitentiary and the **Eastern Penitentiary**. The Eastern prison, in Philadelphia, was the more influential--a prison of single-person cells laid out in blocks like spokes around a hub, with the inmates kept in solitary confinement under a strict rule of silence. Inmates did craft work in their cells, called **outside cells** because they opened to the outdoors and had exercise yards (like a private patio) attached. This was called the "**separate system**." It emphasized keeping inmates totally isolated from each other to avoid contamination, both physical and spiritual. The penitential mood was also supposed to be enhanced by the time alone. Several other prisons were built on the Pennsylvania model, but it was quickly displaced by the Auburn model as the preferred American prison design.

The Auburn System

The New York State Prison at Auburn opened in 1819. The **Auburn system** housed convicts in "**inside cells**," smaller, stacked in tiers, and without exercise yards. Inmates worked together in shops during the day and were isolated in their individual cells at night. Discipline was very strict--silence at all times, the lockstep formation to move around, eating facing another man's back, and quick physical punishment of rule violators. Auburn was called the "**congregate system**," because its offenders worked and ate together, and the "silent system," for the rule of silence that prevailed at all times.

Prison Competition

For several years the argument continued among correctional reformers: which system was better, Pennsylvania or Auburn? The Pennsylvania system seemed more in line with the ideals of the penitentiary. It was a more controlled environment, more penance-inducing, and more individualized. But the supporters of the Auburn model pointed out that their prison was cheaper to build and operate, used space more effectively and, most important, was economically more productive with its group labor. The congregate system thus became the model for the other American states looking to build their own penitentiaries, though the separate system remained influential in Europe.

Rules

The Auburn system worked convicts together under strict discipline. The rules were severely applied--absolute **silence** and noncommunication with other inmates, **lockstep** movements, uniforms of **prison stripes**. Inmates who misbehaved were beaten or whipped, or put on the **treadmill** for exercise, or thrown into **solitary confinement** on a restricted diet. This was "the hole"--what might be called extended lockdown or special housing today, but without the foundation of concern for the prisoner's welfare. Adopting the philosophy of **Elam Lynds**, warden of Auburn and later Sing Sing, this model sought to break the convict's spirit through hard labor, total control, and complete subservience. Even the Auburn prison's massive architectural design, its concrete and iron construction, and its high walls and heavy doors, were intended as much to impress the criminal's mind as to maintain maximum security over his body.

Maconochie and Crofton: A New Approach

In America the reformative aims of the early penitentiary were quickly yielding to the interests of economy and efficient punishment; even brutal punishments, which the penitentiary was intended in part to get away from, were allowed to discourage rule-breakers and maintain perfect control. Some prison officials continued to believe in the use of imprisonment to reform. An English naval officer, Captain **Alexander Maconochie**, was appointed governor of the Norfolk Island penal colony, a thousand miles east of Brisbane, Australia, in 1840. The prison had a terrible reputation, and many cynics hoped the idealistic Maconochie would fail miserably in his reform efforts. He devised what he called the "**mark system**," which allowed the convicts to earn their freedom in stages by performing specified amounts of hard labor. When his regimen appeared to be succeeding, instead of failing, he was replaced by a less imaginative official.

In Ireland **Sir Walter Crofton** developed what was called the "**Irish system**," making use of the **indeterminate sentence**. Prisoners moved through stages of different work conditions, gradually earning more freedom, until they returned to the community on a **ticket-of-leave**, or conditional pardon. Their **conditional liberty**, under supervision, would evolve into the present day practice of parole.

The Reformatory Era (1870 to 1910)

At the first **American Prison Congress** meeting in Cincinnati in 1870, corrections officials from across the country met to discuss the current state of the penitentiary. Many of those in attendance were discouraged at what had happened to the penitentiary in half a century of practical application. The Congress adopted a Declaration of Principles, the first of which promoted "reformation, not vindictive suffering" as the purpose of imprisonment. Influenced by the work of Maconochie and Crofton, the Congress initiated what came to be called the reformatory era in American corrections.

The first reformatory opened at Elmira, New York, in 1876, under the direction of **Zebulon Brockway**. The **Elmira Reformatory** was used for younger first-offenders, those who were believed to be still salvageable. Its program was intended to reform offenders through:
1. increased academic education
2. manual training and trade instruction
3. military training and discipline
4. the most modern standards of operation

The descriptions of the first reformatories sound like promotional brochures for contemporary boot-camp programs or for the military schools where boys used to be sent to be turned into men. The reformatories were the first institutions to latch on to modern-day ideas of correction through programming, and to apply the indeterminate sentence and parole to motivate offenders to change. The more progressive states built reformatories before the time of World War I. These institutions were definitely not for everyone. Their clientele was the select few who did not belong in the expanding penitentiary system.

Post-Civil War Prisons

States in the north continued to build prisons--larger prisons, based on the Auburn model. They emphasized congregate labor in prison factories. Southern prisons were more likely to lease convicts to private contractors or to house convicts on prison farms. Several Southern states built huge farming operations where convicts, mostly black former slaves, labored under working conditions more severe than those found on pre-Civil War plantations.

15

The Twentieth Century and the Industrial Prison

By the end of the 1800s, most of the reform ideals associated with the early penitentiaries had been abandoned. In their place was the ideal of a factory behind walls--the **industrial prison**--where several thousand convicts worked to produce goods that were sold on the open market, thereby paying for part of the cost of the prison's operation. The dream of the efficient warden was to operate his prison "in the black." Prisons grew ever larger. The old prison discipline began to yield to the principles of scientific management.

The role of the prison as a factory had been under attack for a long time, on the grounds that it exploited prison labor and deprived free men of jobs by selling reduced-price products. Labor unions were staunch opponents of prison industries. The Great Depression of 1929 finally accomplished the end of the industrial prison. Congress passed two pieces of legislation, the **Hawes-Cooper Act** of 1929, making the shipment of prison-made goods subject to state laws, and the **Ashurst-Sumners Act** of 1935, amended in 1940 to prohibit the interstate shipment of prison products. By the time World War II began, the industrial prison was dying.

The Period of Transition (1935 to 1960)

With prison work at an end, what would replace it? For a time the best answer was idleness. Convicts had nothing purposeful to do in many prisons. Corrections officials and politicians responded by emphasizing the need for heightened security, a **"lock psychosis"** that kept most inmates under much greater security than they really required. The image of the convicted felon was that of the **"convict bogey,"** a fearful creature who was a menace to society. Under the leadership of **Sanford Bates**, the Federal Bureau of Prisons opened its first superprison, **Alcatraz**, in 1934. This high-security prison was publicized as the institution necessary to confine America's most dangerous criminals. In time it became more the dumping ground for the federal system's misfits.

When the most prolonged period of serious **prison riots** in American history erupted in the early 1950s, the American Correctional Association (what the National Prison Congress eventually turned into) investigated and attributed the causes not to breaches of security or more hardened criminals, but to neglect, idleness, overcrowding, and poor management. Prison riots dramatically increased in number after prison industries were done away with.

The Modern Era

Another round of prison riots and internal turmoil marked the beginning of the modern era of corrections in the 1960s and early 1970s. Prisoners were given expanded legal rights by the courts, and political and civil rights issues in the larger society spilled over into the prison as well.

Internally Sought Reform

Prisons have remained difficult to control ever since. The prison population has tripled in the past fifteen years. Prisons are more secure than ever in terms of preventing escapes, but inside prisons, especially the maximum security facilities called **"total institutions"** because of their insulation from the outside world and their efforts to control all aspects of their inmates' lives, the atmosphere is more volatile than ever. Prison officials have explored several alternatives, including the use of the **ombudsman** to investigate complaints, as ways of alleviating prisoner grievances and conflict. In prisons that are always at capacity, filled with men who have very little of purpose to do, keeping the peace is not a simple function.

The Prison Population Boom

As our corrections system grows ever larger, drawing more Americans into institutions and community supervision, we see that people have many different ideas about what causes offenders to commit crimes and what should happen to these offenders while they are under correctional controls. In the fifteen years since the War on Drugs became a national policy, prison and jail expansion has continued unabated, with no end in sight. What are we trying to accomplish by locking all these people up?

Conflicting Correctional Ideologies

An **ideology** is a systematic set of concepts about human nature and culture. In corrections, ideology refers to ideas concerning the purposes and practices used in treating (or controlling) criminal offenders. Over time certain ideologies become more important and others lose importance. Advocates of one ideology are often in sharp conflict with advocates of another. In America in recent decades, ideological arguments in corrections have often focused on three principal rationales--punishment, treatment, and prevention.

The Punishment Ideology

The **punishment ideology** places the interests of society above the interests of a criminal offender who deserves a penalty to accomplish some worthwhile purpose. **Retribution** is one such purpose, the modern face of the older responses of retaliation and vengeance. One calculates how much harm the offender has done, and he is punished equivalently to restore balance to society.

Another purpose is deterrence. The theory of the **deterrent effect** of punishment is based on the idea that punishing offenders for crimes discourages other would-be criminals from committing similar acts. The **stigma of conviction** marks offenders after they leave correctional control: the term "ex-con" is not an affectionate label. Deterrence theory can be used to justify brutal physical punishments, with the justification that prisoners must be made an example of--to other prisoners and to society.

Incapacitation is yet another purpose of punishing offenders. It protects society by keeping offenders in a place where their actions cannot harm good people. According to the **theory of disablement**, imprisonment effectively disables criminal offenders, at least for awhile. Recent arguments have centered on the idea of **selective incapacitation**, which seeks to use the limited resources of corrections to confine the high-rate offenders who do the most damage to society. Social disablement or isolation of chronic offenders is often suggested as an approach to dealing with violent criminals, as in "three strikes and you're out." **Determinate sentencing**, which seeks to eliminate discretion and make sentence length more precise, can be used in pursuit of incapacitation (and retribution and deterrence as well). **Prediction**, or the use of background characteristics as devices to predict future behavior, is often associated with selective incapacitation as a correctional policy.

Pursuing a policy based on punishment has important social consequences. It involves a commitment to the **brick-and-mortar solution** to crime: building more prisons and jails to confine more and more offenders. This is expensive and draws away resources that could be used for purposes more productive than paying one group of human beings to keep another group of human beings doing nothing. The punishment perspective views criminals as being different from the rest of us and requiring separation for our protection; this makes it difficult for ex-offenders to return to mainstream society. Punishment goes on long after the sentence is over.

In contrast to punishment, the **treatment model** focuses on the offender's needs. It uses programs to attempt to eliminate the causes of the offender's criminal behavior. The treatment model grew out of **positivism**, a school of criminological thought that developed in the latter part of the nineteenth century. Positivists believe that the essential causes of criminality lie in biological, psychological, and sociological forces over which the offender has no control. But if society works with both the offender and his or her environment, these forces can be counteracted, and crime can be controlled.

The views of the positivists are often contrasted with earlier philosophical views of human nature and with the religious view of mankind. The **Quakers**, who were so important to the origins of the penitentiary, clearly believed that crime was sin, and the way out was through God, who would accept the criminal's penance as evidence of contrition for his wrongdoing. If everyone could get right with God and stay there, crime would cease.

For the past century corrections has focused less on the offender's philosophical or spiritual nature and more on his social, mental, and emotional problems. The **reformatory movement**, which placed emphasis on education, vocational training, and discipline, was the first broad-based attempt to apply the modern treatment model in corrections.

Treatment today means offering programs that attempt to change attitudes and behavior, and to give prisoners the basic social skills they will need to make a life outside of prison. A more rigorous approach than this was the **medical model** in corrections, which viewed crime as a sickness and corrections as the therapy necessary to cure the disease. The medical model was emphasized in the federal system and in several of the more progressive states, though not all offenders would ever have been treated in its comprehensive programs. Doubts about the effectiveness of prisons as "hospitals" to cure criminality led to a scaling back of this model after the early 1970s.

As doubts persist about the ability of corrections to eliminate criminal behavior, some aspects of the treatment model have been altered. The **indeterminate sentence**, which left it up to the prison or the corrections department to determine when the offender had been rehabilitated and ought to be released, has been abolished in most states, to be replaced by more determinate sentences. Parole, based on evidence of rehabilitation, has been eliminated altogether in several states and cut back--by declaring certain crimes ineligible for parole, by eliminating repeat offenders from parole consideration, or by requiring offenders to serve more time before meeting eligibility requirements. Good-time laws which give time off the length of sentences for good behavior have also been changed, usually to the detriment of violent and repeat offenders, in many states.

By the late 1960s and continuing through the next decade, many corrections scholars questioned whether the prison setting was even the appropriate place to attempt treatment. Their arguments, making up what came to be known as the **reintegration model**, was that the best place to work with offenders was in the community, since that was where they had come from and where they would return. Prison was the artificial life; the community was the real world. Until support for rehabilitation began to yield to increased public and political pressure for the greater certainties of punishment, reintegration sought to get prisoners out into the real world as much as possible and to keep as many offenders as possible in society, participating in different types of community-based correctional programs.

The **prevention ideology** moves away from the corrections system and its central question about what the system is supposed to do with offenders. Prevention looks at the larger society from which offenders come. It asks what can be done with individuals and the social and physical environment they live in to prevent crime. It may emphasize programs to benefit children particularly, to improve public security in the neighborhood, and to deal with social problems, such as poverty, which are closely related to criminality.

Community corrections programs, which at any given time supervise far more young people and adults than are confined in prison, often apply a combination of prevention and treatment strategies in their efforts to keep offenders from venturing further into the system. These programs keep offenders in their own communities and living their normal lives while they are being "corrected."

Diversion programs, which keep minor offenders out of court altogether by requiring participation in treatment or other alternative programs, have become popular in many areas in the past two decades. The perception is that the formal corrections system, with its emphasis on institutional controls, creates more failures than successes.

The Pendulum Swings

Looking at the past two decades in American society, there is no doubt that the punishment ideology has been the prime force in corrections. The impact of **"get-tough" laws** has been to increase rates of confinement and to promote the continuous expansion of our institutional corrections system. The pendulum has swung to the right, and so far it shows no signs of swinging back to the center.

Restorative Justice

Within the past decade, a new model has emerged to influence criminal justice policy. Most often called **"restorative justice,"** the balanced and restorative justice model (BARJ Model) seeks to add the interests of crime victims and the community to the traditional relationship between the offender and the larger society, as represented by our system of legal authorities. Restorative justice has its origins in the victims' rights movement, but it is not necessarily dedicated to the hard-core persecution of criminals; if it were, the retributive and incapacitative elements of punishment would be sufficient. In restorative justice, the emphasis is on restoration, which means repairing the harm done by crime and rebuilding community relationships. Criminals have wronged other people, but they themselves are often victims of other crimes. The goals of restorative justice are to break down the barriers erected by the criminal law and to reconcile the needs of all members of the community--victims and offenders, criminal justice professionals and private citizens--using a balanced process to heal the damage done by crime. The orientation becomes more holistic than legalistic. The ideas of restorative justice are becoming better known, but we obviously have a long way to go before this new model defines a dominant view of how to cope with crime in 21st century America.

Contemporary Corrections

Since the report of the **President's Crime Commission** in 1967, the American corrections system has been the subject of extensive study and research, much more so in the past 30 years than in the preceding 300. We have learned a lot about what works and does not work in corrections, and we have also learned that corrections is more politics driven than fact driven. Corrections officials set forth the facts, and politicians, driven by the public's fear of crime (and often feeding the fear themselves), disregard the facts and base policies on ideologies instead. The past 30 years have seen a decline in emphasis on treatment in prisons, and the outright abandonment of the medical model; we have also seen a pronounced shift toward determinate sentencing, which by limiting judicial discretion has the effect of sending more people to prison and keeping them there longer. We have explored so-called **intermediate punishments** more, but more as stricter options to probation, which is seen as totally ineffective, and as economically necessary alternatives to prison, than because of any real belief in reintegration as a mode of thought. If we could afford it, we would probably like to have three or four times as many people locked up today as we do, even though incarceration rates are already at an all-time high. We have two million adults behind bars, another four million on probation and parole, yet we remain as ideologically committed to locking people up as we have ever been.

The **"War on Drugs"** of the past fifteen years has driven the continuing expansion of our jail and prison system at a time when rates of violent and property crime have been in decline. If we want to punish more, one way to do so is to redefine who ought to be punished. Our drug problem has not really been affected, but our jails and prisons are now taking in more offenders for drug crimes than for any other type of criminal offense. How determined are we to pursue such policies indefinitely?

SELF TEST

Multiple Choice

1. In Crofton's Irish system, what did it mean to the convict when he got a ticket-of-leave?
    a. He got a full pardon for all crimes.
    b. He was about to be executed.
    c. He got a Christmas furlough to go home.
    d. He was released on conditional liberty under supervision.
    e. He was shipped overseas.

2. Which type of prison system was associated with total isolation of inmates, craft work, and outside cells?
    a. Pennsylvania
    b. Auburn
    c. Virginia
    d. California
    e. Michigan

3. The first federal "superprison," which opened on an island in San Francisco Bay in 1934, was called:
    a. Attica
    b. Armageddon
    c. Terminal Island
    d. Ithaca
    e. Alcatraz

4. In the model of the industrial prison of a century ago, the greatest emphasis was placed on:
    a. inmate education
    b. psychological counselling
    c. economic production
    d. spiritual development
    e. physical conditioning

5. The American Prison Congress meeting of 1870 is considered the start of which era in corrections?
    a. reformatory
    b. work release
    c. corporal punishment
    d. reintegration
    e. deterrence

6. Alexander Maconochie's "mark system" is considered an early predecessor of:
    a. capital punishment
    b. psychotherapy
    c. the indeterminate sentence
    d. solitary confinement
    e. prison uniforms

7. The principal purpose of Red Hannah in the Delaware prison system was:
    a. recreational
    b. conjugal visiting
    c. medical care
    d. corporal punishment
    e. counseling

8. The combined effect of the Hawes-Cooper and Ashurst-Sumners Acts was to:
    a. establish parole in America
    b. prohibit capital punishment except for murder
    c. create the reformatory
    d. end the shipment of prison-made goods
    e. encourage higher education of prisoners

9. Which type of prison system was associated with congregate labor in shops, the rule of silence, and inside cells?
    a. Attica
    b. Indiana
    c. Auburn
    d. Arkansas
    e. Australian

10. One of the practices associated with the prevention ideology is an alternative which seeks to place lesser offenders into treatment programs prior to adjudication; the common name for this alternative is:
    a. parole
    b. waiver
    c. diversion
    d. allocution
    e. integration

11. The reformatory movement is associated with the origins of which one of the following models?
    a. incapacitation
    b. rehabilitation
    c. detoxification
    d. humiliation
    e. regimentation

12. Part of the incapacitation approach in corrections is the concept of _____, which uses background records and other indicators to anticipate whether offenders will continue to engage in criminal behavior.
    a. reversion
    b. obfuscation
    c. labelling
    d. prediction
    e. avoidance

13. Allen and Simonsen suggest that one of the drawbacks of emphasizing the punishment ideology is the _____ of conviction, the legacy of wrongdoing that marks the offender for life.
    a. pain
    b. stigma
    c. lack
    d. catharsis
    e. semblance

14. Punishing one offender as an example to discourage other offenders is called:
   a. nonsense
   b. transference
   c. monasticism
   d. genetics
   e. deterrence

15. The movement of the 1960s and 1970s that shifted emphasis away from prison programming back to community-based correctional programs was called:
   a. indoctrination
   b. structuralism
   c. reintegration
   d. absolutism
   e. institutionalization

16. Which one of the following best states the purpose of indeterminate sentencing?
   a. To keep the prison population as small as possible.
   b. To move all offenders through the system as quickly as possible.
   c. To frighten young people into avoiding lives of crime.
   d. To provide early release for rehabilitated inmates.
   e. To separate the mentally ill from the general prison population.

17. The idea that prison could be used as a place of treatment to cure offenders of their criminal behavior best fits which model:
   a. medical
   b. prevention
   c. sequestration
   d. banishment
   e. sanitorium

18. The Quakers believed that for the convicted offender the key to ending crime lay in:
   a. hard labor
   b. family values
   c. prevention
   d. penitence
   e. banishment

True or False

_____ 19. The most intense period of rioting in American prisons came immediately after the Civil War and gave rise to the creation of the reformatory.

_____ 20. The term "convict bogey" is used to express the idea that inmates pretend to be much tougher than they really are to prevent other inmates from taking advantage of them.

_____ 21. Crofton's Irish system was considered too harsh in its treatment of inmates and was finally prohibited by the British government.

_____ 22. The Eastern Penitentiary was considered the model of the Pennsylvania-style prison.

_____ 23. The use of inside cells was associated with the Auburn-style penitentiary.

_____ 24. The lockstep was a metal device which was attached to the legs of prisoners who tried to escape from the old penitentiaries.

_____ 25. One of the principal reasons the Auburn prison model won out over the Pennsylvania model was that the Auburn model was economically more productive.

_____ 26. In the penitentiary of a century ago, solitary confinement was generally used to reward convicts for good behavior.

_____ 27. American prisons remained virtually unchanged by the period of civil rights and social turmoil of the 1960s.

_____ 28. The President's Crime Commission argued that criminal laws should be made much more punitive to discourage the rising tide of crime in America.

_____ 29. The shift to determinate sentencing is intended to give judges more discretion in tailoring sentences to fit offenders.

_____ 30. An ideology can be defined as a set of concepts that would guide a person's thinking about some aspect of human culture, such as the purpose of imprisonment.

_____ 31. "Get-tough" laws are considered an important part of the treatment model in corrections, in that they give authorities the power to compel change.

_____ 32. The idea of vengeance is most closely associated with the incapacitation theory in corrections.

_____ 33. Selective incapacitation is based on research showing that a small percentage of offenders commit the majority of serious crimes.

_____ 34. The War on Drugs has emphasized the treatment model as the best way of dealing with America's drug problem.

_____ 35. America has stopped building new prisons and jails as the number of people in confinement has levelled off.

_____ 36. As an approach, the treatment model seeks to eliminate criminal behavior by addressing the needs of individual offenders.

Fill In the Blanks

37. Because inmates worked together in the congregate system, prison officials used _____ to prevent contamination.

38. The model of the penitentiary that was considered more reformative was the _____ system.

39. The model of the penitentiary that was considered more economical and efficient was the _____ system.

40. The mark system and the ticket-of-leave are both associated with the idea of the indeterminate sentence and the present day practice of _____.

41. The historical event that led to federal laws banning the interstate shipment of prison-made goods was _____.

42. Many of the problems of American prisons since the end of World War II appear to be related to the condition of _____, which came about after the end of the industrial prison.

43. The major institutional alternative to the penitentiary that developed in the 1800s was the _____.

44. The origin of the term "penitentiary" was in the idea of _____, or feeling sorry for your sins or offenses.

45. In contrast to the Northern industrial prison, the post-Civil War Southern prison was more likely to provide what kind of environment? _____

46. The public policy most responsible for the increase in our prison population over the past fifteen years is commonly called the _____.

47. In the medical model, the prison was to serve the function of a(n) _____, providing therapeutic treatment of "sick" criminal offenders.

48. Allen and Simonsen's symbol of the swinging mood of public opinion in dealing with criminal offenders is the _____.

49. If it worked perfectly well, the _____ approach would probably reduce prison population by identifying and confining the high-rate offenders who commit the majority of serious crimes.

50. "False negatives" and "false positives" are associated with the element of _____ in corrections.

51. In contrast to punishment, which considers the good of society, the treatment ideology considers _____.

52. Restorative justice is predicated on the notion that traditional ideologies focus too much on the offender and do not consider the needs and interests of the _____.

53. The ideology which attempts to make changes in society to keep offenders from committing the crimes that would get them sent to prison is known as _____.

54. In the early penitentiaries, prisoners were marked by being forced to wear prison uniforms that featured _____.

Matching I

_____ 55. In contrast to present day prison cells, these cells opened to a private exercise yard.

_____ 56. The prison official called the father of the Irish system.

_____ 57. The term for an official whose purpose is to investigate inmate complaints against the prison.

_____ 58. The overemphasis on security caused by prison officials' fears of escapes and misconduct by inmates.

_____ 59. The status in the Irish system that is equivalent to the present day condition of parole.

_____ 60. The founder of the Elmira reformatory.

_____ 61. An early device used to punish inmates and burn up energy; you would be more likely to find it in a gym today.

_____ 62. The prison warden given credit for developing much of the model of early prison discipline in America.

_____ 63. The Pennsylvania practice intended to prevent contamination by not allowing inmates to be in contact with each other.

a. Pennsylvania system
b. outside cells
c. Eastern Penitentiary
d. separate system
e. Auburn system
f. inside cells
g. congregate system
h. Elam Lynds
i. silence
j. lockstep
k. prison stripes
l. solitary confinement
m. treadmill
n. Alexander Maconochie
o. mark system
p. Sir Walter Crofton
q. indeterminate sentence
r. Irish system
s. ticket-of-leave
t. conditional liberty

u. American Prison Congress
v. Zebulon Brockway
w. Elmira Reformatory
x. industrial prison
y. Hawes-Cooper Act
z. Ashurst-Sumners Act
aa. Sanford Bates
bb. Alcatraz
cc. lock psychosis
dd. convict bogey
ee. prison riot
ff. total institution
gg. ombudsman
hh. ideology
ii. punishment ideology
jj. retribution
kk. deterrent effect
ll. stigma of conviction
mm. theory of disablement
nn. incapacitation

oo. selective incapacitation
pp. determinate sentencing
qq. prediction
rr. brick-and-mortar solution
ss. treatment model
tt. positivism
uu. Quakers
vv. reformatory movement
ww. medical model
xx. indeterminate sentencing
yy. reintegration
zz. prevention ideology
aaa. diversion
bbb. community corrections
ccc. "get-tough" laws
ddd. restorative justice
eee. President's Crime Commission
fff. intermediate punishments
ggg. War on Drugs

Matching II

_____ 64. The punishment motive based on retaliation or vengeance.

_____ 65. The reintegration model emphasizes these over prisons.

_____ 66. The sentencing structure that provides a minimum and a maximum and lets corrections authorities determine how long the offender stays in custody.

_____ 67. If you were arguing that anyone convicted of three felonies ought to be locked up for life to protect society, you would be arguing for this purpose of punishment.

_____ 68. The term for a more precise sentencing structure that reduces the discretionary authority of judges and corrections officials.

_____ 69. If you were arguing for harsh punishments to discourage other would-be lawbreakers, you would be arguing for which purpose of punishment.

_____ 70. This prison era used discipline, education, and vocational training to provide rehabilitation in confinement.

_____ 71. This ideology is more directed to trying to keep people out of prison by focusing on individuals and conditions in society.

_____ 72. The balanced approach that seeks to reconcile victims and offenders in repairing the harm done by crime.

a. Pennsylvania system
b. outside cells
c. Eastern Penitentiary
d. separate system
e. Auburn system
f. inside cells
g. congregate system
h. Elam Lynds
i. silence
j. lockstep
k. prison stripes
l. solitary confinement
m. treadmill
n. Alexander Maconochie
o. mark system
p. Sir Walter Crofton
q. indeterminate sentence
r. Irish system
s. ticket-of-leave
t. conditional liberty

u. American Prison Congress
v. Zebulon Brockway
w. Elmira Reformatory
x. industrial prison
y. Hawes-Cooper Act
z. Ashurst-Sumners Act
aa. Sanford Bates
bb. Alcatraz
cc. lock psychosis
dd. convict bogey
ee. prison riot
ff. total institution
gg. ombudsman
hh. ideology
ii. punishment idelogy
jj. retribution
kk. deterrent effect
ll. stigma of conviction
mm. theory of disablement
nn. incapacitation

oo. selective incapacitation
pp. determinate sentencing
qq. prediction
rr. brick-and-mortar solution
ss. treatment model
tt. positivism
uu. Quakers
vv. reformatory movement
ww. medical model
xx. indeterminate sentencing
yy. reintegration
zz. prevention ideology
aaa. diversion
bbb. community corrections
ccc. "get-tough" laws
ddd. restorative justice
eee. President's Crime Commission
fff. intermediate punishments
ggg. War on Drugs

Discussion

73. Tell how an inmate's life would differ according to his placement in a Pennsylvania-style or Auburn-style penitentiary.

74. What rules of prison discipline were devised to make it easier to control men in confinement?

75. What reforms did Alexander Maconochie and Walter Crofton contribute?

76. What ideas and practices are associated with the reformatory era in American corrections?

77. Describe the industrial prison in its heyday. What happened to kill it off?

78. What major problems have persisted in American prisons over the past half century since the decline of the industrial prison?

79. How would you describe the impact of the War on Drugs on American corrections?

80. Outline how the prevention ideology would attack the crime problem.

81. Explain the difference between the treatment model and the medical model.

82. Identify the most important purposes served by the punishment ideology.

83. Contrast the philosophy of restorative justice with the punishment ideology.

84. What were the most important findings of the presidential commissions and various task forces that did corrections research beginning in the 1960s?

85. What has been responsible for the dominance of the punishment ideology in corrections over the past two decades?

CHAPTER THREE

From Crime to Conviction

CHAPTER OBJECTIVES

This chapter reviews the crime problem in America today and the role the other parts of the criminal justice system play in processing offenders before they get to corrections. After reading the material in this chapter, you should be familiar with:

1. the distinction between felony and misdemeanor crimes.
2. what our systems of generating crime statistics show about the incidence of crime.
3. arrest patterns for violent and property crimes.
4. the importance of domestic violence, sexual abuse of children, white-collar and misdemeanor offenses to the crime problem.
5. the impact of alcohol on our crime statistics.
6. the flow of offenders into and out of the system.
7. the role of the police in initiating the criminal process.
8. how the prosecutor represents the public interest in processing criminal cases.
9. the judge's place in overseeing the disposition of criminal cases.
10. the layers of the correctional filter as offenders pass through the system.

KEY TERMS AND CONCEPTS

treason
felony
misdemeanor
index crimes
National Crime Victimization Survey (NCVS)
Uniform Crime Reports (UCR)
crimes against the person
criminal homicide
forcible rape
robbery
aggravated assault
domestic crime
spouse abuse
child sexual abuse
white-collar offenses
common drunk

skid row
alcoholic
detoxification center
DWI/DUI
correctional filter
discretion
cleared by arrest
plea bargaining
nolle prosequi (no paper)
no contest
sporting theory
shock probation
incompetent to stand trial
not guilty by reason of insanity
halfway house
drug offenses

28

CHAPTER SUMMARY

Common-Law Origins of Crime

English common law recognized three types of offenses:
1. **treason**, a capital offense against the state.
2. **felony**, a capital offense against a person or property.
3. **misdemeanor**, a non-capital offense with lesser penalties attached.

American laws generally define felonies as crimes providing a punishment of a year or more in a state or federal prison; a misdemeanor is a crime with a punishment of no more than a year in a local jail. There are far more misdemeanors than felonies committed each year in this country, but many Americans, when they think of the crime problem, think only of the worst crimes such as murder, rape, and robbery, and not the most common which are those relating to traffic, alcohol, and disturbances of the public peace.

Most of the public's perception of the overall incidence of crime in America comes from media reports based on two sources: the FBI's **Uniform Crime Reporting (UCR)** system and the Bureau of Justice Statistics' **National Crime Victimization Survey (NCVS)**. The UCR system is based on reports of crimes made to the police. While it includes data on arrests, police employees, and assaults on police, it emphasizes the **index crimes**, eight serious violent crimes (murder and nonnegligent manslaughter, forcible rape, robbery, and aggravated assault) and property crimes (burglary, larceny/theft, auto theft, and arson). Media accounts tend to highlight how much these crimes have gone up or down in specific reporting periods. The NCVS surveys victims directly, using statistical sampling techniques to build a survey population representative of the United States as a whole. The NCVS is a much more comprehensive reporting system than the UCR, which suffers from chronic underreporting of crime. Both sets of crime statistics agree that serious crime in America has levelled off or declined over the past two decades, though you would never believe this if you listened to politicians and most media reports.

Crimes Against Persons and Property

What people fear most are the **crimes against the person**--homicide, rape, assault, and robbery. They make up about 10% of the index crimes reported to police. **Criminal homicide**, which for the FBI's purposes consists of the different degrees of murder and nonnegligent manslaughter, is the least numerous of the index crimes, resulting in about 20,000 deaths a year. The most common homicide situation is a killing committed by a poor, young minority male against another poor, young minority male, as a result of an argument or a dispute over drug trafficking. **Forcible rape**, defined as sexual intercourse without consent, is statistically more numerous, with more than 100,000 reports annually, though many observers believe it remains the most underreported of the crimes against the person. **Robbery** and **aggravated assault** are each responsible for another half million reported crimes each year. Offenders convicted of violent crimes tend to receive the longest sentences.

Offenders convicted of the crimes against property--burglary, larceny/theft, auto theft and arson--actually make up the largest category of admissions of inmates sentenced to jail and prison, though because of shorter sentences they turn over faster. About 90% of the FBI's index crimes reported each year are these crimes against property.

The largest single category of new admissions to state and federal prisons is made up of felons convicted of **drug offenses**, which is not one of the FBI's index crimes categories. There is obviously no way to know how many drug offenses--buying, selling, and using drugs--take place each year in this country; we catch enough drug offenders to make them the fastest growing part of the prison population over the past fifteen years.

Although most Americans are probably more afraid of crimes committed by strangers, certain types of crimes are much more likely to be committed by family members and friends. **Domestic crime** is the name given to crimes committed by persons living together within household units. **Spouse abuse**, or domestic violence, is criminally assaultive behavior involving persons married to each other or cohabiting. Most batterers are men; most victims of battering are women.

Sexual Abuse of Children

Child sexual abuse also much more frequently involves household members rather than predatory strangers: the child molester is much more likely to be lying on your living room sofa than lurking in the park. Most incidents of child sexual abuse go unreported and unprosecuted, though legal changes have been made in recent years to make it easier for child victims to testify. Child abusers are not very popular in prison, but most of them never get there--where they would face likely victimization themselves.

White-Collar and Corporate Crime

White-collar offenses are committed by persons in positions of trust in business and government. Estimated losses--to consumers, businesses, and the public--from white-collar crime far exceed economic losses from the index offenses of larceny and burglary. Evidence suggests that white-collar criminals are being punished now more frequently than before, though with their good backgrounds and non-criminal values they often warrant minimal punishment.

Misdemeanors

Of the estimated twelve million people arrested annually in this country, most faced prosecution for misdemeanors--offenses which carry a maximum punishment of less than one year in jail, usually a local facility operated by a sheriff. As prisons become more full of drug offenders, jails continue to be full of people arrested for abusing alcohol--arrestees charged with public drunkenness (the **common drunk**), DWI/DUI, disturbing the peace, disorderly conduct, and minor assaults and batteries. Thirty percent of misdemeanor arrests involve alcohol abuse. It is estimated that about 5% of the American people are **alcoholics**, many of whom have a long history of arrests for alcohol-related crimes. Some of these habitual drunks can be found on the **skid rows** of America's cities. Their processing through jails and local courts is a repetitive, assembly-line procedure that accomplishes little. **Detoxification centers** found in most urban areas now treat the majority of those people who would once have been arrested for simple drunkenness. They are cared for in hospital settings instead of further overcrowding above-capacity urban jails. But **DWI/DUI** arrests continue to number more than a million each year, as many jurisdictions reduce blood alcohol levels and take special steps to get drunk drivers off the road. More Americans are killed each year in alcohol-related traffic accidents than are murdered by criminals; most other countries take drunk driving much more seriously than we do.

The Correctional Process

Corrections is only one part of a much larger American system (or sometimes more aptly described non-system of independently-operating, mostly local entities) of criminal justice. Corrections is what happens after sentencing. The offenders that corrections takes in are the ones who have passed all the way through the system; most offenders never get that far. What happens to the rest of them? They are diverted from the system at earlier stages through the process Allen and Simonsen call the "**correctional filter**."

Elements of the Criminal Justice System

The police, the criminal courts, and corrections are the three main subsystems of the larger criminal justice system, but each of the subsystems is divided among many independent organizations and offices at four levels of government--municipal, county, state, and federal. Many public officials--and sometimes private persons as well--make decisions about processing criminals before offenders end up in the hands of corrections officials.

The police initiate the criminal process by taking reports of crime, conducting investigations, and making arrests. Policing in America is done mostly through local agencies. America's basic law enforcement officer is a municipal police patrol officer or a county deputy sheriff. These officers enjoy great **discretion** in deciding what cases to investigate and whom to arrest, especially for misdemeanor law violations. They do their work surrounded by a vast sea of criminal offenses, only a small portion of which are ever investigated and cleared by arrest.

One of our two main sets of crime statistics, the UCR or Uniform Crime Reporting system of the FBI, is based on complainant reports of crime made to police agencies. For a crime to exist in this system, it must be officially reported by a citizen or a police officer. The other set of statistics, the NCVS or National Crime Victimization Survey, surveys victims directly. It shows a much greater number of crimes than the figures generated by the UCR. Both sets of statistics show that crime has decreased since the 1970s. In one recent year fourteen million index crimes were reported to the UCR system, while the NCVS estimated forty million serious crimes. Over eleven million persons were arrested, but only half a million people were admitted to prison. The clearance rate, which to police means crimes **cleared by arrest**, for serious crimes in the UCR system is only about 20%; it is much higher for violent crimes but lower for the property crimes that predominate in this system.

For people who are arrested, the prosecutor's office decides who will be charged, and with what. In most jurisdictions, half or more of all felony arrests will be dismissed, mostly on the prosecutor's authority, without a conviction. The prosecutor's decision to drop the charges is called *nolle prosequi* or "**no paper**," meaning that no legal paper is processed.

When a conviction is obtained, it is usually through **plea bargaining**, which gets a conviction but benefits the defendant by reducing the charge or shortening the length of the sentence imposed. About 90% of criminal convictions are obtained through pleas of guilty or **no contest**. The prosecutor's control over the charging decision and the resolution of cases through bargaining makes him the most powerful official in the criminal justice system.

Many outsiders would think that judges are more powerful, but their influence over cases that do not go to trial is limited. Even in cases that do go to trial, the judge's role is more of a referee, overseeing the adversarial relationship of the prosecutor and defense attorney. Trials under common law apply **sporting theory**, meaning that the trial takes on the form of a contest or a game between adversaries. The judge applies the rules. If he rules in error, the case may well be overturned on appeal and be returned for a new trial. Judges are important to sentencing, though with plea bargaining and the pre-sentence investigation reports done by probation officers their discretion is far from absolute.

Most offenders do not go to prison. A few are diverted into the mental health system as **incompetent to stand trial** or **not guilty by reason of insanity** at trial. Many are placed on probation or get a form of **shock probation** combining a short sentence to confinement with a longer period of probation. Many felons end up pleading guilty to misdemeanors. They are sentenced to short jail terms and often qualify for immediate release from jail on credit for time served if they have been held in jail pre-trial. Lesser offenders may also be placed into a number of community corrections alternatives, such as residence in a local **halfway house** where they can be required to work or take part in a treatment program. A money fine, restitution to the victim, and community service are other common options.

Another Look at Crime Statistics

When we take a more thorough look at the correctional filter, we see that most defendants "leak" out of the system long before they reach the prison system. Of every 100 felons arrested in California, only 14 go directly to prison after conviction. Most felony charges are either dismissed (often at the request of the complainant) or reduced to misdemeanors. In other states the percentage may be slightly higher or slightly lower, depending on the norms of the system, but the basic point remains: most people who could go to prison don't, because other dispositions take them out of the system first.

SELF TEST

Multiple Choice

1. Four of the following are FBI index crimes against the person; which one is NOT?
    a. murder
    b. robbery
    c. kidnapping
    d. forcible rape
    e. aggravated assault

2. Four of the following are FBI index crimes against property; which one is NOT?
    a. larceny/theft
    b. vandalism
    c. auto theft
    d. arson
    e. burglary

3. A crime with a maximum penalty of no more than one year in a local jail is called a(n):
    a. infraction
    b. citation
    c. default
    d. canon
    e. misdemeanor

4. In the old days, common drunks were put in a special cell in the city jail called the drunk tank; nowadays they are more likely to be taken to special facilities called:
    a. inebriate wards
    b. filling stations
    c. detoxification centers
    d. therapeutic milieus
    e. treatment pods

5. Of the following criminal victimizations, which is least likely to happen to you?
    a. being murdered
    b. having your car stolen
    c. being robbed
    d. having your home broken into
    e. being the victim of an aggravated assault

6. Of the people serving felony terms in our state and federal prisons, the largest number are there for which type of crime?
    a. murder
    b. rape
    c. burglary
    d. drug offenses
    e. white-collar offenses

7. Four of the following would be considered white-collar criminals; which one would NOT?
   a. Pete Rose
   b. Leona Helmsley
   c. Reverend Jim Bakker
   d. O.J. Simpson
   e. Ivan Boesky

8. Considering the NCVS's value in crime statistics, the key word in its name is probably:
   a. centralized
   b. correctional
   c. new
   d. violent
   e. victimization

9. Who are the most frequent perpetrators of child sexual abuse?
   a. peers of the child at school
   b. church officials
   c. family members
   d. predatory strangers
   e. babysitters and day care employees

10. The plea of "no contest" basically means:
    a. you are pleading insanity
    b. you plan to use the alibi defense
    c. you are indigent and are asking for appointed counsel
    d. you will accept your sentence
    e. you demand your right to a trial

11. If the prosecutor exercises her *nolle prosequi* powers, what happens?
    a. the case is prosecuted as a felony
    b. the charges are dismissed
    c. the judge is changed
    d. the defendant is denied bail
    e. the date of the trial is delayed

12. The term meaning the situational application of professional judgment is:
    a. diversion
    b. discrimination
    c. denouement
    d. disengagement
    e. discretion

13. If you are charged with a crime but your mental state has deteriorated to the point that you cannot help your attorney prepare your defense, the court might rule that you are:
    a. guilty but mentally ill
    b. faking it
    c. incompetent to stand trial
    d. *in pauperis profunda*
    e. a ward of the state

14. What is the basic source of the crimes that get into the FBI's Uniform Crime Reporting system?
   a. newspaper accounts
   b. court records
   c. complainant reports to police
   d. interviews of arrested criminals
   e. police surveys done in the neighborhoods

15. The basic police standard of when a crime is solved is:
   a. prosecutorial acceptance of charges
   b. cleared by arrest
   c. convicted of an offense
   d. "we know you did it"
   e. judicial acceptance for trial

16. The largest number of criminal convictions are obtained through:
   a. plea bargaining
   b. *nolle prosequi* pleas
   c. insanity pleas
   d. jury trials
   e. judge-only trials

17. The idea of sporting theory is best applied to:
   a. police questioning of suspects
   b. probation supervision
   c. a candidate for judge running for office
   d. a criminal defendant pleading to less serious charges
   e. the conduct of a criminal trial in court

18. If we did not have a correctional filter, and all felony defendants made it through the system as charged, what would be the most obvious consequence?
   a. we would need more police
   b. the workload of the courts would go down
   c. we would have to vastly expand the prison system
   d. local criminal justice agencies could be eliminated
   e. the crime rate would be much higher

True or False

_____ 19. Under English common law, a felony was an offense punishable by death.

_____ 20. Someone convicted of a felony alcohol-related offense would be a good prospect for a term in a detoxification center.

_____ 21. NCVS statistics indicate that from 1993 to 1997 the crime rate dropped sharply for household and personal crimes.

_____ 22. As an offense, murder typically involves offenders and victims of the same race.

_____ 23. For the crime of spouse abuse, females are arrested about in equal numbers with males.

_____ 24. The FBI's Uniform Crime Reporting system is often criticized for underreporting crime statistics, because it relies on complainants to make reports to police.

_____ 25. For misdemeanor crimes, alcohol abuse is probably much more significant than drug abuse.

_____ 26. For an offense to be called a "domestic crime," it must take place within the home or residence of an offender and a victim who are married to each other.

_____ 27. If you are convicted of a felony offense and given a term in confinement, you would generally serve that term in a state or federal prison.

_____ 28. It is generally accepted today that police have few opportunities to exercise discretion in their work.

_____ 29. The NCVS shows a much greater pool of serious crimes than does the UCR.

_____ 30. In most jurisdictions, about as many charges are rejected or dismissed as are processed to conviction.

_____ 31. The choice of defense counsel is the most important step in the criminal justice system for most suspects.

_____ 32. In the criminal courts, a person who is found to be insane can expect to be dealt with by being placed in a mental institution rather than a correctional facility.

_____ 33. Most of the states have done away with plea bargaining by passing laws forbidding prosecutors to engage in it.

_____ 34. Most observers agree that the American criminal justice system lacks flexibility because it is too rigidly controlled by the federal government.

_____ 35. For felony defendants in California, the most common sentence involves a combination of jail time and probation.

_____ 36. Halfway houses are most commonly used for pre-trial detainees who do not qualify for money bail.

Fill In the Blanks

37. The Uniform Crime Reporting system counts only those offenses that are _____.

38. Under common law the name for a crime against person or property punishable by a sentence of death was _____.

39. In the United States, probably the most significant ban we could impose to reduce our arrest statistics would be a ban on _____.

40. Treason was considered a more serious crime because it was an offense against _____.

41. Robbery, rape, and aggravated assault are examples of the class of offenses known as _____.

42. A hospital setting for the civil treatment of a person arrested for drunkenness is typically called a(n) _____.

43. Household crime involving physical or sexual abuse is known as _____.

44. If you were convicted of an offense and sentenced to thirty days in a local jail, the offense would have been a(n) _____.

45. The most important reason for the enhanced comprehensiveness of the NCVS is that it gets information directly from _____.

46. In 1975 Alaska became the first state to abolish the practice of _____.

47. The overall clearance rate for the FBI's index crimes in 1997 was about _____ percent.

48. Screening would be another name for the process Allen and Simonsen call the _____.

49. The oldest and most widely-known set of crime statistics in the United States is the _____.

50. The concept of sporting theory views the criminal trial as a contest between two opponents: the _____ and the _____.

51. First you'll serve ninety days in jail; then you'll be on probation for two years. This is an example of the sentence called _____.

52. Plea bargaining is usually focused on one or the other of two important issues: the _____ or the _____.

53. The index crime with the highest clearance rate is _____.

54. As a defendant, your case has just been "no papered" by the prosecutor; this means that the charges have been _____.

Matching

_____ 55. The category of offenders MADD is mad at.

_____ 56. A crime against the security of the state.

_____ 57. The place in a city where drunks and derelicts used to cluster.

_____ 58. The general term for business-related crimes.

_____ 59. A lesser crime involving a sentence of less than a year in jail.

_____ 60. A crime of violence involving sexual intercourse without consent.

_____ 61. Murder and manslaughter make up this category.

_____ 62. Before detox came along, the most numerous "criminal" found in local jails.

_____ 63. The FBI's category of the eight most serious crimes.

_____ 64. The system of crime statistics based on crimes reported to police.

_____ 65. A term for non-secure community-based residential facilities for offenders.

_____ 66. A term applied to the prosecutor's decision to dismiss pending criminal charges.

_____ 67. The system of crime statistics that interviews victims directly.

_____ 68. An idea that sees a criminal trial as a contest between two opposing attorneys.

_____ 69. The term for a short jail term followed by regular probation.

_____ 70. Allen and Simonsen's term for the criminal justice system's screening out of cases at various steps in processing before imprisonment.

_____ 71. The means by which the greatest number of guilty pleas are obtained.

_____ 72. Most authorities agree that the essence of the police officer's role as a law enforcer calls for the situational application of this.

a. treason
b. felony
c. misdemeanor
d. index crimes
e. National Crime Victimization Survey (NCVS)
f. Uniform Crime Reports (UCR)
g. crimes against the person
h. criminal homicide
i. forcible rape
j. robbery
k. aggravated assault
l. domestic crime

m. spouse abuse
n. child sexual abuse
o. white-collar offenses
p. common drunk
q. skid row
r. alcoholic
s. detoxification center
t. DWI/DUI
u. correctional filter
v. discretion
w. cleared by arrest
x. plea bargaining
y. _nolle prosequi_ (no paper)

z. no contest
aa. sporting theory
bb. shock probation
cc. incompetent to stand trial
dd. not guilty by reason of insanity
ee. halfway houses
ff. drug offenses

Discussion

73. What are the most common misdemeanor offenses?

74. Describe the pattern of criminal homicides.

75. How are white-collar criminals different from ordinary street criminals?

76. What do the UCR and the NCVS say about the crime rate in America over the past two decades?

77. Are sex offenders different from other criminals?

78. What are the index crimes, and why are they important?

79. What are the main component parts of the criminal justice system in America?

80. Using California as an example, explain the process of the correctional filter between felony arrest and imprisonment.

81. Although we think of prosecutors as trial lawyers, most prosecutors do trials infrequently; what three main functions do they perform outside of court?

82. Compare the two main systems used for generating crime statistics in the United States today.

83. How do decisions made by the judge narrow the correctional filter?

84. The idea of the "non-system" in criminal justice probably fits the police best of all. Why?

CHAPTER FOUR

The Court Process: Sentencing and Appeals

CHAPTER OBJECTIVES

For the convicted offender, sentencing is a critical phase in the criminal justice process--determining the direction of his life, perhaps, for years to come. After sentencing, the offender's legal case enters the murky realm of the appellate courts, where it may wander for years seeking resolution. After reading the material in this chapter, you should be familiar with:

1. the reasons for recent changes in sentencing laws.
2. the new sentencing practices that have developed in state and federal courts.
3. the differences between judicial and administrative decision-makers in sentencing.
4. the strategies state legislatures have followed in exerting more control over sentencing practices.
5. possible approaches to reforming criminal sentencing.
6. the strung-out appeals process through state and federal courts.
7. what actions the appeals court can take in reviewing trial court decisions.
8. how state and federal appellate courts are structured.
9. how federal court orders and consent decrees have affected state prison administration.
10. measures suggested to help control the volume of appeals flooding the federal courts.

KEY TERMS AND CONCEPTS

bench trial	good-time policies	trial
indeterminate sentencing	Model Penal Code	sentencing
discretionary release	justice model	double jeopardy
selective incapacitation	"stone and razor wire curtain"	affirm
"three strikes and you're out"	due process	modify
just deserts	criminal law revolution	reverse
mandatory sentences	"railroaded"	remand
sentencing guidelines	*Gideon v. Wainwright*	jailhouse lawyers
sentencing disparity	collateral attack	court of last resort
presentence report	Fourteenth Amendment	supreme court
Minnesota Sentencing	initial appearance	Section 1983
Guidelines Grid	recognizance	court order
judicial sentencing	bail	consent decree
administrative sentencing	preliminary hearing	court master
presumptive sentencing	grand jury	screening
plea bargaining	indictment	diversion
determinate sentencing	information	parole guidelines
sentencing commission	arraignment	emergency crowding provisions

CHAPTER SUMMARY

The Sentencing Decision

Each year millions of Americans face criminal sentencing after conviction of misdemeanor or felony offenses. Most have pleaded guilty; the rest have been convicted by a jury or by a judge alone, in what is called a **bench trial**. Most of the misdemeanants will get fines, suspended sentences and probation, or short jail terms. The same options also apply to convicted felons, with the additional possibility of imprisonment. Judges acknowledge that sentencing criminals is their most difficult responsibility. How do we determine that a sentence is appropriate to both the offender and society?

From before World War II until the mid-1970s, most states used a practice called **indeterminate sentencing**. Judges imposed a minimum and a maximum sentence--such as one year to ten years--and then left it up to parole boards using their **discretionary release** authority to determine when the inmate was ready to be released. This approach emphasized rehabilitation; when correctional authorities believed the inmate had reached this state he should be returned to society under supervision.

In the mid-1970s the indeterminate sentence was attacked from several directions at once. Convicts protested rehabilitation "game-playing"--the idea that you had to participate in programs to prove your behavior had changed enough to warrant release. The discretion of sentencing authorities was questioned. Did not too much discretion invite discrimination? How could parole boards predict post-release behavior? The very basis of rehabilitation as an objective of imprisonment was disputed as research indicated that inmates who had been "rehabilitated" often returned to prison at the same rate as those who had not. And many politicians, waging their rhetorical war on crime, argued that we should be more equal and tougher on all criminals--limiting discretion and making sentencing more punitive.

Rehabilitation faded in importance and the language of sentencing changed. **"Selective incapacitation"** meant that high-risk offenders, if they could be identified, ought to get longer sentences. **"Three strikes and you're out,"** a baseball analogy, was applied to habitual offenders, particularly those convicted of repeated violent crimes, as a way of taking dangerous offenders out of society for good. **"Just deserts"** became a new, humane approach for applying the principles of retribution.

Most states changed the way criminal sentences were imposed. The general drift was to limit the discretion traditionally associated with the courts and corrections components of the system. State legislatures passed laws requiring **mandatory sentences**: offenders in certain categories--gun crimes, drug offenses, habitual offenders, or sex criminals, for instance--are required to serve prison terms. Parole was abolished in a dozen states. The **Minnesota Sentencing Guidelines Grid** popularized the practice, now in use in many states and the federal courts, of using scales based on the seriousness of the crime and the offender's prior criminal history, sometimes influenced by other variables, such as his cooperation with authorities--to provide greater structure in sentencing. These **sentencing guidelines** narrow the choices open to judges at sentencing.

Many politicians probably only wanted to lock up more criminals of all types for longer periods of time, in their belief that this would help control crime. Other reformers were bent on reducing **sentencing disparity**, the widely differing sentences applied to similar offenders, often with no apparent reason for the differences.

The approach has been to not only make sentencing more specific to the crime and criminal but also to make it more "scientific." Most courts order **presentence reports**, prepared by probation officers, if they have doubts about the sentences to be imposed on convicted felons (meaning cases where a plea bargain has not already determined the exact sentence to be imposed). The presentence investigation report reads like a summary of the offender's life, including comments from people who know him well. Most reports call for a recommendation from the probation officer, which the judge tends to follow in the great majority of cases. The presentence investigation report, as a comprehensive personal history record, also has long-term value as the foundation of the offender's prison records; later reports often return to its basic matter-of-record information.

As **judicial sentencing** discretion has been limited by legal changes, so has **administrative sentencing** discretion. Administrative sentencing has to do with the authority of officials in the executive branch of government, in this case the corrections system, to affect sentence length. The main ways this is done today is through the parole and executive clemency functions vested in state parole and pardon boards, and through the awarding of good-time credits, time deducted from sentences for good behavior, and sometimes for participation in designated prison programs. Many states, even those retaining parole, have established **parole guidelines** to structure parole decision making. Laws have been changed to make parole or clemency harder to obtain and to reduce the impact of **good-time policies** traditionally used in prisons to give time off for good behavior. The model for the federal system now, for instance, calls for offenders to serve 85% of their sentence before earning good-time release. Sentencing has become so punitive, in sending increasing numbers of men and women to prison, that several states have had to enact **emergency crowding provisions** that kick in when prison capacity reaches a certain level.

The complete package of sentencing changes is made up of many variables combined in different ways in different states. California, for instance, uses **presumptive sentencing** that sets an average penalty for each crime and then a higher and a lower penalty based on the presence of so-called aggravating or mitigating circumstances. **Sentencing commissions** at the federal level and in those states requiring judges to follow a sentencing guidelines grid impose greater outside controls over judges who, frankly, resent this intrusion into their affairs. The state of Alaska and several local jurisdictions have abolished **plea bargaining**, which reduces to some extent the prosecutor's involvement in sentencing. Most states have adopted forms of **determinate sentencing** in which a judge pronounces a penalty of a fixed term of years. A perfectly determinate sentence would be one in which there is no parole, and the only variable affecting sentence length would be the good behavior credits earned by the inmate according to the state's good-time policies. We have almost returned to the early years of the penitentiary when the time imposed on the offender was the exact time the offender had to serve in prison--not a day less.

Problems with Penal Codes

Sentencing of criminals is basically a hodge-podge of practices, lacking a common theme or structure and moving in whichever direction the political winds are blowing. At one time under common law all felonies were punishable by death. American felony offenses are still punishable by severe sentences in comparison to those applied in other countries. The use of long sentences and the greater use of long-term imprisonment are the principal reasons why the United States ranks first or second in the world (depending on prevailing practices in Russia) in the rate of imprisonment. The **Model Penal Code**, proposed by the American Law Institute in 1962, suggested that imprisonment should be used as a last resort. Most Americans today don't see it that way. They think imprisonment should be used more often, not less often.

Models for Sentencing

Suggestions for reforming criminal sentencing have been forthcoming from many directions for a long time; no legislative body has ever tried to incorporate these reforms into a consistent, structured model. David Fogel's **justice model** represents one well-known proposal for completely revamping criminal sentencing; crimes would be grouped in categories and the penalties made much more consistent. Many practitioners and corrections researchers would like to see a model of sentencing that uses shorter sentences and more community-based alternatives; many politicians and private citizens evidently prefer exactly the opposite. To whatever degree disparity has been reduced, the reduction has been accomplished by avoiding leniency and by imposing sentences that are equally severe--as in the growing trend toward the imposition of natural life sentences in many states.

The Issue of Due Process

At one time prison walls were said to be a "stone curtain" (today a **"stone and razor wire curtain"**) isolating prisoners not only from the outside world but from the legal process as well. No more. Since the 1960s many federal court cases have established that prisoners retain the right to due process of law even while serving sentences. Due process applies to both their rights to appeal their conviction and sentence and to the conditions of imprisonment.

What is **"due process"** of law? No simple definition exists, but in practice the term means that a defendant is entitled to a fair and orderly legal proceeding in which the actions of legal officials are monitored by the courts. In what is called the **"criminal law revolution"** of the 1960s, the United States Supreme Court used several landmark cases to establish the basic legal rights of criminal suspects and defendants. These rights had varied considerably from one state to another depending on court rulings within each state. Criminal defendants often claimed that they had been **"railroaded,"** meaning that legal officials had framed them or simply ignored their rights to a fair trial in the haste to get a conviction. The Supreme Court, using the due process and equal protection clauses of the **Fourteenth Amendment**, incorporated the Bill of Rights to the Constitution (which at one time applied only to federal law and the actions of federal officials) and made it binding in the states as well. Thus these major cases set standards for all legal officials all over the country to follow.

One such landmark case was *Gideon v. Wainwright*, which provided for appointed counsel for indigent felons. The expansion of the right to counsel over the next few years brought about major changes in the appeals process. Appointed counsel were available to conduct far more appeals and the issues on appeal were often appealable in the federal courts, which had assumed supervisory authority over state courts. The result was that many appeals and post-conviction proceedings could follow a dual track--one through the state courts and another simultaneously through the federal courts. This dual process is called a **collateral attack**. It is a major reason why appeals take so long.

The basic premise of due process at the end of the twentieth century is that of a set of layers of authority. The trial court judge supervises the conduct of the law enforcement officers and prosecuting attorneys who bring the case to trial. The state appellate courts review the actions of the trial court judge. And the federal courts, up to the Supreme Court, review the actions of the state officials.

The Path of a Criminal Case

This very thorough and time-consuming process begins even before arrest in many cases. If an arrest or search warrant is needed it must be approved by a magistrate before it can be executed by police. When a suspect is arrested and becomes a defendant he must be taken before a judge for an **initial appearance**, typically within two or three days after arrest. At this appearance the defendant will be informed of the charges he faces and bail will be set. He may be released on his own **recognizance** without having to post **bail** if he is known to the court or if the jurisdiction has a program to screen defendants for pre-trial release. The important point is the supervisory authority of the court. The judge is supposed to be seeing that other officials are treating the defendant fairly and properly--that the defendant does not get abused or lost in the system.

The judge continues in this role pre-trial. At the **preliminary hearing** the prosecution has to present enough evidence to show the need for a trial. Or the case may be reviewed by a **grand jury**, which is a group of citizens who review the evidence in secret and make a report to the judge in open court charging the defendant if they believe the evidence warrants a trial. The grand jury's charging document is called an **indictment**. In most jurisdictions a defendant can also be charged through an **information,** or bill of information, initiated by the prosecutor on his own authority. At the **arraignment** the judge accepts the defendant's formal plea.

To begin the **trial** the judge monitors jury selection by opposing counsel. During the trial the prosecution and defense often disagree with each other's questions or presentation of evidence. The judge makes rulings according to her understanding of precedent--the legal procedures established by statute and case law. What the defense is looking for is reversible error, a mistake so serious that the appellate court would have no choice but to reverse the conviction and send the case back for a new trial. This does not happen often, but the defendant and his counsel keep hoping. The judge instructs the jury on the law. When the verdict comes in the judge does the **sentencing**, either at once or at a later hearing after a presentence report has been completed.

The Mechanics of an Appeal

Every step of this process, from the arrest warrant to the jury verdict, can be part of the appeal. Even the sentence can be appealed if it is in error or in many jurisdictions if the defendant believes it is too severe for the crime. The appeal is ordinarily filed by defense counsel shortly after the defendant is convicted. In our system the prosecutor cannot appeal a not guilty verdict. A defendant once acquitted cannot be retried in the same jurisdiction on the same facts. We call this concept "**double jeopardy**."

The basic choices open to the appellate courts are to **affirm, modify, reverse**, or **modify**. The affirmation, which is the most common, lets the decision stand. The modification makes a change, such as sentence reduction. The reversal sends the case back to the trial court to start over. The modification sends the case back to the trial court, usually with an order that the judge reconsider a ruling.

The affirmation of the conviction at one level of the appellate courts can be appealed to the next higher level or into the federal courts. Most states have two levels of appeals courts, a **court of last resort**, often called the state **supreme court**, and an intermediate court of appeals below it. The federal system is structured the same way, with one Supreme Court and thirteen regional courts of appeal below it.

The greater availability of legal counsel and the much greater volume of criminal cases overall have kept both state and federal appellate courts far busier in recent years than used to be the case. Prisons are required to provide law libraries and trained inmate counsel (often called "**jailhouse lawyers**," though this term can be applied even to a self-taught inmate who works only on his own case) to help prisoners doing legal research. Prisoners are far more aware of their legal rights today than they were a generation ago and they have far greater access to the courts now than they did then.

Reform by Judicial Decree

Prisoners can attack their own convictions or they can attack the conditions under which they are confined. The vehicle for attacking conditions of confinement is often a **Section 1983** lawsuit. Title 42 of the U.S. Code, Section 1983, provides penalties for public officials who violate the civil rights of citizens. Convicts are citizens, and prison employees are public officials. Inmates lose far more suits than they win but they have won often enough in recent history to keep many local jails and state prisons--and sometimes entire state prison systems--in hot water with the courts.

Court Orders and Court Decrees

Federal judges exercising their supervisory authority over state officials have issued very detailed and demanding **court orders** requiring specific improvement in jail and prison operations, most often relating to issues of overcrowding and medical care. Corrections officials are often obligated to sign **consent decrees** agreeing to make the changes the courts require. The court will frequently appoint an independent corrections expert to be a **court master**--the authority who actually oversees the implementation of the court order and reports back to the court on compliance (or non-compliance). Jail and prison officials, as you might expect, do not like to be put in this position. They try to resolve disputes about prison conditions short of full-scale legal battles. In the process standards of acceptable prison operations emerge.

Appeals Flood the Courts

As our jails and prisons continue to grow in population, so do the flood of criminal appeals and prisoners' rights cases saturating the appellate courts. The courts have explored ways of reducing the number of cases coming to trial through such options as **screening** and **diversion**. Screening would take weak and unimportant cases out of the system before trial. Diversion is a non-adjudication alternative, meaning that criminal charges are withdrawn if the defendant completes a treatment program instead of proceeding to trial.

The Battle for Rights Continues

These limited measures would not really do much to reduce the workload of the appellate courts. Most of the suggestions that would make bold reductions in the appellate workload have one basic flaw: They are themselves violative of due process. In our system once the legal standards are established they have to be adhered to until they are replaced through subsequent case law. Federal appellate courts and many state court systems have taken a more conservative turn over the last decade or more, declining to expand the rights of criminal defendants further or establish new constitutional rights for prisoners. But criminal defendants keep trying. Every term of the Supreme Court, indeed every term of the state and intermediate federal appellate courts, presents new cases dealing with the rights of criminal defendants and the rights of offenders in confinement. With four times as many inmates in custody now as twenty-five years ago, and with vastly improved legal resources available to prisoners, it is no wonder that the criminal litigation boom continues unabated.

SELF TEST

Multiple Choice

1. A sentence that requires the offender to serve a prison term, such as for committing a crime of violence using a firearm, is called a(n):
    a. preemptive sentence
    b. concurrent sentence
    c. exclusive sentence
    d. reductive sentence
    e. mandatory sentence

2. The purpose best served by the "three strikes and you're out" laws is:
    a. reintegrative
    b. restorative
    c. incapacitative
    d. eclectic
    e. diminutive

3. If you were protesting "sentencing disparity," you would most likely be making which one of the following statements?
    a. Criminals are not given enough help to change their behavior.
    b. Penalties for the same offense vary too much from one offender to another.
    c. Judges ought to have more discretion rather than less in imposing penalties.
    d. Victims have too much influence over sentencing.
    e. It is hard to tell whether a specific sentence has much effect on the offender.

4. Minnesota's Sentencing Guidelines Grid emphasizes these two components as being most important in determining a criminal sentence:
   a. the offender's IQ and the victim's wishes
   b. age and remorse
   c. seriousness of the crime and prior criminal history
   d. substance abuse history and work record
   e. the judge's perception of dangerousness and public opinion

5. Who usually prepares the presentence investigation report?
   a. the judge's law clerk
   b. the deputy court clerk
   c. a police detective
   d. the probation officer
   e. an assistant district attorney

6. If the defendant is convicted in a bench trial, who would do the sentencing?
   a. the trial judge
   b. a panel of three judges
   c. the jury
   d. no one; it would have been set in a plea bargain
   e. there would be no sentence; this is an example of diversion

7. The Model Penal Code suggests that imprisonment should be used:
   a. extensively on the young
   b. as much as possible
   c. primarily for its retributive benefits
   d. only on the weak-minded and immoral
   e. as a last resort

8. California's presumptive sentencing approach establishes an average sentence and then considers what as modifiers?
   a. perversion and innate evil
   b. intelligence and organic disorder
   c. family and community support
   d. aggravating and mitigating circumstances
   e. personality and ability to change

9. Which of the following is probably least important to the concept of administrative sentencing?
   a. the governor's office
   b. the parole board
   c. the prison's deputy warden for security
   d. the trial judge
   e. the pardon board

10. During what decade did the "criminal law revolution," extending due process of law to state court defendants, take place?
   a. 1790s
   b. 1850s
   c. 1930s
   d. 1960s
   e. 1990s

11. The two key provisions of the Fourteenth Amendment, in terms of relevance to the legal process, are:
    a. inalienable rights and burden of proof
    b. civil rights and fair play
    c. due process and equal protection
    d. absolute power and conditional liberty
    e. probable cause and fair trial

12. A court master is most responsible to:
    a. the defendant
    b. the department of corrections
    c. the appointing judge
    d. the public
    e. the district attorney

13. Double jeopardy basically means:
    a. second-time felons can expect longer sentences
    b. a defendant cannot be tried a second time in the same court after an acquittal
    c. a defendant cannot be held both civilly and criminally liable for the same offense
    d. if a defendant wins his appeal, he cannot be retried for the same crime
    e. one defendant can be forced by a grant of immunity to testify against his co-defendant

14. The court of last resort in most states is called the:
    a. High Court
    b. Court of Last Resort
    c. District Court
    d. Circuit Court
    e. Supreme Court

15. An affirmation of a criminal conviction has what effect?
    a. It lets the conviction stand.
    b. It sends the case directly to the U.S. Supreme Court on a constitutional legal issue.
    c. It overturns the sentence only.
    d. It sets the defendant free.
    e. This term has nothing to do with the appellate process.

16. Four of the following are part of the judge's pre-trial supervisory role; which one is NOT?
    a. the initial appearance
    b. jury instructions
    c. a bail hearing
    d. the preliminary hearing
    e. arraignment

17. The best explanation of the term collateral attack is:
    a. a defendant is provided one attorney for trial and another for appeal
    b. a death penalty defendant gets two attorneys
    c. a defendant can attack either his sentence or his conviction but not both
    d. a case can be appealed in both state and federal courts at the same time
    e. a defendant must be in prison before he can file his appeal

18. The case of *Gideon v. Wainwright* dealt mostly with the issue of:
    a. probable cause for search warrants
    b. timely appeals
    c. conditions in local jails
    d. the prosecutor's power to determine criminal charges
    e. appointed counsel for indigents

True or False

_____ 19. Indeterminate sentencing gave correctional authorities a lot of power to determine how long the offender actually remained in custody.

_____ 20. Selective incapacitation would suggest that every felony offender ought to serve at least ten years in prison.

_____ 21. The rate of imprisonment is remarkably similar from one state to another across America.

_____ 22. Although parole standards have been toughened in a few states, the Supreme Court has ruled that every state must allow every inmate a parole hearing before a parole board.

_____ 23. Sentencing today emphasizes rehabilitation to a greater extent than it ever has previously.

_____ 24. Parole decisions today are based more on "risk to the community" than on the length of time imprisoned.

_____ 25. Studies show that judges more often than not disregard the findings of the presentence investigation report and base the sentence more on their own intuition and experience.

_____ 26. Federal drug laws punish people dealing small quantities of crack cocaine much more severely than they punish people dealing similar quantities of powder cocaine.

_____ 27. A prison inmate would typically file a Section 1983 lawsuit to claim that he had been wrongfully convicted.

_____ 28. The appeals courts are much busier today than they were twenty years ago.

_____ 29. If the U.S. Supreme Court turns down your appeal, the only higher appeal is directly to the Court of Final Appeal.

_____ 30. An indictment is the product of grand jury deliberations.

_____ 31. The federal courts have no authority to order changes in state prison operations.

_____ 32. For a defendant, the principal advantage of a diversion program is that he gets to avoid the stigma of a criminal conviction.

_____ 33. "Truth-in-sentencing" laws generally lengthen the amount of time inmates spend in prison before release.

_____ 34. If the appeals court finds any error whatsoever, it must overturn the conviction and order a new trial.

_____ 35. Of the felony convictions obtained in formal trials, only about a third of them are appealed.

_____ 36. The appellate delays in the federal courts over the past decade have been blamed almost entirely on the growing number of prosecutions for white-collar crimes.

Fill In the Blanks

37. When parole is done away with, the principal remaining way for a convict to get early release is _____.

38. The most notable feature of so-called mandatory sentences is that they require _____.

39. The general argument against discretion in sentencing suggests that allowing too much discretion results in _____.

40. The Model Penal Code identified _____ and _____ as the two worst features of our present sentencing laws.

41. David Fogel's simplified sentencing model, which makes use of flat sentences and divides offenses into five categories, is often called the _____.

42. The indeterminate sentence was intended to emphasize _____, by providing for the offender's release when correctional authorities believed his behavior had changed.

43. Maine has the lowest rate of imprisonment, 121 persons per 100,000 population; the state at the other end of the scale, imprisoning people at a rate almost six times higher, is _____.

44. If a state legislator was making a speech about "imperialism" in sentencing, he would probably be criticizing the power of _____.

45. Under presumptive sentencing, those features of a crime that make it worse than the average offense are called _____ circumstances.

46. The key legal phrase that appears in both the Fifth and Fourteenth Amendments is _____.

47. A federal court might assume the authority to monitor state prison conditions by issuing a legal directive called a(n) _____.

48. If the court lies between the trial court and the court of last resort in a state, it is most likely to be called the _____.

49. If the appellate court decides to let the lower court decision stand as is, it issues an opinion called a(n) _____.

50. The citizens to whom the term "stone and razor wire curtain" had the most application were _____.

51. An expert appointed by the federal court to monitor a prison system's compliance with a court order would be called a(n) _____.

52. The practice of a collateral attack means that (if you have been convicted in a state trial court) while your case is under appeal in the _____ courts you can also initiate an appeal in the _____ courts at the same time.

53. The key legal official in ensuring due process through the time of the trial is the _____.

54. Allen and Simonsen suggest that the term of the Warren Court in the 1960s saw the criminal law pass from a state of evolution to a state of _____.

Matching I

_____ 55. The idea that offenders being sentenced for the same crime get widely divergent sentences, often without any meaningful reason why.

_____ 56. The practice of confining high-risk offenders for longer periods of time to better protect the public.

_____ 57. A popular state model used to guide judicial sentence selection.

_____ 58. A sentencing model that imposes fixed terms on offenders and allows only limited opportunities for early release.

_____ 59. Practices related to the prison reducing the inmate's sentence for good behavior.

_____ 60. The retributive concept that looks at the harm done by the crime and at the offender's moral culpability in deciding the appropriate penalty.

_____ 61. This more finite model, popular in California and several other states, sets forth an average sentence and longer and shorter options based on the circumstances.

_____ 62. A public body, usually consisting of both lawyers and laymen, with authority to monitor the guidelines judges use in imposing criminal sentences.

_____ 63. The basic document used by the court to review the defendant's background before sentencing.

a. bench trial
b. indeterminate sentencing
c. discretionary release
d. selective incapacitation
e. "three strikes and you're out"
f. just deserts
g. mandatory sentences
h. sentencing guidelines
i. sentencing disparity
j. presentence report
k. Minnesota Sentencing
   Guidelines Grid
l. judicial sentencing
m. administrative sentencing
n. presumptive sentencing
o. plea bargaining
p. determinate sentencing
q. sentencing commission

r. good-time policies
s. Model Penal Code
t. justice model
u. "stone and razor wire curtain"
v. due process
w. criminal law revolution
x. "railroaded"
y. _Gideon v. Wainwright_
z. collateral attack
aa. Fourteenth Amendment
bb. initial appearance
cc. recognizance
dd. bail
ee. preliminary hearing
ff. grand jury
gg. indictment
hh. information
ii. arraignment

jj. trial
kk. sentencing
ll. double jeopardy
mm. affirm
nn. modify
oo. reverse
pp. remand
qq. jailhouse lawyers
rr. court of last resort
ss. supreme court
tt. Section 1983
uu. court order
vv. consent decree
ww. court master
xx. screening
yy. diversion
zz. parole guidelines
aaa. emergency crowding
    provisions

Matching II

_____ 64. Dropping weak or unimportant criminal cases early in the legal process.

_____ 65. A slang term for being pushed through the legal process without regard for your due process rights.

_____ 66. The term for what an appellate court does in sending a case back to the trial court to change the judgment in some way.

_____ 67. A mini-trial conducted by the judge to establish that enough evidence exists to proceed on to trial.

_____ 68. A derogatory term for prison inmates who initiate appeals and lawsuits from behind bars.

_____ 69. The phrase from the Fourteenth Amendment that was used to give federal courts authority over state criminal court proceedings.

_____ 70. What each state's highest court and the U.S. Supreme Court represent in the legal process.

_____ 71. The idea that prison confinement once cut the offender off from access to outside courts.

_____ 72. The court proceeding at which the judge accepts the defendant's formal plea.

a. bench trial
b. indeterminate sentencing
c. discretionary release
d. selective incapacitation
e. "three strikes and you're out"
f. just deserts
g. mandatory sentences
h. sentencing guidelines
i. sentencing disparity
j. presentence report
k. Minnesota Sentencing Guidelines Grid
l. judicial sentencing
m. administrative sentencing
n. presumptive sentencing
o. plea bargaining
p. determinate sentencing
q. sentencing commission

r. good-time policies
s. Model Penal Code
t. justice model
u. "stone and razor wire curtain"
v. due process
w. criminal law revolution
x. "railroaded"
y. _Gideon v. Wainwright_
z. collateral attack
aa. Fourteenth Amendment
bb. initial appearance
cc. recognizance
dd. bail
ee. preliminary hearing
ff. grand jury
gg. indictment
hh. information
ii. arraignment

jj. trial
kk. sentencing
ll. double jeopardy
mm. affirm
nn. modify
oo. reverse
pp. remand
qq. jailhouse lawyers
rr. court of last resort
ss. supreme court
tt. Section 1983
uu. court order
vv. consent decree
ww. court master
xx. screening
yy. diversion
zz. parole guidelines
aaa. emergency crowding provisions

Discussion

73. What does sentencing disparity mean, and how can we get rid of it?

74. How does the use of a sentencing guidelines format (such as the Minnesota Grid) structure judicial discretion?

75. Compare judicial sentencing authority to administrative sentencing authority.

76. Explain the rationale of the shift from indeterminate to determinate sentencing.

77. If you were a judge looking over a presentence investigation report on an offender you knew nothing about, what information in the report would you find most important?

78. How does a judge in a state trial court see that a defendant is provided due process?

79. How does an appeal move through the courts, from the time it is first filed until it is finally over?

80. How do the federal courts end up issuing court orders to improve conditions in state prisons?

81. Why has the volume of appeals and prison lawsuits increased so much in the past thirty years?

82. What are some ways (wise and otherwise) that have been suggested to reduce the volume of criminal appeals and prison litigation?

CHAPTER FIVE

Jails and Detention Facilities

CHAPTER OBJECTIVES

The jail is the entry point into the correctional system, the only correctional institution most offenders ever see. Jails hold an eclectic mix of adult offenders (and a few juvenile offenders) at all stages of the criminal process. After reading the material in this chapter, you should be familiar with:

1. the jail's place in corrections history.
2. the legal status of jail inmates.
3. the changing nature of jails and jail design.
4. problems associated with jail overcrowding.
5. the characteristics of jail inmates.
6. the background of jail staff.
7. alternatives to jail.
8. the mental and physical health concerns of jails.

KEY TERMS AND CONCEPTS

detention
gaol (jail)
lockup
jail inmates
presumption of innocence
first-generation jails
second-generation jails
third- (new-)generation jails
direct supervision jails
pods
detention centers
arrested adults
pretrial jail incarceration
unsentenced
"rabble"
holdback jail inmates
mental health issues

overcrowding
bullpen
drunk tank
fee system
per diem
sheriff
price-tag justice
day fine
weekender
community service
pre-trial alternatives
detoxification center
John Howard Society
criminal history data
small jail facilities
admissions to jails

CHAPTER SUMMARY

Jails: A Grim History

Detention is the part of corrections that takes place before trial. The English institution that provided this function was called a **gaol**. The American pronunciation is the same but the spelling is **jail**. Each year more than ten million people are booked into (and most quickly discharged from) county and city jails across America. Several hundred thousand more juveniles are detained in separate facilities called juvenile detention centers, detention homes, and halls. An untold number of arrestees are held briefly in police-operated facilities called **lockups**, which differ from jails in that they do not keep custody of prisoners for more than 48 hours. Lockups hold short-term prisoners for questioning, transfer, or release. The 3,000 jails in the United States (according to the latest jail census of the department of justice) book in more than 10,000,000 persons a year, most of them staying for a short time but some remaining for months or years until their charges are resolved.

The jail is the oldest correctional facility, though some would argue vehemently against the idea that the jail has ever had much of a correctional purpose. Early English and colonial American jails, as we have already seen, were places of brutality, exploitation, disease, and despair. Their only correctional motivation was avoidance: NO ONE would want to come back.

American jails today continue to be defined by extremes--from very small to very large; from primitive to ultra-modern; from one short tier of cells to multi-story high rises; from isolated rural settings to locations in the middle of big cities; from no services at all to services equal to the best provided in state prisons. Jails run the gamut.

Jail inmates are very diverse--felons, misdemeanants, transients and the mentally ill, drunks, drug addicts, and DWI offenders, juveniles in many jails, probation and parole violators under detainer, federal and state prisoners in many jails, material witnesses--anyone who can be locked up can be found in a jail. Most of the pre-trial offenders who make up the largest single portion of the jail population get released on bail or other forms of pre-trial release after a few hours to a few days in jail. But many offenders charged with felony offenses are kept in jail for months or years because they cannot afford to meet bail requirements. For them the **presumption of innocence** really does not apply; they simply start serving their sentences before conviction, often pleading guilty in bargains that count their jail time and turn them loose on probation.

Inmates in most jails are confined under maximum security conditions with very little to do, like lockdown conditions in a state prison. Jails have long been criticized for enforced idleness--the absence of meaningful work, programs, or activities to keep inmates productive and busy. Experts and activists have suggested an expanded role for the jail--as a community correctional center providing a wide variety of confinement and non-confinement supervision to local pre-trial and sentenced inmates--but most jails remain focused on one purpose only: keeping inmates securely locked up. Jails have been very difficult to improve, because most of them are operated at the local level by county sheriffs who lack the resources and skills to make them better.

Jails come in all types and designs. The oldest, called **first-generation jails**, were often found on the top floor or basements of county courthouses. These jails featured multi-man cells arranged in long tiers like prison cellblocks. Guards walked up and down the corridors outside the cells observing inmates through the bars. These jails featured such cells as the **bullpen**, which might hold from half a dozen to twenty or more inmates in a single cell; the **drunk tank**, a foul, smelly cell where drunks were kept until they sobered up; a padded cell for mental cases; and separate cells or tiers for juveniles and women. These jails practiced little classification of inmates; a middle-aged businessman arrested for traffic violations might be thrown into a bullpen with murderers and rapists who had been in jail for years.

Second-generation jails were designed to provide indirect surveillance of inmates by jailers who watched from glassed-in control booths. Cells were arranged in groups commonly called **pods**, sharing a common floor space used for eating and other group activities; inmates spent most of their time in this common area, not locked in their individual (usually two-man or larger) small cells. One jailer would typically be watching a pod that contained twenty or more inmates. Jailers were only in direct contact with inmates when they went into the pod.

Most jails built today are of the type called **third-** or **new-generation**, or **direct supervision jails**. In this design, the jailers are locked inside the pods with the inmates. The jailer mans a console or a desk where he can observe and talk to inmates directly at all times. This approach increases security and also promotes interaction between jail guards and inmates. Guards know much more about what is going on inside the jail.

Jail Populations and Characteristics

At any given time about half a million inmates are locked up in over 3,000 local jails, most of them at the county level. The **sheriff** is America's principal jailer today. Six less populous states have combined jail and prison systems that are state operated. The average jail would appear to hold about 160 inmates, which sounds like a cozy, manageable group, but in fact there is no such thing as an average jail. The great majority of American jails are small town and rural jails designed to hold fewer than fifty inmates. Larger metropolitan jails, such as the Central Jail in Los Angeles County, hold several thousand inmates each. The 500 largest jails, holding more than 100 inmates each, house over 80% of all jail inmates. Several of these have populations larger than most state prisons.

The Problems of Overcrowding

Because of their mix of inmates and their dearth of resources, jails are often called dumping grounds or, in Ronald Goldfarb's book, "the ultimate ghetto." The problems of urban jails are aggravated by **overcrowding** problems. Many of the largest jails are always at or over capacity; many are under federal court order to control overcrowding or improve other jail services--most often medical care, food services, physical conditions, security, classification and segregation, or mental health services. Inmates in urban jails live together in jammed together idleness, their existence defined by the culture of overcrowding.

Problems with Personnel

Most people who work in American jails are deputies who are employed by local sheriffs. Most of them have no particular qualifications or interests in corrections. Many of them would rather be working in some other function within the sheriff's department; they will move on to do so when an opening comes up. Most jail employees are guards whose job is to maintain security. Jails do not provide nearly as many counselors or professional staff as prisons do; most jails provide minimal programs for which professional staff would be needed. Jails are much cheaper to operate than prisons. The ratio of guards to inmates is lower, and fewer support staff are needed. In England, jails operated for centuries under a **fee system**, in which inmates were charged for their daily room and board and upkeep. Someone had to pay their fees before they could be released. In most American jails today sheriffs are paid a **per diem** rate by county government for housing local prisoners. This rate is typically pitifully small; sheriffs use their own revenues, often supplemented by payments from state and federal authorities for housing their prisoners, to maintain decent living conditions. Many improvements have been made in the quality of jail staff, particularly in regard to training, but many jails remain both understaffed and badly staffed by employees who, like the inmates, would much rather be someplace else.

Alternatives to Jail

As overcrowding and other problems persist in local jails, authorities explore alternatives that would reduce jail populations. Confinement in jail is a perfect example of **price-tag justice**. Offenders with money or property get out of jail on bail. Poor people stay in. "Ten days or a hundred dollar fine," judges used to say. People with money paid their fines and went home; poor people went to jail, often repetitively, for drunkenness and other minor offenses. Several American jurisdictions have experimented with a European practice called the **day fine**, which equalizes the economic impact of the fine by tying it to the offender's income. Other jails have explored such alternatives as intermittent sentences, in which offenders called **"weekenders"** spend weekends in jail and weekdays at home working, and **community service**, which obliges offenders to put in hours on public service projects. **Pretrial alternatives** and expanded sentencing options administered by a full-service community correctional center would provide increments of increased control over offenders, who could replace idle time with time spent more productively in the community.

Jail Clients Vary Widely

Most **arrested adults** will be booked into jails--most of them locally operated but a few state or federal--as their entry point into the legal system. Juveniles are generally housed in separate **detention centers** or detention homes, but some facing adult trials or living in rural areas where juvenile facilities are not available may continue to be confined in adult jails. **Admissions to jails** numbered more than 14,000,000 in 1993. Most of them do not stay long; the total jail population at any given time now numbers about 600,000. Jail populations have increased rapidly in recent years, though not as fast as prison populations. The number of people in jail has gone up two-and-a-half times over the past 15 years, whereas the number of people in prison has more than tripled.

Most American jails are small, the largest portion being rural jails built to house fewer than 50 inmates. But the biggest urban jails, holding more than a thousand prisoners each, are like compact, high-density prisons. Jails were originally designed to detain persons awaiting trial or execution of sentence, and later it became common to sentence misdemeanor offenders to short jail terms. This has also changed in recent years, as state prison overcrowding has caused a backup of state prisoners in local jails. Many states have changed their laws to allow convicted felons to serve their sentences in local jails, adding one more divergent element to an already jumbled population mix.

A big urban jail is probably the most diverse correctional facility in the country. The majority of its inmates are confined in **pretrial jail incarceration**. They are supposed to be detained and not punished, since they are not yet convicted, but it is not easy to tell the difference in many jails where they are mixed with other inmates serving sentences. Except for the ranks of the **"holdback" jail inmates**--those felons serving state time--the sentenced inmates are misdemeanants, which means large numbers of people convicted of DWI, theft, assault, and minor drug crimes. But many misdemeanants were originally charged with felonies, such as burglary, drug distribution, grand larceny, auto theft, robbery, and aggravated assault. They pleaded their crimes down to misdemeanors to avoid prison terms. Another category of jail inmates has been convicted but remain **unsentenced**, or if sentenced, not yet transferred to state or federal custody to begin serving the sentence. Jails also hold large numbers of probation and parole violators under detainer, meaning that they cannot be released until a revocation hearing is held. In the miscellaneous category, you might find a few material witnesses, a few people in contempt of court, and, more recently a growing number of people behind on their child support payments--so-called "deadbeat dads." Finally, jails hold inmates awaiting transfer to other state prisons or to federal facilities, including alien deportation centers and military jails. Little wonder that the big city jail (which more often than not is operated by the county sheriff's department) has been called the bus terminal to the rest of the corrections system. It's here that people make connections to wherever they are going.

Why Are They in Jail?

Many minor offenders never go any further than their one local jail, though they may go in and out of it many times during their lifetimes. Chronic drunks in many cities in the old days might have hundreds of arrests spread out over half a century. The old image of the jail was of a "dumping ground," where people the police needed to get off the streets could be placed temporarily. This included drunks, the mentally ill, vagrants and derelicts (before they became "homeless people"), juvenile runaways, and anyone else the police wanted to detain until they could decide what to do with them. Even today, when other placements are more likely to be available for some of these categories of offenders, the study of **criminal history data** justifies Allen and Simonsen's use of such terms as **"rabble,"** "losers of society," and "marginal people" to describe the jail population.

Jails today are more likely to house offenders formally charged with "real" criminal offenses, as opposed to the made-up and nuisance charges of the past. Mental health clinics and crisis intervention centers deal with mentally disordered people who would have once ended up locked in jail. Homeless shelters house and feed people who would once have been confined or run out of town as vagrants. **Detoxification centers** have had great impact in removing habitual drunks and some offenders high on drugs from the drunk tank to the treatment ward.

But as some classes of offenders move out of the jail, others move in. As local jurisdictions crack down on DWI and domestic violence offenders, more of them find their way into jail populations. Urban jails are now full of men and women arrested on drug charges--not drug dealing, necessarily, just simple possession of various illegal drugs. And more homeless people are finding their way back into jail as police crack down on disorderly conduct in public places--trying to drive transients off the streets.

One Virginia sheriff described his "neighborhood"--meaning his jail--as having the highest concentration of substance abusers and chronically mentally ill people in the city. His statement is true for practically all jails. If you went through the jails and eliminated the offenders without serious, documented problems with alcohol and drugs and without a history of **mental health issues**, you would not have many people left in most jails. This is not to say that their crimes are excusable simply because they have other underlying problems; it does suggest that prevention and treatment programs may offer more hope of reducing criminality than repetitive processing through the legal system. Jails deal with many troubled people, as you see in jail death statistics--suicide trailing only natural causes as the leading cause of inmate deaths, and AIDS deaths increasing rapidly. Allen and Simonsen suggest that the analysis of jail inmates' criminal history data indicates that these inmates are a "marginal group of mostly male offenders who have had a lengthy but not necessarily serious involvement in criminal activity."

Jails continue to evolve as the nature of their inmate population changes. Drug crimes have brought more women to jail. AIDS, tuberculosis, and hepatitis, all of which are strongly associated with drug usage and unhealthy lifestyles, have brought a lot more sick inmates into jails, and have escalated the costs of jail medical care. Jails are still cheaper to operate than prisons, because of lower guard-to-inmate ratios and the lack of rehabilitation and support services, but the cost differential is narrowing. Reform groups, such as the **John Howard Society**, named after the English sheriff who was the leading jail reformer of his day, advocate a much broader role for the jail in dealing with criminal behavior. Jails touch far more lives than prisons do. As they continue to move further away from their original narrow detention function, they can begin to address more effectively the problems that direct the lives of their disparate clientele.

The underlying difficulty, in hoping the jail will do more than keep people locked up securely, is that jails are mostly locally operated facilities. The majority of these jails, the so-called **small jail facilities**, have the most meager resources to work with. Housing the holdback inmates sentenced to serve felony time in other jurisdictions is actually economically beneficial to county jails. The per diem rates sheriffs are paid are typically higher than daily per inmate costs, so sheriffs get extra money to use in jail operations. The trend of housing more state prisoners in local jails is an important one. Louisiana, the state that has the highest per capita jail population, has gone the farthest with this practice. It has almost as many convicted felons in local jails as it has local prisoners, and its sheriffs are consequentially enjoying an unprecedented economic boon. They have seen the future of housing felons as a business enterprise, much like the fee system in England centuries ago. Whether the felons are happy to be there, in facilities offering far fewer services than state prisons offer, is another question altogether. But most jails don't ask inmates whether they like the facilities and services. Prisoners are known to be difficult to please, especially when they are mostly dopeheads, drunks, and nuts to start with.

SELF TEST

Multiple Choice

1. If you were in a cell with three other inmates in a long row of fifteen cells fronting onto a corridor, which type of facility would you be in?
   - a. a halfway house
   - b. a first-generation jail
   - c. a second-generation jail
   - d. a third-generation jail
   - e. a generation X jail

2. Most jails are operated by which authorities?
   - a. county sheriffs
   - b. municipal police departments
   - c. state corrections departments
   - d. the Federal Bureau of Prisons
   - e. private contractors

3. This English practice put the cost of jail operation on the offenders housed in it:
   - a. the day-fine
   - b. transportation
   - c. wergeld
   - d. the bounty
   - e. the fee system

4. Another name for the newest or third-generation jail is the:
   - a. lockup
   - b. direct supervision jail
   - c. treatment facility
   - d. work release center
   - e. correctional clinic

5. What was the basic purpose of the early jail?
   - a. rehabilitation
   - b. reformation
   - c. deterrence
   - d. diversion
   - e. detention

6. The most pervasive problem resulting in federal court supervision of local jails has been:
   - a. overcrowding
   - b. lack of recreation
   - c. brutality by guards
   - d. lack of screening for HIV
   - e. limitations on visiting

7. Most jail inmates are in which legal category?
    a. probationers and parolees under detainer
    b. sentenced to state custody
    c. pretrial
    d. sentenced to federal custody
    e. convicted and awaiting sentencing

8. The greatest number of American jails have a rated capacity of how many inmates?
    a. over 1,000
    b. 501-1,000
    c. 251-500
    d. 51-250
    e. 1-50

9. The concept of "price-tag justice" is most closely tied to:
    a. fines
    b. deputy salaries
    c. jail construction costs
    d. medical care
    e. attorney fees

10. A living unit of a new jail is most often called a:
    a. pod
    b. hub
    c. tank
    d. wheel
    e. cage

11. The largest jail system in America is found in:
    a. New Orleans
    b. Los Angeles
    c. Chicago
    d. San Antonio
    e. Houston

12. By their use of the term "rabble," Allen and Simonsen are suggesting that most jail inmates are:
    a. mean and rebellious
    b. infected with diseases
    c. poor and unimportant
    d. not going to stay in jail very long
    e. known to have long criminal histories

13. The leading cause of death in jails in 1997 was:
    a. AIDS
    b. homicide
    c. natural causes
    d. suicide
    e. accidents

14. The John Howard Society would best be described as an organization that promotes:
    a. more rights for victims of crimes
    b. a return to the fee system
    c. legalization of drugs
    d. jail reform
    e. abolition of the federal prison system

True or False

_____ 15. John Howard became famous as the inventor of the fee system, which raised money to finance better jails.

_____ 16. Jails generally have a better physical environment and better services for inmates than prisons do.

_____ 17. A second-generation jail would practice indirect monitoring of inmates, typically with a guard in a glassed-in control booth.

_____ 18. The majority of American jail inmates are convicted felons serving their terms in jail because of overcrowding in state prisons.

_____ 19. The twenty-five largest jail systems in the United States hold almost a third of all jail inmates.

_____ 20. The concept of price-tag justice insists that poor people deserve bad treatment by the criminal justice system because they lack the economic resources to control their fate.

_____ 21. Arrests for DWI have declined steadily in recent years.

_____ 22. In the city jails of the modern era, the "tank" was considered the nicest cell, where trusty inmates were put to reward good behavior.

_____ 23. Most of the new jails feature inmate living quarters that keep individual offenders in extended isolation, much like the early Pennsylvania penitentiary.

_____ 24. Although the number of female inmates is rising, males continue to make up 90% or more of the population of jail inmates.

_____ 25. Jails have more people locked up at any one time than do prisons.

_____ 26. The largest jails in America are at over 100% of capacity.

_____ 27. In most states, the state corrections department is taking over jail operations to improve the quality of services provided inmates.

_____ 28. Allen and Simonsen suggest that the use of detoxification centers has virtually eliminated people with alcohol problems from local jail populations.

Fill In the Blanks

29. The English sheriff, as the principal jailer, was economically dependent on _____ to maintain his jail on a day-to-day basis.

30. Holdback inmates are supposed to be in _____.

31. One option often used for misdemeanor offenders in lieu of a jail term and sometimes a fine is an assignment to some type of public works project. This is called _____.

32. The most distinctive identifying feature of the third-generation jail is the concept of _____.

33. In 1973 the National Advisory Commission on Criminal Justice Standards and Goals wrote: "If cleanliness is next to godliness, most jails are securely in _____."

34. The best-known jail reformer in eighteenth century England was the sheriff named _____.

35. The employees patrolling the pods of most American jails today wear the uniforms of what governmental agency? _____

36. If you were a drunk-driving offender who stayed at home during the week and checked into the jail on Friday night to stay locked up until Monday morning, you would be called a(n) _____.

37. For the pre-trial inmate, the purpose of jail confinement is supposed to be _____.

38. If you had to pinpoint the one most significant problem of jail inmates, you would point to _____.

39. The other major problem of jail inmates, according to Allen and Simonsen, is most noticeable in the larger urban jails, where large numbers of inmates have _____ concerns.

40. Allen and Simonsen point out that one of the major problems in the jail is the extended confinement of defendants who are supposed to be _____.

41. The reason most sheriffs would want to house "holdback" inmates in their jails is _____.

42. Each year about _____ million people are booked into jail.

Matching

_____ 43. The typical living arrangement of both second- and third-generation jails.

_____ 44. A new type of economic sanction based on the offender's ability to pay.

_____ 45. The original name for a pretrial facility in England.

_____ 46. A daily rate that the jail operator would be paid for housing certain types of offenders today.

_____ 47. The worst problem of the largest urban jails.

_____ 48. Allen and Simonsen suggest this basic legal precept does not really apply to inmates who remain in jail because they cannot afford bail.

_____ 49. The term often applied to a small, short-term detention facility such as might be found in the back of a police station.

_____ 50. The official you would call if you wanted to talk to the person in charge of your local jail.

_____ 51. Rows of cells with bars and inmates who were not under the direct surveillance of guards would be found in this generation of jails.

_____ 52. The basic clientele of local jails in America.

_____ 53. The jails that have the poorest resources in providing services to inmates.

_____ 54. The term for state prison inmates serving their terms in local jails.

_____ 55. An illness associated with drug use that has become a leading cause of death in jails today.

_____ 56. The term for those inmates who have been convicted but not yet had their court disposition pronounced.

a. detention
b. gaol (jail)
c. lockup
d. jail inmates
e. presumption of innocence
f. first-generation jails
g. second-generation jails
h. third- (new-)generation jails
i. direct supervision jails
j. pods
k. detention centers
l. arrested adults
m. pretrial jail incarceration
n. unsentenced
o. "rabble"
p. holdback jail inmates
q. mental health issues

r. overcrowding
s. bullpen
t. drunk tank
u. fee system
v. per diem
w. sheriff
x. price-tag justice
y. day fine
z. weekender
aa. community service
bb. pre-trial alternatives
cc. detoxification center
dd. John Howard Society
ee. criminal history data
ff. small jail facilities
gg. admissions to jails

Discussion

57. What problems are traditionally associated with jail operations?

58. Describe the operation of a "typical" American jail today.

59. How have jail designs changed in recent decades? What is the dominant thinking in jail design at present?

60. How is the jail population different from the prison population?

61. What are the worst problems of large urban jails?

62. What alternatives are commonly used to reduce jail populations?

63. As someone who has just been arrested and booked into a county jail, you are put into a pod with about two dozen other inmates. What are their backgrounds like?

64. What problems might be expected to develop as more and more "holdback" inmates accumulate in local jails?

65. Imagine that you were a progressive sheriff who really wanted to do something to help jail inmates with their problems. What circumstances do you see that would limit your ability to do so?

66. If you could change one thing about the behavior of jail inmates that would reduce their involvement in criminality, what would you change and why?

67. One author years ago titled his article "Our Sick Jails." He could have been referring to the inmates as easily as the institutions. Explain.

CHAPTER SIX

Probation

CHAPTER OBJECTIVES

Probation is the principal option to imprisonment used in American corrections today. After reading the material in this chapter, you should be familiar with:

1. early predecessors of probation.
2. the development of probation in America.
3. how probation services are provided in the states.
4. what the workload of the probation officer consists of.
5. the conditions commonly imposed on probationers.

KEY TERMS AND CONCEPTS

probation	statutory restrictions
suspended sentence	conditions of probation
right of sanctuary	tourniquet sentencing
benefit of clergy	felony probation
stigma	technical violation
surcease (*surcis*)	probation revocation
John Augustus	*Gagnon v. Scarpelli*
juvenile probation	special conditions of probation
presentence investigation report	co-morbidity
risk and needs assessment	family empowerment intervention
state probation	War on Drugs
county probation	bricks and mortar solution
caseload	front-end solutions
casework	back-end solutions

CHAPTER SUMMARY

Suspended Sentence and Sanctuary

As an alternative to imprisonment, **probation** is considered a modern sentence, but it has its roots in earlier forms of withholding punishment--what we often refer to as the **suspended sentence**. The **right of sanctuary**, under church doctrine, set aside holy places for offenders to seek protection from secular laws. **Benefit of clergy** similarly allowed religious officials to avoid punishment in the criminal courts, thus avoiding the **stigma** attached to a criminal conviction. Predecessors of probation in use in English and early American courts allowed judges to withhold punishment for deserving offenders. In practice the suspended sentence came to have a more narrow meaning than contemporary probation; it did not require supervision or impose conditions on the offender, as probation does. The European model of **surcease**, or *surcis*, withholds punishment if the offender commits no new crime during the period of suspension.

The History of Probation

The origins of modern probation in America are often traced to the work of **John Augustus**, a Boston shoe manufacturer and civic leader of the 1840s and 1850s. Although probation was not then a legal sentence, Augustus often persuaded judges in Boston courts to assign offenders to his care. He helped almost 2,000 people straighten out their lives over two decades. Massachusetts, encouraged by his example, passed the first probation statute in 1878. Several other states followed, and the rise of the juvenile court in the early twentieth century promoted the continued expansion of formal probation services.

Juvenile probation spread more quickly than adult probation, but in both courts the concept of probation as the principal alternative to imprisonment gradually gained widespread legal acceptance. Probation began informally in many jurisdictions, often making use of volunteers who reported directly to local judges. As time went on, probation became more of a governmental function. Full-time agents were expected to perform the functions of pre-sentence investigation, report writing, supervision, and caseload management that define probation work today.

Probation Services

State probation, in which probation officers work for a state agency, usually the state department of corrections, is the more common model in American corrections today. In several states, such as Texas, **county probation** prevails. Probation officers in these states work for county governments. In both models probation officers work for local judges--either the judge in the state trial court or typically a city court of limited jurisdiction. The judge imposes probation on the offender, and the probation officer provides the mechanism for executing the sentence.

A typical probation officer in a state or county probation office carries a caseload of 100 or more probationers. The term **"caseload"** refers to the number of clients supervised by the probation officer. **"Casework,"** on the other hand, applies to an approach or methodology, typically a treatment-oriented model associated with the medical model in corrections. Because most probation officers lack the training, time, and inclination to "treat" offenders, probation has tended to move away from this model in recent years. Probation at the federal level and in many state and local jurisdictions is more likely to employ instead a team approach--a model in which probation officers specialize in performing one part of the process or in supervising one particular type of client. One officer might only do presentence investigations, for instance, or handle revocation hearings. Another might only supervise intensive probationers or DWI offenders.

The team approach also develops team members' expertise in regard to specific client needs, such as mental health services or substance abuse counselling. The **War on Drugs** has further increased the number of probation clients with substance abuse problems, often with other mental health, physical health, and interpersonal issues. Probation officers have had to learn a whole new lingo, the language of drug treatment, if not to treat then to understand the treatment their clients are undergoing. The officers are dealing with many clients who suffer from **co-morbidity**, or drug abuse in combination with other intrapersonal problems. They must also be familiar with many different treatment modalities, including some, such as **family empowerment intervention**, that involve not only the client but also other family members as well. As if life were not complex enough.

The probation officer's job today is very demanding. Supervising a caseload is only a part, in many offices a small part, of a much larger function. The officer does **pre-sentence investigation reports** for the court; the information in these reports often makes up the basis of the offender's permanent file, used in later cases and in parole- and clemency-related matters. The officer spends time in court, at sentencing hearings and at probation revocation proceedings. Probation officers complete paperwork to transfer offenders from one jurisdiction to another, and they must complete reams of forms to bureaucractically manage the clients of today. Probation work is caught up in the effort to provide greater accountability based on outcomes. Many probation agencies use some type of **risk and needs assessment** instrument in determining how to manage their clients most effectively. Caseloads are structured by level of supervision, based on frequency of contact, from minimal to intensive.

In many states, probation officers have also been saddled with the responsibility for monitoring offenders to whom intermediate sanctions are applied. Probation is typically combined with these other options--house arrest, electronic monitoring, halfway house residency, out-patient treatment, day reporting, and other options. The probation officer thus becomes the overall supervisor of all forms of community corrections.

Conditions of Probation

Not all offenders are eligible for probation. Many states use **statutory restrictions** to deny probation to certain violent criminals and to repeat offenders. Offenders placed on probation are subject to both general and special conditions. The general **conditions of probation** include such provisions as obeying the law (the first rule of probation), maintaining a job and a residence, not leaving the jurisdiction without permission, meeting with the probation officer, and sending in required reports. **Special conditions** applicable to individual offenders often deal with such matters as substance abuse or domestic violence counselling, avoiding contact with specified persons, performing community service hours, restitution, and, the most common special condition in a recent national survey, paying supervision fees.

Violation of any of these conditions can lead to **probation revocation**. The sentencing judge to whom the probationer is responsible is required by the Supreme Court decision of *Gagnon v. Scarpelli* to hold a due process hearing before revoking probationary status. Being rearrested for a new crime is highly likely to result in revocation. Failing to follow other conditions results in so-called **technical violations**, which are important in a pattern of behavior but less certain to result in revocation and imprisonment. If offenders are brought back to court as probation violators, judges often practice **tourniquet sentencing**, tightening the rules, such as through curfews and drug testing, to control unlawful behavior. It is apparent that many probationers do not take probation at all seriously; they make little effort to change their lifestyles and avoid wrongdoing. Judges and probation officers today have more tools to use to get the attention of these offenders, who, if they are convicted felons, could just as easily be serving time in prison.

Felony Probation Today

In the early years of the penitentiary, probation for convicted felons was the exception. Now **felony probation** is an accepted practice. In most jurisdictions, more felons get probation, either directly or after a short jail term, than go straight to prison. But is probation a real sentence, a serious punishment, or did the criminal "get away with it"? There is no doubt that both the conditions of probation and probation supervision in practice have gotten tougher in recent years. Probation is more restrictive and more costly to the probationer, and probation violation rates are up in most jurisdictions as probationers are monitored more closely. Probation's success rate, measured by terminations without revocation, was once in the range of 75 to 80%. Today it is generally lower, one recent national study showing a success rate of 62%. The courts want to make probation seem more punitive, to both inattentive criminals and a disapproving public, and corrections authorities know that probation may be ten to twenty times less costly than locking the criminal up.

Probation has come to be the most frequently used sentence for serious misdemeanor and felony offenders in America today. More than twice as many offenders are on probation as are confined in state and federal prisons. In most jurisdictions first-time non-violent offenders, and some repeaters and less serious violent criminals, are routinely put on probation as a second chance. In many states probation is combined with a short jail term in what is called a split sentence. In practice probation has come to mean:
    1. a disposition, with different provisions for controlling the offender's behavior.
    2. a status, which allows the offender to remain in the community under supervision.

3. a subsystem of criminal justice.
4. a process, involving such elements as investigating, reporting and supervising.

Probation is one of the "**front-end solutions**" to the increasing rate of incarceration in America. If you decrease the use of probation, you must emphasize either the "**bricks-and-mortar solution**" of building new jails and prisons, or the "**back-end solution**" of releasing criminals under control after they have been in confinement. Many authorities in corrections believe that the front-end solutions, including various forms of probation, have the most to offer to long-term crime control policies. The present task is to make probation appear to work well enough, in terms of controlling and changing criminal behavior, to make it politically acceptable.

SELF TEST

Multiple Choice

1. Probation is basically a contract between the offender and the:
    a. warden
    b. probation board
    c. district attorney
    d. victim
    e. judge

2. If an offender on probation did not like his probation officer and refused to stay in contact with him, the offender could be brought back into court for this _____ violation.
    a. administrative
    b. legalistic
    c. derivative
    d. technical
    e. structural

3. Which one of the following circumstances is the most frequent reason cited in holding disciplinary hearings for adult probationers?
    a. being found drinking in a bar
    b. staying out past curfew
    c. being fired from a job
    d. being found in the company of someone with drugs in his possession
    e. absconding or failing to keep in contact with the officer

4. Probation is founded on the idea of:
    a. the suspended sentence
    b. continuous surveillance
    c. prosecutorial discretion
    d. banishment
    e. executive clemency

5. Benefit of clergy and sanctuary in the early days were both tied to the authority of:
    a. the ruler
    b. the prosecutor
    c. the school
    d. the victim
    e. the church

6. Where is probation best placed among these options?
   a. executive sanctions
   b. brick-and-mortar solutions
   c. back-end solutions
   d. front-end solutions
   e. institutional refinements

7. John Augustus' success in applying informal probation led this state to be the first to officially legalize probation as a sentence in 1878:
   a. Maine
   b. Ohio
   c. Illinois
   d. Virginia
   e. Massachusetts

8. The most commonly used special condition of probation is:
   a. paying supervision fees
   b. electronic monitoring
   c. domestic violence counseling
   d. restitution
   e. a lobotomy

9. In which one of the following statuses would you find the most offenders under correctional supervision?
   a. federal prison
   b. state prison
   c. jail
   d. probation
   e. parole

10. The idea of tourniquet sentencing basically means that if the behavior of an offender on probation begins to slip, the court will:
   a. revoke his probation and make him serve the full prison sentence
   b. try a different probation officer
   c. recommend mental health treatment
   d. impose stricter controls on the offender
   e. send the case to a more punitive judge

True or False

_____ 11. Drug offenses are the most common crimes among felony probationers today.

_____ 12. Most probation services are provided by officers who work for state agencies.

_____ 13. The trend in probation services today is to emphasize the role of the probation officer as a therapist doing individual casework.

_____ 14. The courts have ruled that every convicted felon is legally eligible for probation.

_____ 15. Although its success rate has declined recently, probation still has more successful terminations than failures.

_____ 16. The responsibility for the preparation of presentence investigation reports has generally been transferred from probation officers to the police in recent years.

_____ 17. Under the more restrictive sentencing provisions currently being adopted, only misdemeanants, NOT felons, are eligible for probation.

_____ 18. Juvenile probation was a legal sentence in every state before adult probation was.

_____ 19. The number of people on probation has begun to decline as sentencing turns more punitive.

_____ 20. A probationer who is arrested for a violent felony offense would ordinarily be taken straight to prison without a hearing first.

Fill In the Blanks

21. The two key features of active probation, in contrast to the suspended sentence, are _____ and _____.

22. The man called the "Father of Probation" in America for his work with the courts in Boston is _____.

23. Kentucky is the state with the lowest per capita rate of probation; the state with the highest rate of probation is _____.

24. The English practice allowing offenders to avoid punishment if they could recite Psalm 51 was called _____.

25. The common felony offense for which offenders are most likely to get probation is larceny; the common felony offense for which offenders are least likely to get probation is _____.

26. If a probationer was marked by a serious personality disorder in combination with a substance abuse problem, she would be said to be suffering from _____.

27. *Gagnon v. Scarpelli* is still considered the landmark Supreme Court case dealing with the issue of _____.

28. Other than the time spent working with the probationers in his or her caseload, the generalist probation officer is likely to spend most of the remaining time performing the function of _____.

29. Allen and Simonsen use the term _____ to mean the judge's tightening the conditions of probation until the offender changes his behavior to avoid more punitive conditions.

30. Probably the principal motivation for expanded use of felony probation in most states has been _____.

Matching

_____ 31. The term for the social work or therapeutic approach in probation.

_____ 32. The mark of shame or disgrace that would be attached to a felony offender, especially one who has been imprisoned.

_____ 33. The European model of suspended sentence, obliging the offender only to avoid criminal conduct.

_____ 34. The term for a conditional sentence that is not served in confinement.

_____ 35. An instrument that would be used to predict the future behavior of an offender.

_____ 36. Among the possible strategies for reducing prison populations, probation is counted among this group.

_____ 37. The most important influence on the judge in the sentencing hearing, according to Allen and Simonsen.

_____ 38. A Biblical predecessor of probation that allowed the offender to take refuge from the law in a holy place.

_____ 39. An approach recommended for female juvenile drug abusers.

_____ 40. "Don't break the law." "Report in." "No drugs." "Keep in touch with your P.O." What are these examples of?

a. probation
b. suspended sentence
c. right of sanctuary
d. benefit of clergy
e. stigma
f. surcease (*surcis*)
g. John Augustus
h. juvenile probation
i. presentence investigation report
j. risk and needs assessment
k. state probation
l. county probation
m. caseload
n. casework
o. statutory restrictions
p. conditions of probation
q. tourniquet sentencing
r. felony probation
s. technical violation
t. probation revocation
u. *Gagnon v. Scarpelli*
v. special conditions of probation
w. co-morbidity
x. family empowerment intervention
y. War on Drugs
z. bricks and mortar solution
aa. front-end solutions
bb. back-end solutions

Discussion

41. What were important early practices that provided a historical foundation for probation?

42. How did probation develop in America?

43. What does a probation officer actually do?

44. What general and special conditions are typically applied to probationers?

45. How is the role of probation changing within the legal system of today?

46. Is probation a punishment? How can it be made more punitive?

CHAPTER SEVEN

Intermediate Sanctions

CHAPTER OBJECTIVES

Intermediate sanctions fill the gap between prison and probation. They provide greater controls over offenders while stopping short of secure custody. After reading the material in this chapter, you should be familiar with:
1. the impetus for stricter controls over offenders left in the community.
2. the range of controls provided by intermediate sanctions.
3. the features of intermediate sanctions leaving the offender at home or in community-based residential centers.
4. the use of accelerated or "shock" programs as intermediate sanctions.

KEY TERMS AND CONCEPTS

intermediate sanctions	community work orders
day attendance centers	community service
restitution orders	home detention
risk management	house arrest
community corrections	furlough
desistance	electronic monitoring
restitution	electronic parole
day fine	halfway houses
punishment units	community residential treatment centers
tourniquet sentencing	day reporting centers
intensive supervised probation (ISP)	shock probation
drug court	shock incarceration
enhancement programs	boot camp

CHAPTER SUMMARY

Overview

For many years the courts faced a simple "either/or" choice in sentencing convicted felons--either non-secure probation, allowing offenders to roam free under minimal supervision, or secure imprisonment, which isolated offenders from society. The past two decades have seen the development of a wide range of **intermediate sanctions** which impose more controls and restrictions over offenders. Most intermediate sanctions are considered a part of **community corrections**, keeping offenders at home or in a community-based residential facility. But some involve placement in jail or prison settings for short periods, in combination with other periods of supervision in the community. Intermediate sanctions can be seen as providing more individualized controls matched to the offender's behavior; these sanctions also make the probation function more punitive by imposing greater costs on the offender's liberty. They are sometimes referred to as **enhancement programs**, because they enhance both the treatment options for the offender and the control options for the state. Their objective is to achieve **"desistance**," which is defined as the system's effort to get the offender to cease criminal behavior.

Overcrowding

In the early 1970s America's rate of imprisonment began a sharp climb that has continued for a quarter-century. With more than a million-and-a-half adults in jails and prisons, our rate of incarceration has climbed to over 500 per 100,000, a figure exceeded only by Russia, a country in far greater social and political turmoil. The costs, both economic and social, of pursuing the "bricks-and-mortar" solution to the crime problem have spurred interest in other less costly and less severe options. What are these intermediate sanctions that have developed in response to the notion that for many offenders prison is too much and probation is too little?

Intermediate Sanctions

James Byrne has represented common sentencing options on a continuum or scale of controls, from least to most punitive. The idea of a scale of options fits the scheme of **"tourniquet sentencing**," tightening controls over the offender until desistance occurs. The corrections system is put in the business of **risk management**, which has to do with assessing risk and providing structured controls appropriate to the degree of risk the offender is believed to represent.

Restitution is at the low end of this scale. Restitution, which is akin to the old practice of wergeld, is accomplished through **restitution orders** that require the offender to repay the victim for economic losses; it is used more often in property crimes but can be used in violent crimes where injury also results.

Next on the scale is the **day fine**, which has been in use in European countries for some time. Instead of a flat fine, such as $500 for DWI that all offenders pay, the fine is expressed as a part of the offender's income. Each crime is worth so many **punishment units**. The judge sets a number of units for this specific offense, and these units are multiplied by a standard percentage of the offender's income (such as 1/1000th of his annual income) to come up with a specific financial obligation. A number of American jurisdictions are using this method of equalizing the economic impact of fines.

Community service or **community work orders** are next up on Byrne's scale. Offenders are ordered to put in so many hours of time devoted to some public service or charitable work. Sometimes the work is skill-related, as a doctor who might provide free medical care; more often it involves social services, such as visiting a nursing home, or manual labor, such as picking up trash in a park. The idea is that the community work is more productive and more morally effective than being locked up or being let off with a fine or a suspended sentence.

Standard probation remains an option, though with typical caseloads of greater than 100 it provides minimal supervision. Many jurisdictions now structure probation supervision from routine (or low) to intermediate to high, with the highest level termed **intensive supervised probation**, or **ISP**. Georgia pioneered intensive probation starting in 1974, and it has subsequently spread nationwide. Intensive probation has several standard features--small caseloads, frequent, sometimes daily, contacts between probationers and probation officers, drug testing, supervision fees, curfews, and participation in treatment programs. In some states those offenders assigned to intensive supervision would otherwise have been sent to prison. They are usually repeat property or drug offenders. In other states intensive supervision in part of an enhancement program; that is, it provides stepped-up supervision for regular probationers or parolees who have failed to comply with the conditions of less-intensive caseloads. Their supervision is enhanced as an alternative to imprisonment.

Other intermediate sanctions center on confinement at home. Many states once used **furloughs** to allow inmates short visits home, often during the holidays or prior to release from custody. Furloughs have been less popular in recent years, primarily because political officials cannot take the heat when a criminal on furlough commits a new crime. Violent crimes committed by Willie Horton, a Massachusetts prisoner on work furlough, became an important issue in the 1988 Presidential election, with George Bush using the issue to claim that Michael Dukakis, then governor of Massachusetts, was "soft on crime." Furloughs are still around in most states and the federal system, but the number of inmates who get them is much reduced.

House arrest, or **home detention**, is an intermediate sanction now used in many states and local jurisdictions. It may be a part of probation or a sentence in itself, as it is in Florida's Community Control Program (FCCP). Home detention can be very restrictive, particularly when it is combined with **electronic monitoring** to impose even stricter controls over the offender's movements and whereabouts. The use of technological devices to monitor offenders was proposed in 1964 as **electronic parole**, but it has only come into general usage within the past decade. About one-third of offenders on house arrest nationwide are monitored through various types of electronic systems--some of which now have video and breath-testing capabilities.

Programs of these types are sometimes criticized as "net widening," meaning that lesser offenders are caught in a wider net of supervision and subjected to more intrusive controls than they deserve. But in many jurisdictions, the offenders on house arrest and electronic monitoring are people who would otherwise be sent to prison under existing sentencing standards. Thus house arrest and electronic monitoring probably keep as many people out of prison, at substantially reduced cost, than they bring into the system under higher degrees of supervision. Success rates for electronic monitoring tend to be in the same range as for routine probation, around 75% or higher.

If offenders cannot live at home, the next step up the scale is to place them in a non-secure residential facility. These facilities were typically called **halfway houses** at one time. They became popular in the mental health field and spread to community corrections in the 1960s and 1970s, when the reintegration era was in vogue. Their name came from their place--halfway between freedom and confinement. They were used both for offenders exiting the system, on pre-release, parole, or discharge, and for probationers who required stricter supervision. **Community residential treatment centers** today are almost always tied to employment, education, or treatment programs of some sort. Their emphasis is on making offenders productive and on providing intensive services that offenders cannot get as easily at home.

In some jurisdictions the latest twist on the halfway house is the **day reporting center** (called the **day attendance center** in Australia and in some other models). Offenders live at home, but they report to another site each day to report in and take part in specific programs, usually treatment-, education-, or vocation-focused. They then go home at night under curfew; with telephone checks or electronic monitoring added on, day reporting centers can be made nearly as restrictive as community residential centers.

Intermediate sanctions are usually tied to the community, as in recent **drug court** programs now proliferating in many urban areas, but there are variations that involve confinement in secure jails or prisons. Intermittent or "weekend" jail sentences and split sentences involving prison and probation are common in many jurisdictions. Accelerated or "shock" programs are another recent sanction combining time in secure custody with time under supervision--often intensive supervision--in the community. **Shock probation** was established in Ohio in 1965. The Ohio model uses a three- to four-month prison term followed by the offender's return to probation in the community. The judge is the official with authority to recall the inmate from prison and set the conditions for probation.

Georgia (1983) and Oklahoma (1984) were the first states to establish a different kind of shock program-- **shock incarceration** or **boot camp**. Most states and many local jurisdictions have set up boot camp programs within the last decade, even though evidence of their effectiveness is so far inconclusive. People like the *idea* of boot camp, whether it works or not. Most boot camps follow a similar regimen: they are short term, three to six months, featuring military dress and discipline, including drill instructors yelling at offenders and lots of physical exercise. Some boot camps add in physical labor, education and training, and counseling, particularly for substance abuse.

Boot camps are slanted toward young offenders, and their popularity is based on the premise that a taste of military life is just what young criminals need to motivate them to straighten out. This premise ignores the fact that the military has plenty of criminals of its own and no longer allows confirmed criminals to enlist on active duty. Free-world criminals tend to make bad soldiers. They create disciplinary problems and end up getting early discharges.

Shock incarceration is said to be a new approach, yet its regimen is very similar to the first American reformatories of a century ago. Reformatories did not achieve remarkable success rates, and so far boot camps have not done so either. Offenders may be shocked by the nature of the boot camp experience, but the shock effect apparently wears off soon. Recidivism rates for boot camp graduates resemble those of ordinary convicts over time. But at least boot camp is quicker and cheaper, so corrections officials keep hoping its effectiveness can be substantiated. On James Byrne's scale, boot camp is the most severe of the intermediate sanctions, and the closest to imprisonment. Fail here, and you're already in prison. All you have to do is take off your fatigues and put on the uniform of an ordinary convict.

SELF TEST

Multiple Choice

1. The European intermediate sanction recommended because it specifically adjusts for income inequality among offenders is the:
      a. enhancement
      b. split sentence
      c. community service
      d. day fine
      e. furlough

2. The only nation that we are aware of with a higher incarceration rate than the United States is:
      a. Japan
      b. France
      c. Canada
      d. Mexico
      e. Russia

3. On James Byrne's scale of sentencing options, which of these provides the lowest level punishment?
      a. jail
      b. intensive probation
      c. restitution
      d. house arrest
      e. split sentence

4. Which one of the following did NOT fit Georgia's model of intensive supervised probation?
      a. only violent offenders were accepted
      b. mandatory curfew
      c. unannounced alcohol and drug testing
      d. five face-to-face contacts each week
      e. community service

5. Florida's Community Control Program (FCCP) is an example of which type of intermediate sanction?
   a. halfway house
   b. shock probation
   c. home detention
   d. boot camp
   e. day fine

6. Assessing the individual offender to determine how much control is needed to maintain public safety would be part of the process called:
   a. net widening
   b. restitution orders
   c. risk management
   d. altruistic servitude
   e. deprivation mode

7. Allen and Simonsen (citing the research of Parents) suggest that the main focus of day reporting centers is:
   a. deterrence
   b. victim compensation
   c. retribution
   d. treatment
   e. incapacitation

8. The objective of shock probation programs is said to be:
   a. retribution
   b. selective incapacitation
   c. penance
   d. diversion
   e. specific deterrence

9. The boot camp regimen is basically similar to the elements of which earlier institution?
   a. the English Bridewell
   b. the Walnut Street Jail
   c. the Elmira Reformatory
   d. the Eastern State Penitentiary
   e. Alcatraz

10. In the theory of tourniquet sentencing, more restrictive intermediate sanctions can be applied until the goal of _____ is achieved.
   a. strangulation
   b. centering
   c. crimogenesis
   d. desistance
   e. recidivism

True or False

_____ 11. Most local jurisdictions now operate an integrated network of intermediate sanctions using the full range of sanctions on Byrne's scale.

_____ 12. Enhancement programs would generally apply stricter sanctions to those offenders already under some lesser degree of control.

_____ 13. Imprisonment rates have begun to decline as more states emphasize intermediate sanctions.

_____ 14. Every offender on home detention is hooked up to some kind of electronic monitoring system.

_____ 15. Allen and Simonsen use the term "high-commitment years" (between 29 and 39) to mean the period when offenders are best suited to community corrections alternatives.

_____ 16. Research suggests that fines may be more effective in reducing recidivism than jail sentences.

_____ 17. The typical offender in an intensive probation caseload, in the Georgia model, is someone who would probably be locked up if IPS were not available.

_____ 18. Furloughs were an early form of house arrest in which the offender lived at home while serving a felony sentence.

_____ 19. A day reporting center generally provides programs and monitoring but does not require the offender to live on the premises.

_____ 20. Authorities agree that for shock probation to be effective, the offender must be incarcerated for at least a year.

Fill In the Blanks

21. Allen and Simonsen suggest that the greatest impetus from within the system toward greater use of intermediate sanctions is _____.

22. Tourniquet sentencing suggests the need to apply progressively greater degrees of _____ over the offender until his or her behavior becomes legally acceptable.

23. The state whose model of intensive probation (ISP) was most influential was _____.

24. The state whose Community Control Program is considered a model of home detention is _____.

25. If an offender was violating curfew as part of a sanction to a day reporting center, the next sanction up the line that he might be moved to would be a(n) _____.

26. If you were protesting "net widening," you would probably argue that intermediate sanctions ought to be used less and _____ ought to be used more.

27. The official who makes the decision about which offenders are put on shock probation is the _____.

28. The most important thing that boot camp is intended to teach the young offender is _____.

29. The most widespread model of intensive probation assigned a small caseload to a team of two officers, one of whom was called a probation officer and the other a(n) _____ officer.

30. A dentist convicted of a white-collar crime might be assigned to perform eight hours of work each week at a free dental clinic for the poor; this type of sanction is called _____.

Matching

_____ 31. The requirement that the offender provide compensation to the victim of his crime.

_____ 32. Once called halfway houses, these facilities provide a non-custodial place for offenders to live under supervision.

_____ 33. The term applied to those criminal penalties that fall between probation and imprisonment.

_____ 34. The popular name for a short-term correctional program similar to military basic training.

_____ 35. The measure of penalties that can be applied to offenders who commit specific offenses in a day fine system.

_____ 36. A program, started in Georgia, that features small caseloads and frequent contacts with offenders.

_____ 37. The first form of electronic monitoring, proposed back in the early 1960s.

_____ 38. A new type of diversion or sentence-reduction alternative that involves judicial monitoring of substance-abusing defendants.

_____ 39. If you were a second-time DWI offender who got a sentence of 90 days in prison and two years under supervision in the community, this is the term for your sentence.

_____ 40. This is an option which allows prisoners in a secure facility to leave it for short periods of time to visit home or for other approved purposes, such as school or vocational training.

a. intermediate sanctions
b. day attendance centers
c. restitution orders
d. risk management
e. community corrections
f. desistance
g. restitution
h. day fine
i. punishment units
j. tourniquet sentencing
k. intensive supervised probation (ISP)
l. drug court
m. enhancement programs

n. community work orders
o. community service
p. home detention
q. house arrest
r. furlough
s. electronic monitoring
t. electronic parole
u. halfway houses
v. community residential treatment centers
w. day reporting centers
x. shock probation
y. shock incarceration
z. boot camp

Discussion

41. What purposes are served by ordering the offender to provide restitution?

42. Why are day fines said to be more fair than ordinary flat fines?

43. Describe the elements of a typical intensive probation program.

44. Why is boot camp such a popular idea at present?

45. If an ordinary felon was sentenced to regular probation but continued to get into trouble, what other intermediate sanctions might be applied to him before he was revoked and put in prison?

46. What would seem to be the advantages of leaving the offender under intermediate sanctions living at home, as opposed to confining him in a secure jail or prison?

CHAPTER EIGHT

Imprisonment

CHAPTER OBJECTIVES

Offenders convicted of felony crimes may be sentenced to imprisonment in a local, state, or federal prison. After reading the material in this chapter, you should be familiar with:
1. the reasons for the growth of prison populations in recent years.
2. the use of classification for inmate management and treatment in prison.
3. the differing environments of maximum, medium, and minimum security prisons.
4. the consequences of emphasizing imprisonment as a public policy.

KEY TERMS AND CONCEPTS

"get-tough" legislation	high-close security
"War on Crime"	Sing Sing
prison	Gothic-style monoliths
overcrowding	prisonization
baby boom	supermax
classification	special housing unit (SHU)
progressive prison	medium security
correctional treatment	minimum security
segregation	open institutions
maximum security	

CHAPTER SUMMARY

Prison Populations Continue to Climb

Over the past two decades, as the **"baby boom"** generation has matured, America's prison population has climbed to heights never reached before in our nation's history. Americans fear crime, and politicians turn fear into **"get-tough" legislation** that sends more people to prison and keeps them there for longer terms. The **"War on Crime,"** particularly its off-shoot "War on Drugs," has tripled jail and prison populations in just fifteen years. Almost half of the increase is for drug crimes alone. We need about 1,100 new prison beds--the equivalent of a full-sized prison--each week to keep up with the current prisoner population growth rate. America's present rate of imprisonment is over 400 per 100,000, though this rate varies considerably from state to state--from Minnesota at 117 to Louisiana and Texas at 700+. The South has the highest regional incarceration rate. **Prisons**, which are defined as institutions intended to house felons serving sentences of longer than a year, are primarily operated by state governments, although the Federal Bureau of Prisons confines federal offenders, four large cities operate their own prison systems, and county jails in many states now hold felons serving long sentences alongside pre-trial defendants and sentenced misdemeanants. **Overcrowding**--housing inmates above the designed capacity--is a continuing problem in most state prisons. Prisoner health and safety suffer when overcrowding persists.

Classification: A Basic Element of Corrections

Prisons of today are very different from the early penitentiaries. Prisoners are treated more humanely by prison officials, and prison living conditions are much better. Prisoners are also subject to **classification**, which differentiates them into categories according to the institution's custodial needs and the prisoner's treatment needs. Classification is associated with rehabilitation in corrections, but in most prison systems it probably has as much to do with security, inmate housing, and work assignments as with treatment programming. In the ideal "**progressive prison**," classification was to ensure that the inmate would be matched with the **correctional treatment** and training programs necessary to correct his deficiencies.

As a management tool, classification is the basis of **segregation** or grouping of inmates in like categories. The most important categories in prison are not needs based, focusing on individualized treatment (though some states do have specific institutions for treating offenders such as substance abusers or sex offenders); rather, they are custody based, focusing on the institution's security needs. The most important designation the prisoner gets is his security level. It defines in large part the nature of his prison existence. The five most common security designations for American prisons are maximum, high/close, medium, minimum, and open. More inmates are housed today under medium security than any other custodial level.

Maximum Security Prisons

Early penitentiaries practiced **maximum security**; indeed, our mental image of a "prison" is derived from the architecture of these institutions--high walls, guard towers, cellblocks stacked in tiers, massive concrete and steel construction. The early American prisons not only maximized security, they also practiced isolation and intimidation to a high degree. Allen and Simonsen call these institutions **Gothic-style monoliths**, because of their fortress-like appearance. About 60 of these prisons built in the 1800s remain in use today, including **Sing Sing**, the 1825 New York prison that institutionalized the features of the Auburn penitentiary model. It is these prisons--the oldest, largest, and most secure--that define imprisonment in America. It is these prisons to which Donald Clemmer applied the term "**prisonization**," meaning the inmate's adaptation to the culture of the penitentiary. The more profoundly artificial and different the prison is from the outside society, the more the prison inmate is set apart from the values of conventional society. The prison culture becomes more important as inmates remain in prison to serve long sentences; prisonization becomes so complete that prisoners lose sight of the normal society beyond the walls. Maximum security and its cousin one step down, **high-close security**, continue to house more than 20% of American prison inmates.

Supermax: The Next Notch Up on Security

In the decade of the 1990s, the term "supermax" entered the prison management vocabulary. Although Alcatraz, which opened in 1934, is often said to be the first supermax prison, the concept of a special prison or housing unit above maximum security became more prevalent during the continued expansion of the prison system in the 1980s. With the increase in the number of inmates overall, the number of inmates considered unmanageable, dangerous, or high-risk increased also. Most states already have a supermax prison or unit, and most of the rest, except for the smallest, have looked at the idea for the future.

Supermax refers to the highest level of security that can be applied to a prison housing unit. Inmates are kept in single-person cells, generally locked down twenty-four/seven. It is an earned status, based mostly on what the inmate does *after* he gets to prison, rather than what he has done before. Most supermax inmates do not have work assignments, nor do they have access to ordinary prison recreation, inmate organizations, or programming. Visiting is restricted. Privileges are minimal. Contact with other people, including staff, is very limited. The inmate is isolated in his cell as much as possible, with brief outdoor exercise periods in a small, individual exercise yard. Supervision is very high, higher in many states than that provided inmates on death row. Some entire prisons are designated supermax; other prisons have cellblock units so designated. The rules and procedures vary from state to state. Supermax refers as much to a type of inmate (who cannot be controlled in maximum security) as it does to a particular prison architectural or management style. Less than two percent of the American prison population is confined in supermax housing.

Many prisons have a **special housing unit (SHU)** with security conditions similar to supermax, but housing disciplinary offenders for shorter periods rather than long-term security and control problems. Special housing would once have been called "the hole," where inmates were subject to physical punishments, restricted diets, and sensory deprivation. Some supermax prisons also have special housing units within them, and some special housing units use a level system where the worst-behaved inmates are kept on the lowest level. Somewhere in this country, buried deep in the bowels of our supermax prisons and special housing units, are probably the half dozen "baddest" inmates in America; but they are so buried and isolated that even if we could identify them we could not get to them to ask them just how bad they are.

Medium and Minimum Security Institutions

We continue to build new maximum security prisons today, including such supermax prisons as Pelican Bay in California, and Florence, Colorado, in the federal system. But most of the new prisons built in the twentieth century have incorporated lower levels of security--**medium security, minimum security**, and open. Once fences began to replace walls in defining prison perimeters, the look of prisons began to change. For one thing, people could actually *see* into the prisons, which had some effect on the traditional seclusion of inmates behind impenetrable walls. The mode of housing changed from cellblocks to dormitories and rooms. The ratio of guards to inmates was reduced, and the new prisons became more open, making it easier for inmates to move around. The absolute controls that were so much a part of the old-style penitentiary were relaxed, which tends to reduce the impact of prisonization on inmates. Medium and minimum security prisons also tend to be much smaller than the old penitentiaries, and because they are of more recent construction they are much more modern in their design and amenities. At the low end of the security scale are so-called **open institutions**, which are not secure facilities at all in the conventional sense. Open institutions may include pre-release centers, work release centers, prison farms or camps (which can also be maximum security facilities on the other end of the scale), or specialized treatment facilities. To escape from an open facility, all an inmate has to do is run away; of course, when he is recaptured, he will not be returned to the open facility to serve the remainder of his sentence. Most corrections officials agree that only about 15 to 20% of prisoners require maximum security; the rest do fine with less.

Alternatives to Prison Overcrowding

As we face a continuing influx of new prisoners, amounting to an increase of between 50,000 and 100,000 new prison beds annually, we have to ask about the wisdom of pursuing the bricks-and-mortar solution in corrections. Prisons are very expensive to construct. The more secure they are, the more expensive they are to build and to operate after opening. Furthermore, prison beds, once made available, are very difficult to empty. We continue opening new prisons, but we rarely shut down old ones--until they fall down from old age. The more we pursue building new prisons as the appropriate way to punish convicted felons, the more we commit to a future mind-set that encourages high rates of incarceration instead of alternative community-based programs or other crime prevention alternatives. If we have the prison beds available, we are highly likely to fill up the empty spaces first before we consider other options.

SELF TEST

Multiple Choice

1. The biggest increase in the number of new prison inmates over the past fifteen years has been in inmates convicted of:
    a. sex offenses
    b. white-collar crimes
    c. crimes against the elderly
    d. crimes of violence
    e. drug offenses

2. After the prison is built, it is estimated that the cost of confining one prisoner for a year averages about:
    a. $ 3,500
    b. $ 8,000
    c. $12,800
    d. $20,200
    e. $31,300

3. Four of the following fit the environment of the supermax prison. Which one does NOT?
    a. dormitory-style housing
    b. increased staff supervision of inmates
    c. no work assignments
    d. restricted contact with outsiders
    e. loss of privileges

4. At current growth rates, the United States needs about how many new prison beds each week?
    a. 10
    b. 100
    c. 500
    d. 1,100
    e. 5,500

5. Allen and Simonsen argue that prison overcrowding has the most severe effect on:
    a. recreation
    b. treatment programs
    c. visitation
    d. health and safety
    e. work assignments

6. Donald Clemmer's term for the inmate's adaptation to the culture of the maximum security penitentiary is:
    a. incapacitation
    b. derivation
    c. prisonization
    d. absolution
    e. calcification

7. The largest number of prisoners today are in which security classification?
    a. open
    b. minimum
    c. medium
    d. high/close
    e. maximum

8. The prisons built in the 1800s were generally designed to apply which level of security?
    a. open
    b. minimum
    c. medium
    d. high/close
    e. maximum

9. Allen and Simonsen give what warning about open prisons?
    a. They are bad for public safety.
    b. They often fail to provide services inmates need.
    c. Most prisoners do not like them.
    d. Prisons will lose their deterrent value if we make them too nice.
    e. They have higher levels of inmate violence than more secure prisons.

10. The authors would argue that overreliance on the bricks-and-mortar solution promotes four of the following consequences. Which one does NOT fit with the others?
    a. public opposition to prison building
    b. continuing high costs of prison construction
    c. underuse of non-secure alternatives
    d. increasing rates of incarceration
    e. high recidivism rates among ex-offenders

True or False

_____ 11. Most imprisoned felons are confined in institutions operated by the states.

_____ 12. Allen and Simonsen argue that the "War on Drugs" has had virtually no impact on prison population increase.

_____ 13. Blacks are incarcerated at a rate that is about double that for whites.

_____ 14. The death rate in prison increases as prison population density increases.

_____ 15. Classification was developed originally to improve prison security by removing troublesome inmates from the general population.

_____ 16. Allen and Simonsen suggest that in practice the needs of the prison take precedence over any idea of correcting the offender.

_____ 17. The old maximum security prisons tended to be located in cities to be closer to high-crime areas.

_____ 18. Only one penitentiary built before 1900 remains in operation today.

_____ 19. Prison authorities believe that half or more of all prisoners should be kept confined under maximum security conditions.

_____ 20. Prison building in America has peaked out and the number of new prisons opened has gone into decline as the number of incoming and outgoing prisoners balances out.

Fill In the Blanks

21. Allen and Simonsen argue that the part of the "War on Crime" that has had the most impact on prison population growth is the _____ .

22. In the contemporary prison, classification often serves as the basis of both _____ and _____ .

23. If you were an inmate confined in a supermax prison and you were found guilty of a disciplinary violation, you might be moved to an even more restricted place of confinement called the _____ .

24. Allen and Simonsen suggest that the treatment model has a place in corrections, but not in _____ security prisons.

25. In the history of American prisons, the year 1926 is cited as an important date because the first _____ was opened in that year.

26. Although Minnesota is thought of as a progressive state with a relatively small prison population, it shows up at the top of the list on what punitive scale? _____

27. If the prison has high walls, guard towers, individual cells, and extreme regimentation, what security level is it? _____

28. Of police officers, private security guards, and correctional officers, the least likely to be victims of workplace violence are _____ .

29. _____ is measured by calculating the prison's square feet of floor space per inmate; it is an important measure of prison crowding.

30. The expanded use of classification in imprisonment is associated with the changed emphasis from punishment to _____ in operating prisons.

Matching

_____ 31. The New York prison that practiced a refined version of the Auburn model of prison design.

_____ 32. The idea that the post-World War II generation of young people is responsible for our high rates of crime and imprisonment today.

_____ 33. The term for the old-style penitentiaries easily recognizable by their massive appearance.

_____ 34. The idea that prisoners ought to be put into categories after classification, based on such criteria as age, gender, and treatment needs.

_____ 35. Allen and Simonsen's term for the modern prison that offers programs of treatment and training to change behavior.

_____ 36. The experience of new inmates in adapting to the environment of the maximum security prison.

_____ 37. The level of security characteristic of the oldest, largest American prisons.

_____ 38. The level of security characteristic of most American prisons built in the last decade.

_____ 39. The term for non-secure facilities that house low-risk inmates, often late in their sentences.

_____ 40. A process, usually carried out in a prison reception center, that serves as the basis for inmate management and treatment planning.

a. "get-tough" legislation
b. "War on Crime"
c. prison
d. overcrowding
e. baby boom
f. classification
g. progressive prison
h. correctional treatment
i. segregation
j. maximum security
k. high-close security
l. Sing Sing
m. Gothic-style monoliths
n. prisonization
o. supermax
p. special housing unit (SHU)
q. medium security
r. minimum security
s. open institutions

Discussion

41. What are the major reasons for the sharp increase in prison population over the past two decades?

42. What is the purpose of classification in the contemporary prison?

43. How does overcrowding affect the environment of the maximum security prison?

44. Why do Allen and Simonsen use the term "Gothic-style monoliths" to describe the old penitentiaries?

45. How would you explain the movement to medium-security prisons in recent years?

46. Describe the process of "prisonization" as a new inmate would experience it.

47. Describe the nature of inmate life in a supermax prison unit.

CHAPTER NINE

State and Local Prison Systems

CHAPTER OBJECTIVES

The more than 1,500 federal, state, and local prisons in America held about one-and-a-quarter million convicted felons at the end of the 1990s. State prisons systems, differing greatly in philosophy, institutional makeup, and prison conditions, hold the great majority of these inmates. Each state's system is the product of many influences over a long period of historical development, and no two systems are exactly alike. After reading the material in this chapter, you should be familiar with:

1. state institutions by security level.
2. the different types of state prisons.
3. the background of offenders in state prisons and their offenses.
4. the legal environment of contemporary state prison operations.
5. how prisoners are classified and assigned.
6. staff training and accreditation in corrections today.

KEY TERMS AND CONCEPTS

maximum security prisons
close/high security prisons
medium security prisons
minimum security prisons
"cosmetic" security
human resource organization
alternative to death
Thomas Beever
Gaol at Wymondham
Pennsylvania Prison Society
Prison Journal
Jeremy Bentham
panopticon
industrial prison
agricultural prison

work camps
security threat group (STG)
supermax prison
Big Four
Cook County Department of Corrections
New York City Department of Corrections
Washington, D.C., Department of Corrections
Philadelphia Prison System
privacy
cruel and unusual punishment
conditions of confinement
initial classification
institutional needs
American Correctional Association
accreditation

CHAPTER SUMMARY

State Correctional Institutions: The Core of the System

Although both the federal government and several large cities operate prisons for sentenced felons, the bulk of America's convicted felons--well over one million men and women--are confined in institutions operated by state governments. The most common name for this network of prisons, as a state bureaucracy, is the "Department of Corrections." It usually consists of all prisons for adult felons as a core, and it may also include probation and parole for adults and juveniles, juvenile training schools, work release and halfway house facilities, juvenile group homes, and other special purpose facilities. In about half a dozen states with smaller populations, the state department of corrections also operates jails and juvenile detention facilities holding pre-trial prisoners. In several other states, the state has assumed a greater role in promoting (and controlling) community-based alternatives through the passage of what are called "Community Corrections Acts," which prescribe a more comprehensive approach combining state, local, and private correctional agencies that provide a wide variety of non-secure correctional services.

The heart of the state's correctional system (and by far its most expensive component) is its adult prisons. The number of prisons in each state ranges from two, in North Dakota, to well over 100 in Texas. Most states started their prison systems with one institution, a penitentiary based on the Auburn model, and then expanded the system by building additional prisons as the population increased and the need for special purpose facilities (such as those for women, younger offenders, or drug addicts) was accepted. Today prisons are graded according to security levels:

1. **maximum security prisons**. These are often the older, larger, walled penitentiaries with the most rigorous security procedures and the lowest ratio of inmates to guards. They hold about 12 percent of state inmates, almost entirely in one- or two-man cells. There is one step up from this level, the "**supermax prison**," which is permanent lockdown--isolated confinement to a cell under the most restricted conditions in perpetuity.

2. **close/high security prisons**. In some states, considered a kind of maximum security, though the security measures are less restrictive and the ratio of inmates to guards may be higher. About 14 percent of state inmates are held in this classification.

3. **medium security prisons**. Usually the smaller, newer prisons, with double fences instead of walls and dormitory or pod housing rather than cells. The inmate-to-guard ratio may be twice that of the maximum security prison. About 37 percent of state inmates are held in this classification, which is now the usual starting place for new inmates who are not perceived as dangerous or escape risks.

4. **minimum security prisons**. Even newer, smaller prisons with minimal perimeter security and fewer internal controls. The inmate-to-guard ratio is even higher, and inmates may live in rooms or dorms with more privacy and more amenities. About 32 percent of state prison inmates are held in minimum security. They have usually worked their way down from higher classifications; many are "short-termers" approaching release. The public and political fear of criminals has recently resulted in "**cosmetic**" security changes at some of these facilities, such as increasing perimeter fencing to make the public think they are safer, even though it remains very easy to escape from this type of facility. Many inmates are already outside the prison part of the time on work details or other assignments.

5. open security facilities. Not usually called prisons at all, these are non-secure facilities such as work release centers, pre-release centers, halfway houses, and other types of community-based facilities. They have no armed guards and no fences; to escape all you have to do is walk away and not come back. When they catch up with you later, you will be put in maximum security as an escape risk. About four percent of state inmates are in this classification.

Many state prisons are called multi-level institutions because they provide two or more of these levels of security within the same institution. Inmates can change from one grade to another without having to transfer to another prison. The general trend today is toward expanding the lower security grades, especially medium security, though now a greater number of prisoners are held in maximum and close security than were confined in all American prisons only 25 years ago.

Organization of State Systems

A few states, which are predominantly the ones with smaller populations, have very highly centralized corrections bureaucracies; others are very decentralized. There is no standard model that shows how a department of corrections should be structured or how the relationship of the various state, local, and private correctional agencies should be organized. There is in fact no objective way to measure the effectiveness of a state corrections system. "Recidivism," defined as returning to custody, is the standard measure of correctional success or failure, but the definition of recidivism is so variable and the scope of violations so subjective (as in California where most parole violators have failed drug tests) that it is nearly impossible to compare rates from one state to another. We do not have a national corrections system with one set of policies and practices. We have 50 state systems, interacting with thousands of local systems, and a separate federal system, each with policies and practices that have developed in their jurisdictions over a long period of time. As a **human resource organization**, it has been practically impossible to measure the outcome of the correctional process with empirical data. We need much more evaluative research to tell us how we can better manage the complex set of alternatives that make up the modern corrections process.

Development of State Systems

The state systems of today were founded on the nineteenth century penitentiary, which was itself based on the legal reforms of the eighteenth century Age of Enlightenment. The scholars were looking for a more humane and reform-oriented **alternative to death** and the other corporal punishments of the day. What they got, over a half century of development, was the penitentiary. **Sir Thomas Beever** opened the **Gaol at Wymondham**, in Norfolk, England, in 1785, incorporating principles of isolation, work, and penitence to change the nature of confinement. The Philadelphia Society for Alleviating the Miseries of Public Prisons, led by Dr. Benjamin Rush and other civic reformers, incorporated Beever's ideas into the design of the Walnut Street Jail, the first so-called penitentiary in America, which opened in Philadelphia in 1790. As the **Pennsylvania Prison Society**, this organization remains active in corrections reform today. It continues to publish *The Prison Journal*, a leading corrections periodical.

Jeremy Bentham, the Utilitarian philosopher, proposed his model "**panopticon**," a huge prison with a glass top for improved lighting and better supervision of inmates. But what developed in practice was the Pennsylvania or separate system, and then the Auburn penitentiary, which became the American model because of its cheapness and economic productivity. The Northern and Midwestern states perfected the model of the **industrial prison** that lasted into the Great Depression of the 1930s. The Southern states of the post-Civil War developed the model of the **agricultural prison**, the giant prison farm applying the plantation mentality to managing prison labor. States in the South and West also developed prison **work camps**, in which inmates worked on public roads, cleared forests, and completed other public works projects as "slaves of the state."

People borrowed ideas and then built institutions to try to apply the new ideas. The people who built the next generation of institutions tried to improve upon the existing institutions of their time. Thus what we have, in the prison system of today, is an ongoing social experiment in which men and women of "good intentions" use confinement of criminals as a principal means of controlling crime. Does it work? We cannot really say, but nothing else really seems to work either, so we keep on with current practices until the next new idea comes along, and then we incorporate it into the experiment too, looking for any kind of sign that anything we're doing is actually having the desired result, when in truth we might be just as well off still whipping criminals and having mass hangings in the town square on Saturday afternoons, if only these practices were not so "uncivilized."

State prison systems range in size from North Dakota, which has fewer than 1,000 people in prison, to the huge systems of California and Texas, each with more than 100,000 in prison. Rates of imprisonment vary greatly as well. They are highest in the South and lowest in the North. A vast gulf separates Minnesota, with an imprisonment rate of 117 per 100,000, from Louisiana and Texas, both with rates over 700 per 100,000. The state average is about 415 per 100,000.

Who are the people confined in these prisons? They are predominantly young men, mostly poor, undereducated and underemployed, and disproportionately minorities (two out of three are black or hispanic) who have been in trouble before. About 40% are confined for violent crimes, which means the majority are imprisoned for non-violent drug and property crimes. Most prisoners are basically "unattached," not a member of a close family unit, and most identify themselves as having a history of alcohol or drug abuse. Many also have physical and mental health problems. Prisons hold the real failures of American society. As it costs more and more to keep this most troublesome one-half of one percent of our population locked up, we pursue other alternatives but remain committed to one central idea: The worst criminals ought to be locked up for the good of society. The rest of corrections, and the rest of what happens to offenders in society, is just superstructure.

City-Operated Prisons

Allen and Simonsen point out that not all felons sentenced for state crimes end up in state prisons. In another of those historical anomalies, four large cities--the **Big Four**--operate their own prison systems independent of the state. The Big Four are:
>   the **Cook County Department of Corrections**
>   the **New York City Department of Corrections**
>   the **Washington, D.C., Department of Corrections**
>   the **Philadelphia Prison System**

These cities operate prison systems larger than the systems of many states. Their prisons are solely for sentenced felons, who are held in local rather than state custody. It has also become much more common, over the past decade, for felons to serve state time in the local jails of other states. This practice is due primarily to overcrowding of state prisons and to the economic incentive for local sheriffs to house the overflow of state prisoners in their county jails.

The Legal Environment

State prisons operate today in a much more complicated legal environment than was once the case. Prisoners still do not have much of a right to **privacy**, because of the predominant need for security, but they do have important rights in other areas. Developments over the past 30 years have brought about much closer federal court supervision of conditions of confinement. The legal avenue to federal court intervention has most often been the **cruel and unusual punishment** clause of the Eighth Amendment. The **conditions of confinement**, whether in a single prison or in an entire system, have often been found to be so bad that the institutions were ruled to be in violation of the U.S. Constitution. Many state prisons, including the entire prison system of most of the states in the South, have been under federal court order at one time or another. Louisiana's state penitentiary, Angola, was under federal court supervision for almost 25 years, beginning in 1975. Prisoners have far greater access to the courts than they once did, and even though the courts are no longer as attuned to prisoner complaints as they were a few years ago, the threat of litigation remains a powerful force motivating administrators to maintain constitutional standards in prison operations.

Much of today's prison litigation is filed by inmates challenging the institution's control and disciplinary processes. The new supermax prisons around the country have faced numerous lawsuits challenging their severe regimens and the selection of those inmates to be housed there. The efforts of prisons in many states to stifle the influence of prison cliques or gangs, now more often called by the term "**security threat groups**," has also resulted in legal complications. Members of these groups, which are typically organized along racial and ethnic lines and often affiliated with neighborhood street gangs outside, seek to dominate the inmate subculture within the prison. They are involved in selling contraband, extortion, violence, and corruption of prison staff. But prison officials often have difficulty coming up with the evidence to charge them with crimes or internal disciplinary violations; it is not easy to get other inmates to talk about gangs, when they have to go on living with the people they are snitching out. Members of the security threat groups often challenge the arbitrariness of the institution's intervention in their lives. "Why me, man? I wasn't doing nothing." They probably used the same line with the police on the street.

Classification and Assignment in State Prisons

In the complex, multi-level state prison system of today, incoming inmates usually go to a specific facility for classification upon entry into the system. These facilities are called by various names--reception centers, diagnostic centers, reception and evaluation centers, or classification centers, for instance--but what they have in common is a process. Inmates are tested, interviewed, and monitored; their criminal history files are reviewed and prison records brought up to date. The prison attempts to determine the state of their physical and mental health, their educational and program needs, and any specific skills they may possess. Most of all, the **initial classification** is geared toward determining the level of security the inmate should be placed in. Is he an escape risk? A protection case? Is he dangerous to himself, to other inmates, or to staff?

Classification was originated as a tool to match the institution's programs to the needs of the prisoner, but it became over time more a device of security--to match the inmate to the **institutional needs** of the prison. Classification only takes a few weeks in most state systems, but to the prisoner the outcome is tremendously important. It determines what prison he will be sent to, what security level he will be housed in, what his work assignment will be, and what programs he will be allowed to take part in. Classification determines which road you will be allowed to follow in prison; take a wrong turn, and it may be impossible to ever get back on the right track.

Training in State Systems

Contemporary state prisons are emphasizing staff training as never before. Training is viewed as the way to standardize workplace practices and to avoid the kind of inept actions that result in civil liability. With the growth of state corrections bureaucracies, many correctional policies, procedures, and practices are standardized among all state prisons, which means that all new correctional officers can be sent to one centralized academy for their five or six weeks (or more or less) of preservice training before they report to their assigned prison. The standards and guidelines of the **American Correctional Association** (ACA) are very important here. The ACA, founded as the National Prison Association in 1870, is the leading professional organization in corrections today. The training materials prepared by the ACA and other professional organizations have done much to put better trained correctional staff on the job, and once they get there inservice training is far more abundant as well. Training and education are far more important in state prison systems today than they have been at any previous time in corrections history. The ACA has also pushed for **accreditation** of correctional organizations. Accreditation is an ongoing process involving review by outside experts to determine that corrections agencies are meeting professional standards common to the field.

SELF TEST

Multiple Choice

1. Agricultural prison were found predominantly in:
    a. the South
    b. the Far West
    c. New England
    d. the North
    e. the Midwest

2. William G. Nagel, in his book *The New Red Barn*, identifies the major assumptions upon which the modern prison system was built. Four of the following are part of these assumptions; which one is NOT?
   a. The cause of crime is in the individual offender.
   b. Isolated institutions are the best way to modify behavior.
   c. Minimum security is best for changing behavior.
   d. The offender should be punished for his criminal acts.
   e. Behavior is modifiable.

3. In which security classification are the greatest number of state prisoners held?
   a. open
   b. minimum
   c. medium
   d. close/high
   e. maximum

4. The minimum security prison provides a model for those inmates who are:
   a. near the ends of their sentences
   b. mentally unstable in larger prisons
   c. too young and weak to mix in general population
   d. first-time offenders
   e. serving life sentences

5. Which prison model predominated in the Midwest and the New England states in the first part of the twentieth century?
   a. agricultural
   b. local option
   c. transfer
   d. medical
   e. industrial

6. Which state's entire prison system consists of two prisons holding under a thousand inmates?
   a. Idaho
   b. North Dakota
   c. Rhode Island
   d. Delaware
   e. Maine

7. The state of Missouri's legal action against prison inmate Darryl E. Gilyard is indicative of a trend toward:
   a. punishing inmates who file frivolous lawsuits
   b. putting disciplinary problems in long-term lockdown
   c. filing new criminal charges against inmates who attack guards
   d. imposing greater controls on HIV inmates
   e. making inmates pay for the cost of imprisonment

8. The Philadelphia Society for Alleviating the Miseries of Public Prisons eventually evolved into what organization of today?
   a. the American Correctional Association
   b. the John Howard Society
   c. the Pennsylvania Prison Society
   d. the Vera Institute of Justice
   e. the Fortune Society

9. Which one of the following is NOT one of Allen and Simonsen's "Big Four" cities that operate prisons for adult felons?
    a. Cook County (Chicago)
    b. Houston
    c. New York City
    d. Washington, D.C.
    e. Philadelphia

10. In calling the issue of privacy in prison "almost an oxymoron," the authors are suggesting that:
    a. prisoners should be supervised more closely
    b. prisoners have almost no right to privacy
    c. prisoners spend too much time alone
    d. almost all prisoners have trouble getting along with other people
    e. no one wants to die in prison

True or False

_____ 11. Most convicted felons serving prison terms are in the custody of the states.

_____ 12. The trend today is toward increasing the percentage of inmates confined in maximum security.

_____ 13. Each state has at least one maximum security prison housing unit.

_____ 14. The Auburn penitentiary is considered the model of the modern American maximum security prison.

_____ 15. More than half of all offenders in prison have been sentenced at least twice before.

_____ 16. Classification is an action taken with a prisoner just prior to his release from prison.

_____ 17. Drug offenders serve longer prison terms than any other class of offenders.

_____ 18. With the continuing expansion of state prison systems, prison overcrowding is no longer considered a serious problem.

_____ 19. Most of the medium security prisons in use today have been built within the past 30 years.

_____ 20. The term "security threat group" is most commonly applied to international terrorists who have been convicted of political crimes.

Fill In the Blanks

21. The two states with the largest numbers of inmates confined in their prison systems are _____ and _____ .

22. The process through which the American Correctional Association determines that a prison is meeting the accepted policy and procedural standards of the correctional field is known as _____ .

23. The institution called the first penitentiary in the United States was located in the city of _____ .

24. The average age of the state prison population in 1992 was about _____ years of age.

25. Other than its large size, the most distinctive feature of Jeremy Bentham's panopticon was its _____ .

26. William Nagel has suggested that the American penitentiary was created to test the theory that confinement could accomplish _____.

27. The administration of corrections at the state level is the responsibility of an organization most often called the _____.

28. The prohibition against "cruel and unusual punishment" often used as the basis of inmate lawsuits against the prison is found in the _____ Amendment to the Constitution.

29. When the prisoner first enters the custody of the state, he is usually sent to a reception center to undergo a process called _____.

30. The old penitentiaries built in the 1800s were intended to house inmates under _____ security conditions.

Matching

_____ 31. The grade of security just under maximum security on the scale.

_____ 32. The name for the big factory prisons that developed by the early 1900s.

_____ 33. The general term for the grounds for prison lawsuits under the Eighth Amendment's "cruel and unusual punishment" clause.

_____ 34. A large glass-topped prison designed by Jeremy Bentham.

_____ 35. The English institution often called the first penitentiary for its new principles.

_____ 36. What has become the predominant concern of the prison classification process.

_____ 37. The idea that less secure prisons are made to appear more secure to appease the public.

_____ 38. What the first penitentiaries represented, in the context of punishments of the time.

_____ 39. The modern professional organization that evolved from the National Prison Congress of 1870.

_____ 40. Allen and Simonsen's term for why the corrections system is so difficult to analyze and manage effectively.

a. maximum security prisons
b. close/high security prisons
c. medium security prisons
d. minimum security prisons
e. "cosmetic" security
f. human resource organization
g. alternative to death
h. Thomas Beever
i. Gaol at Wymondham
j. Pennsylvania Prison Society
k. *Prison Journal*
l. Jeremy Bentham
m. panopticon
n. industrial prison
o. agricultural prison

p. work camps
q. security threat group (STG)
r. supermax prison
s. Big Four
t. Cook County Department of Corrections
u. New York City Department of Corrections
v. Washington, D.C., Department of Corrections
w. Philadelphia Prison System
x. privacy
y. cruel and unusual punishment
z. conditions of confinement
aa. initial classification
bb. institutional needs
cc. American Correctional Association
dd. accreditation

Discussion

41. Give a brief profile of the inmates confined in state prisons.

42. Explain the purposes associated with each of the major levels of security you would find in a typical state prison system.

43. How did the model of the American penitentiary develop?

44. Why is the classification process so important to the inmate?

45. A state legislator says, "We ought to make all prisons maximum security again." What criticisms can you direct at his proposal?

46. Explain what Allen and Simonsen mean about the difficulties of managing corrections as a "human resource organization."

CHAPTER TEN

The Federal System

CHAPTER OBJECTIVES

The Federal Bureau of Prisons confines felons convicted of federal crimes; it also houses pre-trial defendants in federal jails in several large cities. It is a newer, well-financed system that in many ways is a model of how a prison system ought to operate. But it has suffered from many of the same problems that state systems have in recent years, as an influx of drug offenders has strained its capacity to effectively manage its inmate population. After reading the material in this chapter, you should be familiar with:
  1. the early history of federal prisons.
  2. the establishment of the Bureau of Prisons.
  3. recent changes in federal prison policy.
  4. the different types of federal prisons.
  5. federal prison industries.
  6. the changing nature of the federal prison population.

KEY TERMS AND CONCEPTS

Federal Bureau of Prisons
Justice Department
Fort Leavenworth
McNeil Island
Atlanta
U.S. penitentiary
Alderson
Sanford Bates
Alcatraz
Oakdale
Mariel boatlift
master plan
gender-neutral
unit management

medical model
regional offices
minimum security
low security
medium security
high security
administrative security
Federal Prison Industries, Inc.
UNICOR
mandatory literacy
CCOs
"cream of criminals"
U.S. Sentencing Commission

CHAPTER SUMMARY

Early Federal Prisons

The **Federal Bureau of Prisons** was created by an act of Congress signed into law by President Herbert Hoover on May 14, 1930. It was established as an office within the federal **Justice Department**, where it remains today. Before this legislation was enacted, there were federal prisons but no central office managing them; before the first federal prison was opened in the 1890s, there were federal prisoners but they served their time in state and local institutions.

95

At one time there were few federal crimes and few criminals serving federal prison time. After the Civil War, the numbers of both offenses and offenders began to climb. Many state prisons and local jails that had previously housed federal prisoners experienced overcrowding problems, and it became more difficult to place federal prisoners in these facilities. In 1891 Congress authorized the construction of three prisons. The first **U.S. penitentiary** was the old military prison at **Fort Leavenworth**, Kansas, which began to house federal prisoners in 1895. **McNeil Island**, Washington, an older prison already in use, was designated a U.S. penitentiary in 1907. The third penitentiary, **Atlanta**, was the first newly-constructed federal prison. It opened in 1899. In the 1920s Congress authorized a reformatory for young men at Chillicothe, Ohio, and the first federal prison for women at **Alderson**, West Virginia.

The Bureau of Prisons Is Born

Institutions were being added one at a time, but no overall plan existed. A U.S. House Special Committee in 1929 studied federal corrections and made a series of recommendations, one of which was to establish a centralized administration of federal prisons at the bureau level. In May of the next year, the Bureau of Prisons was officially created. Prison building continued at a quick pace during the thirties. The first director of the Bureau of Prisons, **Sanford Bates**, was widely regarded as one of the most progressive prison officials of the time. Under his leadership, other penitentiaries, jails, and a hospital were built. The old military prison on Alcatraz Island in San Francisco Bay was converted to confine civilian prisoners; **Alcatraz** became the first "supermax" prison, though its reputation for both the meanness of its clientele and the impossibility of escape was always exaggerated.

The BOP, as it was known in correctional circles, developed into a first-class organization. With its history of strong directors, men like James V. Bennett, Myrle E. Alexander, and Norman Carlson, it had professional leaders of vision and character. It was insulated from the political instability that plagued many state systems, where philosophies and priorities changed every time the governor's office changed hands. Its employees, from prison guards up to wardens, enjoyed strong civil service protection; they were career people. And with the financial resources of the federal government, the BOP could afford the best-- in facilities, equipment, programs, and staff. Its operation was much admired by state departments of corrections, who were always borrowing its ideas and trying to steal its people away.

Recent Policy Changes

Federal prisons have often been referred to as "country club prisons." The popular conception, never really valid, was that federal prisons were too nice, and that federal prisoners were mostly white-collar offenders-- the "**cream of criminals**." Some federal prisons might have tennis courts and picnic tables, but they also had cells and guard towers, and through the early 1980s more federal inmates were doing time for bank robbery than for any other crime. Federal prisons are still nicer than most state prisons, particularly because they are newer prisons, but they are hardly country clubs. Their clientele has changed, too. Today almost two of every three federal offenders are doing time for drug offenses. The neoclassical ideology that has prompted an unprecedented expansion of state prison systems has made its effects known in the federal system as well. From just over 20,000 inmates in the early 1970s, the federal system has grown to hold an estimated 140,000 inmates in custody by the year 2000.

The Bureau of Prisons has long had in effect a **master plan**--a set of principles establishing the direction in which it wished to be moving. It still follows this plan--which is revised periodically--today. The Bureau administers almost 100 separate facilities from its central office in Washington, D.C., and six **regional offices**. Its current prison management model includes these features:

    1. **unit management**, in which the larger prisons are broken down into smaller operating units, and security, treatment, and other staff are expected to work closely together within these autonomous units.

    2. **mandatory literacy**, starting with the target of sixth grade literacy in 1983 and increased to high

school equivalency in 1991. Inmates must participate in literacy training to get better work assignments within the federal prison system.

3. **gender-neutral** hiring, in which women are hired for all staff positions in every institution solely on their perceived ability to do the job.

4. deemphasis on the **medical model**, which had been the brainchild of long-time director James V. Bennett, with the substitution of a more balanced approach combining rehabilitation, deterrence, retribution, and incapacitation.

5. increased training of correctional staff and improved working conditions.

6. expanding the prison system to keep up with the steady increase of new inmates.

Despite its best efforts, the Bureau of Prisons has suffered the pains of too-rapid growth. Several institutions, especially the older, larger prisons, have been badly overcrowded for a long time. Drug offenders, many of whom are lower class minorities, have brought their own brand of problems to the federal system. The two federal prisons at Oakdale, Louisiana, and Atlanta suffered major riots in 1987. In both institutions Cuban inmates--at **Oakdale**, those awaiting deportation and at Atlanta, those serving federal prison sentences--rioted for a most curious reason: They wanted to stay in federal prisons rather than being sent back to Cuba. Many of the rioting inmates had come to the U.S. in the **Mariel Boatlift** of 1980, involuntarily deported from Cuba as undesirables; many did not want to go home. The Oakdale riot destroyed most of the Alien Deportation Center, which was rebuilt as a regular prison (and then the deportation center rebuilt next door). The BOP has wanted to close all three of its original penitentiaries but has so far been able to shut down only McNeil Island, which the State of Washington is now using as a prison. Atlanta and Leavenworth remain very much a part of the system--and are also very much overcrowded.

A Model Inmate Classification System

Since 1979 the Bureau of Prisons has used a five-level security classification system for inmates. From lowest to highest, with inmate-to-staff ratios decreasing steadily up the line, the levels are:

1. **minimum security**. These are the federal prison camps, usually located adjacent to other federal prisons or military bases.

2. **low security**. Called federal correctional institutions (FCIs), these prisons feature double fences and dormitory housing.

3. **medium security**. These FCIs have stronger perimeters, cell housing, and greater internal control over prisoners.

4. **high security**. These are the U.S. penitentiaries (USPs), which look very much like everyone else's penitentiaries.

5. **administrative security**. This category includes special-purpose inmates, such as illegal aliens awaiting deportation and medical cases. It also includes the few hundred federal prisoners held in extended lockdown in the two supermax federal prisons--Marion, Illinois, and Florence, Colorado. Marion was built to replace Alcatraz in the 1960s, and Florence was built in the 1990s to handle the overflow from Marion.

The federal system's classification philosophy is to place inmates in the least restrictive security level in the institution closest to home. In 1999, almost two out of three federal inmates were confined in either low (36%) or minimum (27%) security.

UNICOR: Federal Prison Industries, Inc.

One of the features the federal prison system has long been known for is its work program. **Federal Prison Industries, Inc.**, operating under the corporate name **UNICOR**, is an industry operating within federal prisons. Prisoners work at many different kinds of jobs, for which they are paid reduced hourly wages, making products for use by the military and by federal offices all over the world. UNICOR also offers hundreds of occupational training programs in various trades throughout the system. In contrast to the state prison inmates who often complain of idleness and "make-work" job assignments, the federal system employs its inmates in productive labor and keeps them busy with educational, rehabilitative, and recreational programs when they are not on the job. The federal system stresses that inmates are expected to use their time productively--to help others and to help themselves. Federal prisons have the resources to see that prisoners are provided with such opportunities.

Community Corrections in the Federal System

The Bureau of Prisons is responsible for many pre-trial and convicted offenders who are not in federal prisons. One of the tenets of its master plan is that program alternatives should be available for offenders not in confinement. Offenders in this category are managed through 33 community corrections offices (**CCOs**) spread across the country. Each CCO has a community corrections manager, whose job it is to deal with contract agencies such as local jails, halfway houses, prerelease centers, and other organizations-- both public and private--that provide services to federal offenders outside of prison. Community-based alternatives have not been emphasized in the federal system until recently, and changes in sentencing practices have restricted the authority of federal judges to use intermediate sanctions in lieu of confinement, but the BOP is expanding new options as best it can within these legal limitations.

Changing Population of Federal Institutions

The nature of the federal prison population has changed significantly over the past 15 years. Three of every ten federal inmates are foreigners, from Mexico and Central and South America foremost, but really from around the world. A visit to a federal prison is like attending a session of the Criminal United Nations. Far more illegal aliens are held in detention awaiting deportation, some of them Cubans in custody for almost two decades. The "war on drugs" has brought into the federal system a large number of drug users and street-level drug dealers who would once have gone to state prisons. These offenders bring with them their medical problems and the gang affiliations they had on the outside. As the profile of federal inmates has become more like that of state inmates, violence has become an increasing threat in federal prisons.

Another feature complicating imprisonment over the past decade is the sentencing guidelines adopted by the **U.S. Sentencing Commission** in 1985. These guidelines have limited the use of probation for federal offenders and increased the length of sentences applied to many offenders, particularly those convicted of crimes of violence and drug offenses, by narrowing the sentencing discretion of federal judges. Federal good-time provisions have been changed as well; inmates sentenced now will serve 85 percent of their actual sentence, getting no more than 15 percent sentence reduction for good behavior. The federal system abolished parole in the 1980s, but most judges now impose a condition called "supervised release" on offenders after their release from secure custody. Supervised release, performed by federal probation officers, is practically identical in its effects to parole; it just happens to be imposed by the court instead of by a discretionary parole board.

Changes in public policy enacted as changes in federal law have resulted in a 700 percent increase in the federal prison population in the last three decades. There is no end to this expansion in sight. Federal prisons remain well above 100% capacity at present, and new prisons are being built as fast as Congress appropriates the funds. The federal prison system is still looked to as a leader in the corrections field, but today it is no less driven by the same punitive mood that affects state corrections systems. Good management can only do so much to counterbalance hard sentencing. The Bureau of Prisons will be in an expansion mode for at least the next decade.

SELF TEST

Multiple Choice

1. The first federal penitentiary was located at:
   a. Lewisburg, Pennsylvania
   b. El Reno, Oklahoma
   c. Fort Leavenworth, Kansas
   d. Marion, Illinois
   e. Springfield, Missouri

2. Four of the following were federal laws adopted in the early 1900s that brought more prisoners into federal institutions. Which one was NOT?
   a. Dyer Act of 1919
   b. Hawes-Cooper Act of 1929
   c. Volstead Act of 1918
   d. White Slave Act of 1910
   e. Harrison Narcotic Act of 1914

3. The Mariel group of federal prisoners is most closely associated with which one of the following?
   a. prison riots in two institutions a decade ago
   b. a prison literacy program that started in 1983
   c. the federal death penalty
   d. a contemporary religious movement sweeping through the federal prison system
   e. a terrorist group that carries out attacks against prison guards

4. Which model was officially deemphasized by the Bureau of Prisons after 1975?
   a. brutality
   b. work
   c. medical
   d. counseling
   e. confinement

5. For which category of offenses are the most prisoners confined in federal prisons today?
   a. robbery
   b. white-collar
   c. interstate theft
   d. homicide
   e. drugs

6. In which security classification are the largest number of federal prison inmates confined?
   a. minimum
   b. low
   c. medium
   d. high
   e. supermax

7. Linda Allen is best known as:
   a. the wife of the "Birdman of Alcatraz"
   b. the first woman warden of a federal prison
   c. the originator of the social casework model in federal prisons
   d. a lawyer who represents illegal aliens in federal custody
   e. the first female correctional officer in a high-security federal prison

99

8. In which federal department is the Bureau of Prisons located?
    a. State
    b. Interior
    c. Treasury
    d. Justice
    e. Health and Human Services

9. A small number of federal inmates are housed in state prisons; the most common reason for this is:
    a. They asked for it.
    b. They are protection cases.
    c. There is no room in federal prisons.
    d. They are in programs the federal prison system cannot provide.
    e. The federal system could not control them.

10. For the inmate, the best reason to participate in the federal prison's literacy program is that participation is directly tied to:
    a. early release
    b. conjugal visiting
    c. better food
    d. trusty status
    e. work assignments

True or False

_____ 11. The federal prison system was established before any state prison systems were in existence.

_____ 12. The federal system has announced plans to do away with its high security penitentiaries as being unnecessary to maintaining adequate control over prisoners.

_____ 13. The Oakdale federal prison is best known as the replacement for Alcatraz.

_____ 14. Congress has done away with the Bureau of Prison's "master plan" as being too kind to inmates.

_____ 15. Only those inmates who volunteer are given work assignments in the federal prison system.

_____ 16. The first federal prison for women opened at Alderson, West Virginia, in 1927.

_____ 17. One of the greatest limitations of the federal prison system is that it has no hospital facilities for sick inmates.

_____ 18. The unit management system used in federal prisons means that the prison is broken up into smaller, semiautonomous operating units featuring a team management approach.

_____ 19. A federal prison camp is a minimum-security institution.

_____ 20. The classification philosophy of the BOP is to start the inmate off in the most secure placement available as far away from his home as possible.

Fill In the Blanks

21. The Federal Bureau of Prisons was officially established by an act of Congress signed into law by President Herbert Hoover in the year _____.

22. FCIs would basically provide either _____ security or _____ security.

23. Of minimum, low, medium, and high security classifications, the smallest number of inmates are in _____ security.

24. To complete the BOP's mandatory literacy program, the inmate must be functioning at what grade level? _____

25. FCI Danbury, FCI Butner, FPC Alderson, and FCI Dublin are alike in that all house what demographic group of federal offenders? _____

26. The organization responsible for adopting the sentencing guidelines used by the federal courts is the _____.

27. The largest number of foreign citizens in federal prisons come from the country of _____.

28. Alcatraz and Leavenworth are alike in that both were used as _____ prisons before they became part of the federal prison system.

29. The most destructive prison riots in federal prison history took place in 1987 at the prisons located in _____ and _____.

30. The basic training requirement of new federal correctional officers is that they must complete _____ weeks of formal training shortly after being hired.

Matching

_____ 31. Several thousand Cubans who later ended up in federal custody entered the United States during this flotilla.

_____ 32. An unfenced federal institution where inmates lived in dormitories and worked at the military base next door would be this security level.

_____ 33. The first director of the Federal Bureau of prisons.

_____ 34. The level of security that would be applied to someone who was so dangerous and escape-prone that he had to be kept in permanent lockdown.

_____ 35. If you picked up an item that had been manufactured in a federal prison, it should be marked with this corporate symbol.

_____ 36. The idea--no longer valid--that the federal prison system held only the most elite offenders.

_____ 37. The offices that supervise federal offenders not confined in federal prisons.

_____ 38. The term for an institution that would house an inmate classified in high security.

_____ 39. The Bureau of Prison's statement of its long-term policy objectives.

_____ 40. The term that refers to the educational policy applicable to federal prisoners.

a. Federal Bureau of Prisons
b. Justice Department
c. Fort Leavenworth
d. McNeil Island
e. Atlanta
f. U.S. penitentiary
g. Alderson
h. Sanford Bates
i. Alcatraz
j. Oakdale
k. Mariel boatlift
l. master plan
m. gender-neutral
n. unit management

o. medical model
p. regional offices
q. minimum security
r. low security
s. medium security
t. high security
u. administrative security
v. Federal Prison Industries, Inc.
w. UNICOR
x. mandatory literacy
y. CCOs
z. "cream of criminals"
aa. U.S. Sentencing Commission

Discussion

41. How are federal prison inmates different from state prison inmates?

42. As an inmate, how is federal prison life different from state prison life?

43. Why was the Federal Bureau of Prisons created?

44. What is the importance of Federal Prison Industries, Inc.?

45. How has the management of federal prisons become more complicated over the past 15 years?

46. Briefly outline the different security levels used in the federal prison system.

CHAPTER ELEVEN

Private Sector Systems

CHAPTER OBJECTIVES

Privately operated correctional facilities and services have long been important in providing community-based, non-secure alternatives for adults and juveniles, and in providing selected services within institutions. But over the last 15 years, private corrections has moved aggressively into the business of confinement-- now operating close to two hundred private prisons, jails, and juvenile institutions, with more coming on line every year. Privatization is among the most controversial issues in corrections today. After reading the material in this chapter, you should be familiar with:

1. the early history of private enterprises in corrections.
2. treatment services often privately provided.
3. the recent expansion of private prisons.
4. the arguments for and against private prisons.
5. the evaluation of private prisons to date.
6. privately managed juvenile facilities.

KEY TERMS AND CONCEPTS

private for-profit
private nonprofit
charitable organizations
contractors
Correctional Recovery Academy
CiviGenics
convict leasing
"slaves of the master"
employer model
privatization
technologies for surveillance
low-security custodial facilities

electronic monitoring
growth industry
punishment for profit
correctional/industrial complex
monetary colonization of criminal justice
correctional complex
corporate demon
Corrections Corporation of America
Wackenhut Corrections Corporation
consequential risks
self-insured
Esmor Correctional

CHAPTER SUMMARY

The Private Sector in Community Corrections

The involvement of the private sector in corrections is far from a new idea. In the community, private persons and organizations have operated residential facilities for both juveniles and adults and have provided other non-residential services such as counseling, monitoring, treatment, and medical care. There have been three main forms of private involvement:

103

1. **private for-profit**. A few halfway houses and many drug and alcohol treatment facilities are operated for the profit of their owners. Many individual service providers--such as therapists and counselors--simply contract or bill for their services, often at an hourly rate.

2. **private nonprofit**. This is a corporation organized to perform a specific function, such as operating a work release facility for inmates completing state prison sentences. The corporation is managed by a board of directors that gets no income from their civic work.

3. **charitable organizations**. Often a branch of a larger national organization, such as the Salvation Army or Boys Town, this organization usually has a broader funding base and operates a network of related programs.

Above the community level, many other individuals and organizations are corrections **contractors**. They contract with jails or prisons to provide services the institutions either cannot or do not want to provide--often because the service is only part-time or because no one at the institution is able to provide it. Examples would include medical care, psychiatric treatment, specific types of counseling, education and vocational training, and food service. Allen and Simonsen discuss the operation of the **Correctional Recovery Academy**, a program operated by **CiviGenics**, a private corrections corporation headquartered in Massachusetts. CiviGenics has expanded nationwide to become the leading privately operated business offering program alternatives to imprisonment. Correctional Recovery Academy is an intensive, privately operated therapeutic program intended to prevent criminal relapse among inmate-addicts. In this and many other ways, public funds have been used to pay people in the private sector for their corrections services for many years.

Some Historical Considerations

The role of the private sector in corrections has not always been a happy story. Early English sheriffs were essentially profiteers who operated their jails to make money from the fees charged inmates. In this country, as long as we have had penitentiaries we have had people trying to make a profit from prison labor. Private businesses once operated factories within prison walls and contracted for prison labor. This is a practice similar to the so-called **employer model** of today, in which businesses move production centers to prisons and hire prisoners to work in them. **Convict leasing**, primarily in the South, rented out convicts to private lessees, who in effect owned the convicts lock, stock, and barrel. Convict leases--in which mostly black inmate populations labored as "**slaves of the master**" at agricultural labor, railroad building, levee building, cutting trees, building roads, indeed any form of labor they were directed to by the private businessmen who owned them--lasted into the early years of the twentieth century. Local jail inmates labored on private property at the direction of their sheriffs until very recently. The exploitation of prison labor for the profit of prison officials, politicians, and sharp businessmen is a principal reason for the poor image of privatization in corrections today. Mention "**privatization**" and people immediately think of profiteering, politics, and penal servitude. They forget about the involvement of many private businessmen, such as John Augustus in Boston, who worked to help individual offenders, and the role private organizations have played in community corrections.

More Recent Developments in Privatization

In recent years privatization has been argued mostly as an issue in its application to secure custody, especially medium and maximum security jails and prisons. There has been an increase in private operation of facilities at these levels of security. But the principal impact of privatization in corrections has been felt in other applications, most notably:
    1. treatment programs.
    2. **low-security custodial facilities** and non-secure residential settings.
    3. **technologies for surveillance** of offenders not incarcerated.

Private sector treatment programs can be either residential or non-residential. Many are directed at chronic substance abusers. Adolescents are most often the targeted clientele, particularly for those "life experience" programs that remove young offenders from familiar environments and place them in wilderness areas. Many of the programs for adults feature a combination of job training, social skills, and a practical treatment modality, such as transactional analysis or reality therapy. By contracting with public agencies, these programs can in theory be precisely matched with the perceived needs of the offenders who are referred to them for treatment.

Low-security custodial facilities are the greatest part of the institutional business of private corrections. Private management firms have concentrated on low security and minimum security prisons; they have also targeted other short-term residential facilities providing work release, prerelease, and other functions in the community.

Private contractors have also moved quickly into the application of surveillance and control technologies. Private drug-testing labs support many community-based corrections programs. A number of electronics firms offer **electronic monitoring** devices--everything from bracelets to home video monitors with breath-testing capabilities--to suit many levels of supervision. In some jurisdictions, the monitoring itself is done by private firms who contract with the courts and work under the direction of the local probation and parole office.

The Era of Expansion of Privatization

Twenty years ago there were no privately operated secure correctional facilities in America. Today there are nearly 200, with steady expansion planned for the next several years. Two percent of the prisoner population was confined in privately operated facilities in 1995, with an increase to about six percent projected by the year 2000. And the number of non-secure facilities, treatment programs, and independent contractors has dramatically increased as well. What is responsible for this boom in private corrections?

The most obvious circumstance is that the corrections system itself has gotten huge in the past 25 years. Starting in the early 1970s, corrections has become a major **growth industry**. If you had bought corrections stock three decades ago, your investment would have multiplied several times over by now. Most of the growth of corrections has occurred in the public sector, and it has taken place without any apparent effect on the crime problem in America. This has focused attention on two major corrections related issues: cost and management effectiveness. Why does corrections cost so much to accomplish so little? The American people are constitutionally very skeptical about services provided by government and they believe just as strongly in the superiority of private enterprise.

It seems natural that corporations, many of which were already involved in selling equipment and security technology to correctional facilities, and private investors, many of them former political officials and corrections officials with expertise in the field, would come forth to argue two basic points:
    1. Corrections can be better managed by private initiative than it has been by the public bureaucracy.
    2. Substantial cost savings, in the range of 10 to 15 percent, can result from privatization.

Critics, including political officials, corrections officials, and social scientists, have been quick to respond. They most often attack the motivation of **punishment for profit** and cite the danger of a **correctional/industrial complex** that promotes public policies to continue the growth of the corrections industry. How does corrections grow? By bringing more people into the system. How does it operate more cheaply? By cost-cutting measures, particularly those that have to do with the levels of services and staffing, which are the most significant parts of the correctional budget. In much the same way that the military/industrial complex is blamed for the perpetuation of the Vietnam War, the **correctional complex** is blamed for the continuation of the "War on Crime." War is always good for business.

Critics sometimes conjure up images of a **corporate demon** (Charles W. Thomas's term), scheming in the boardroom to keep the public afraid of crime, to keep politicians passing new laws getting tougher on criminals, to keep widening the net of offenders brought under formal control, and to keep locking up more offenders in secure facilities. Robert Lilly and Mathieu DeFlem, in their article "Profit and Penality: An Analysis of the Corrections-Commercial Complex," warn of the **monetary colonization of criminal justice**. Profit supersedes human values, and economic interests drive justice decisions.

Correctional Privatization: Issues and Evidence

The proponents of privatization strongly resist efforts to portray them as the dark side of the force. They point out, first, that government and not private entrepreneurs establishes corrections priorities, and, second, that they are only an alternate means to achieving public goals. "It's worth a try," they would say. "Let's experiment to see if private corrections can operate better than public corrections." Though some may argue that the involvement of private contractors looking for public bucks drives net-widening, placing minor offenders under greater social controls, no one has seriously attacked the role of private corrections in providing community-based non-custodial services or specific called-for services within institutions. What the opponents of privatization focus on is the private operation of secure prisons and jails.

The foundation for private operation of secure prisons was laid in 1983 with the formation of **Corrections Corporation of America** (CCA) in Nashville, Tennessee. CCA made a bid to take over the operation of the Tennessee prison system, which the state rejected. CCA went ahead with its plans to operate secure prisons, if not a whole system then one prison at a time. More than a decade later, it remains the largest private prison operator in America; it is about twice the size of **Wackenhut Corrections Corporation** (WCC), its nearest competitor. Together CCA and Wackenhut dominate the private prison business, but they have a growing number of competitors. More than a dozen other corporations operate private prisons, most of them with only a few units each but with plans for future expansion.

Several important questions were asked as corporations made bids and signed contracts to build and operate prisons as a private enterprise:
    1. Is it legal?
    2. Will public bodies take the **consequential risks** of contracting with private businesses to operate prisons which are already so litigation-prone?
    3. Will private operation save money?
    4. Will the services provided be comparable to those provided by publicly operated organizations?
    5. Will cost savings results in a decrease of service levels?
    6. Will private corrections only work in certain types of settings--such as the lower security facilities?

The preliminary results, after a decade of private prison operations, suggest that some of the early concerns were unfounded. Litigation in privately operated prisons occurs no more often (and usually less often) than in public prisons. These prisons have been able to maintain liability insurance coverage or to maintain **self-insured** status to cover liability claims. No overall decline of services has occurred. Private prisons do seem to operate more cheaply than public prisons, though the difference is not as great as some of the advocates of privatization had hoped for. Management problems have occurred in some facilities, but management problems occur in public prisons, too. Wardens get fired and key staff members are replaced in public prisons. The same things happen in private prisons.

To the proponents of privatization, the first decade of private prisons has been encouraging. About two-thirds of the states have at least one privately operated secure facility for adults, led by Texas with 43 and California with 24. Private operators have moved to larger prisons, with Wackenhut opening a 2,200 bed prison in New Mexico. They have also moved from lower security to higher security prisons, including a few maximum security prisons or maximum security units of multilevel prisons. The bulk of the privately operated institutions are low or minimum security, but private corporations are confident enough of their track record now to go after contracts to operate higher security prisons as well. Private prisons still have a very small share of the market, but their outlook for the future is bullish. They would be happy to sell you stock if you are looking for a good investment.

The five publicly traded private management corporations (including CCA, Wackenhut, and **Esmor Correctional**) that operate secure facilities for juveniles (a total of 34 facilities housing over 4,300 juveniles in 15 states in 1996) believe that the increasing demand for more secure beds for juveniles will keep them in an expansion mode well into this century, particularly if serious juvenile crime increases at the rate predicted. This does indicate one important difference of perspective: public corrections officials say they want crime rates and incarceration rates to go down; if this should happen, private corrections would lose their contracts and go out of business. Unless by the time it happens, private corrections has the long-term track record to establish that privatization is both cheaper and more effective than public corrections, in which case it may be that public corrections may be the operation with the "going out of business" signs up. Private corporations are bullish on the future of corrections.

SELF TEST

Multiple Choice

1. Correctional recovery, the goal of the Correctional Recovery Academy, is the crimogenic equivalent of:
   a. corporal punishment
   b. higher education
   c. career enhancement
   d. psychotherapy
   e. addiction recovery

2. The worst abuses of convict leasing took place in which part of the country?
   a. the West
   b. New England
   c. the Midwest
   d. the South
   e. the Rocky Mountains

3. Allen and Simonsen suggest that the most important part of the business of private, for-profit contractors is:
   a. mental health facilities
   b. low-security custodial facilities
   c. maximum security prisons
   d. juvenile training schools
   e. local jails

4. The idea of the correctional/industrial complex refers to:
   a. the policy influences of corrections-connected companies
   b. a policy of more private usage of prison labor
   c. a giant prison housing all types of security levels
   d. the warped mental condition of the opponents of private prisons
   e. the lack of public control over private prison operations

5. In 1980, how many private jails and prisons were operating in America?
   a. 0
   b. 17
   c. 43
   d. 81
   e. 152

6. Two of the main fears opponents voiced about private prisons were increased litigation and:
    a. rampant homosexuality
    b. shoddy construction
    c. deficient services
    d. poor training
    e. staff racism and brutality

7. The oldest and largest private corrections corporation is:
    a. Prison Enterprises Group
    b. Secure America
    c. Lock and Key, Inc.
    d. Corrections Corporation of America
    e. Devil's Island Special Tours, Inc.

8. In his use of the term "corporate demon" Charles W. Thomas is suggesting that:
    a. the opponents of private prisons view them as evil
    b. private prisons will always be worse than public prisons
    c. the love of money is the root of all criminal behavior
    d. America's crime problem is not like that of any other country
    e. white collar criminals should be allowed to run prisons

9. Private prison management contracts have been awarded in only two nations other than the United States:
    a. Russia and China
    b. France and Italy
    c. Sweden and Norway
    d. Australia and the United Kingdom
    e. Colombia and Mexico

10. The "employer model" has the most application to:
    a. prison industries
    b. inmate social skills training
    c. private residential treatment facilities
    d. work furloughs
    e. halfway houses

True or False

_____ 11. In the 1980s, the state of Tennessee considered privatizing its entire adult prison system.

_____ 12. Allen and Simonsen argue that privatization of correctional services was a radical new idea that came out of the conservative think tanks in the 1980s.

_____ 13. By law, prison health care must be provided by doctors who are public employees.

_____ 14. If the prison operation is contracted to a private corporation, the government cannot be held legally responsible in any way for what happens within the prison.

_____ 15. Lilly and DeFlem argue that as a motivator for positive change in corrections, "Greed is good."

_____ 16. Private prisons have thus far been sued by inmates at a lower rate than public prisons have.

_____ 17. Houses of refuge were early shelters for female victims of domestic violence and their children.

_____ 18. There are at present no maximum security prisons that are privately operated.

_____ 19. The number of secure adult prison beds in private facilities almost tripled in the period from 1990 to 1999.

_____ 20. Two large corporations operate most of the private prisons in America.

Fill In the Blanks

21. CiviGenics is best known for founding the _____.

22. Allen and Simonsen suggest that electronic monitoring can supplement or replace _____ facilities.

23. The government's control over the private prison is exercised through the _____ that both parties sign to ratify their agreement.

24. The economic monolith formed by business interests and prisons is known by the term _____.

25. The state which has the most private prisons is _____.

26. Moore Haven and Middle Tennessee are examples of _____.

27. Of all types of correctional institutions, the greatest controversy is in regard to the privatization of _____ facilities.

28. Physicians, psychologists, or counselors who maintain a private practice while working part-time through an arrangement with a correctional institution would be called _____.

29. Allen and Simonsen suggest that the _____ between alternate service providers (public and private) is actually in the best interest of corrections.

30. Corrections Corporation of America is the largest private prison management firm. Number two and "trying harder" is _____.

Matching

_____ 31. A phrase suggesting that the profit motive can defeat the corrections organization's pursuit of humane reformative goals.

_____ 32. The legal position of inmates under the old system of convict leasing.

_____ 33. The potential legal and political dangers faced by public bodies who contract with private corporations to operate prisons.

_____ 34. The improper motive often ascribed to the operators of private prisons.

_____ 35. As control devices, what drug testing and electronic monitoring would be considered.

_____ 36. An old form of privatization once in fashion in the Southern states.

_____ 37. The term used today for a private business that would take its operation inside prison walls to hire convict workers.

_____ 38. The term a stockbroker might use in describing corrections as an enterprise over the past quarter-century.

_____ 39. The type of prison most important to the business operation of private prisons.

_____ 40. The evil business spirit responsible for all the ills blamed on the private prison.

a. private for-profit
b. private nonprofit
c. charitable organizations
d. contractors
e. Correctional Recovery Academy
f. CiviGenics
g. convict leasing
h. "slaves of the master"
i. employer model
j. privatization
k. technologies for surveillance
l. low-security custodial facilities
m. electronic monitoring
n. growth industry
o. punishment for profit
p. correctional/industrial complex
q. monetary colonization of criminal justice
r. correctional complex
s. corporate demon
t. Corrections Corporation of America
u. Wackenhut Corrections Corporation
v. consequential risks
w. self-insured
x. Esmor Correctional

Discussion

41. As a student of history, why might you be skeptical about the involvement of private business in corrections?

42. What main advantages of privatization did proponents of private prisons put forth?

43. Explain what the consequences of the correctional/industrial complex might be, if such a thing existed.

44. What role does the private sector play in the provision of intermediate sanctions?

45. What does Charles W. Thomas's analysis of the supposed ills of private corrections reveal?

46. If you were in charge of approving the contract with the operators of the first private prison in your state, what points would you be most insistent about?

CHAPTER TWELVE

Custody Functions and Tasks

CHAPTER OBJECTIVES

Maintaining secure custody of inmates is the most important function of a prison or jail. In a prison, more people work in custody or security than in all other functions combined. After reading the material in this chapter, you should be familiar with:

1. the importance of custody in a bureaucratic prison.
2. the correctional officer's role in maintaining secure custody.
3. how the inmate social system affects security.
4. the methods of secure custody in a prison.
5. reasons for conflict between custodial and treatment staff.

KEY TERMS AND CONCEPTS

bureaucratic control
custody
supermax custody
maximum custody
close custody
medium custody
minimum custody
general population
graduated release
"the Captain"
"screw"
correctional officer
turnover rate
bureaucratic-legal order
unionization
blue flu
total institutions
prisonization
prison gangs

lockdowns
the count
sally port
prison rules
preservice training
inservice training
contraband
frisk search
strip search
"keester"
body cavity search
shakedown
escape
electrified fence
paramilitary model
minimum critical staffing
unit team management
"use of force"

CHAPTER SUMMARY

Custody: A Twenty-Four-Hour Impact

From their origins as small, highly individualized institutions intent on salvation and humane penance, penitentiaries evolved into large, highly structured formal organizations intent on applying measures of **bureaucratic control** to hundreds or thousands of human beings. The modern prison is a prime example of Max Weber's characteristics of bureaucratic organization--hierarchical authority, job specialization, and formalized rules.

In the modern prison, the principal means of applying control is **custody**. Institutions are custody graded, with inmates classified from **supermax custody** at one extreme to open at the other, depending on the terms and practices of each state. The three most common custody grades are maximum, medium, and minimum. **Close custody** is sometimes added as a grade between maximum and medium. **Maximum custody** generally features inmates living in cells, a low inmate-to-guard ratio, very restricted movement by inmates, and the strictest security procedures. Maximum custody institutions are often the oldest and largest prisons, so they often have the high walls, guard towers, and steel-and-concrete construction we associate with Allen and Simonsen's "gothic monoliths" or medieval castles. **Medium custody** and **minimum custody** prisons are usually newer and smaller, with fences instead of walls. Medium and minimum custody have higher inmate-to-guard ratios, dormitory and room housing, more freedom of movement, less strict security, and easier access to the outside world. Minimum custody inmates are often called trusties (not trustees, who are financial overseers). Inmates at any custody level may be part of what is called the "**general population**," meaning the most open inmate society; but the closeness of supervision over the general population decreases as the custody level is reduced. Inmates typically start out at a higher level of custody and work their way down over time (or some go up and down over the years like an irregular pulse), heading for the least restrictive environment and "**graduated release**," allowing them reentry into the outside world. Custody shapes the inmate's passage through the prison system.

Correctional Officers and Jailers: On the Front Lines

The people who work in custody run the prison. In the old days, the chief guard was often called "**the Captain**." While the warden was a mythical political official on about the same level as God, the captain ran the prison day to day. He interacted with inmates, made assignments, disciplined and punished, and saw to it that the work got done. No one was sure what the warden did, but everyone saw the fruits of the captain's labor. Guards in the old-style prison had total power over inmates--and used it. The inmate nicknames for the guard--"**screw**," "**bull**," "**hack**"--express the adversarial nature of the guard/inmate relationship in the maximum custody penitentiary (and they express as well the contempt for the guards that marked the inmate subculture). Prisons were often located in rural areas. The guards were often farmers working in the prison to make ends meet. The convicts were most likely to be street criminals from the big city. These cultural differences were often heightened by differences of race and ethnicity as well. The old-style convict and the old-style prison guard were different in just about every way, except for two points: they were both on the bottom level of society, and neither of them wanted to be in prison.

The **correctional officer** of today is a different kind of animal from the guard of a hundred years ago. Correctional officers are men and women (20% of custodial officers in prison are women), white, black, and hispanic. They are better-educated than in the past, and thanks to civil service they are much more career oriented. Correctional officers in several states are unionized. **Unionization** has not been as strong in corrections as it has been in other public sector vocations, but it has thrown the fear of worker solidarity into prison administrators. Prison employee groups have sometimes used sick-outs or attacks of "**blue flu**" to support their demands for recognition or improved working conditions. Prison employees are not allowed to strike.

Prison administrators, for their part, want correctional officers to be better trained and more legally aware. They do not want to lose lawsuits and incur the wrath of politicians and public because of inept, brutal guards. All states have some requirement for **preservice training** for new correctional officers (the state average in 1998 was 232 hours), and requirements for **inservice training** have increased steadily also, averaging more than 40 hours per year. Despite the increasing professionalization of the correctional officer's role, the **turnover rate** for COs remains high. The simple truth is: prisons are unpleasant places to work, and many people cannot handle the work hours, the **bureaucratic-legal order**, with its premium on holding employees accountable for following detailed rules, and the tense relationships with inmates. The average annual turnover rate for prison custodial officers is about 12%, with some states having much higher rates. This is actually good news for COs in many places: The faster the turnover the better the opportunity to move up. Advancement opportunities in corrections, with the comparatively high turnover rate and the continuing expansion of the system to deal with overcrowding problems, make corrections an attractive career field for the time being.

Inmate Organization: The Social System

Prisons, especially maximum security penitentiaries, are **total institutions**. They take away individual responsibility and autonomy, which is what we need to operate in the outside world, and attempt to make the inmate completely submissive to prison authority and totally dependent on prison routine. Prisoners enter most prisons naked, without any possessions of their own. They are as dependent as newborn babies. Babies grow and mature, but prisoners will still be treated like babies--like very bad babies--years later. This infantilization of inmates is a serious limitation of the custodial approach in corrections. Inmates do not progress much while they remain infantilized.

The inmate subculture, at whatever strength it remains today, divides the prison into the keepers and the kept. The subculture opposes the dominant culture imposed by custody; it tries to work around the rules and procedures and maximize the inmates' pleasure and control over their own lives. They seek through the subculture what they are denied by the formal organization. **Prisonization**, or the adaptation to the subculture, not only affects inmates; it affects correctional officers as well. They must learn to get along with the inmates in a long-term relationship. A career correctional officer will spend much more time locked up than most prisoners will.

The social system of the prison has been significantly effected in recent years by two circumstances. First, prisons in most states are at or over capacity. Overcrowding aggravates the natural conflicts that would occur in prison, it escalates tensions and the potential for violence, it gives prison officials fewer choices about how to place individual inmates (especially the ones who cause trouble), and it makes the task of keeping the prison safe and secure more difficult. Second, the rise of **prison gangs** has divided the social system into competing (sometimes warring) factions and further heightened the violence potential. Prison gangs are predominantly a problem in the Southwest, where hispanics are found in prison in greater numbers. The most influential gangs are the hispanic gangs with such names as the Mexican Mafia, Mexikanemi, Texas Syndicate, and Nostra Familia. Whites, in the omnipresent Aryan Brotherhood, and blacks, in gangs typically associated with Crips and Bloods street gangs, often organize to protect their own interests in the conflict with the hispanic gangs. Prison gangs demand a lifetime commitment, and death is said to be the only way out. Most prison violence occurs for personal reasons that have nothing to do with gang affiliation, but those states that have serious gang problems recognize that inter-gang and intra-gang conflicts make the problem of prison violence worse.

Custody as a Way of Life

The deputy warden for custody (or security) remains a very important figure in the daily life of the modern prison. He has more people under his authority than any other prison official below the warden. The custodial staff have many devices and techniques available to them as they attempt to maintain secure control of inmates. Among these measures are:

1. **the count**. The most important task of the custodial staff, according to Allen and Simonsen, is counting inmates to determine their whereabouts. The count goes in to a control center, and it must be verified. Until it is, prison life stops. The frequency of counting varies with the prison and the custody level.

2. the **sally port**. Basically a double gate, a sally port is used to control vehicle and pedestrian traffic into a prison. Only one gate can be open at a time; in theory prison security is always maintained.

3. **prison rules**. Usually provided to the newly arrived inmate in a handbook during classification or orientation, the rules define categories of offenses, disciplinary actions, and grievance procedures. Prisoners in violation of the rules may get a report, sometimes called a "write-up" or a "ticket." Serious incidents, such as "**use of force**" events, always warrant a report for the file.

4. control of **contraband**. Contraband is anything not authorized by prison rules, including items that are allowed but of which the prison has too many: six spare batteries when only four are allowed. Contraband may come in through the mails, or it may be carried in by visitors or other inmates. Most contraband comes into prison through guards. Common contraband items smuggled in would include drugs, alcohol, pornography, weapons, and money.

5. searches. Three basic searching techniques prevail in prisons. The **frisk search** is most commonly used. It is a pat down search of the inmate's outer clothing. The **strip search** requires the inmate to remove his clothing so that both his body and the clothing can be inspected more closely. Inmates suspected of hiding contraband in their rectum--a practice called "keestering," meaning to hide in one's "**keester**"--may be subjected to a **body cavity search**, which is supposed to be done by medical personnel rather than a guard with a fat angry finger.

6. tool and key control. To prevent inmates from gaining access to items that could be used as weapons or as tools of escape. Inmate trusties or orderlies who once had keys, which allowed them to control access to other inmates and to supplies, no longer have them in the modern prison.

7. shakedowns. A **shakedown** is a search of an area, such as a cell or tier of cells, a dormitory, a work place, or a communal area such as the library, the dining hall, or the chapel. Any contraband item can be hidden anywhere in the prison. Prisons have shakedown crews of guards whose job it is to carry out thorough searches. Shakedown crews do not find everything, but they do contribute a lot of useful anxiety to prisoners with contraband in their possession.

8. walls and fences. Old prisons have walls; new prisons have fences, usually double fences topped with razor wire. Guards armed with rifles man towers that surveil stretches of wall or fence. Several states are using **electrified fences**, which can be as lethal as a rifle shot. This is called perimeter security to distinguish it from internal security within the walls.

9. **lockdowns**. A lockdown means that one or more inmates, from a cellblock to a dormitory to an entire prison, are confined to their living quarters for a period of time. This may often be done after an incident of violence or when trouble is anticipated. It is seen as a preventive measure. Extended lockdown is used to hold the most troublesome inmates in long-term isolation.

To the custodial staff, the worst event in prison is an **escape**. In the old days, when there were fewer guards and inmate trusties were often involved in helping maintain security, prison escapes were common. Now they are rare events, and most escapes are from minimum custody or open facilities where they are more like walkaways than breakouts. About three-quarters of escapees are recaptured quickly, picking up new criminal charges upon recapture.

Custodial Models

The history of custody in American prisons is the history of the **paramilitary model**. Guards wear uniforms and use military rank and like to imagine they are imposing military discipline. One of the traditions of this model is that custodial staff remain separate and apart from inmates. In American prisons, this has led to two key ideas:

1. custody rules. All facets of prison life, including treatment, are subordinate to the custody function. Custody prevails over all over functions. One important concept is that of **minimum critical staffing**, which means that sufficient numbers of custodial staff must be on duty to fill all critical posts,

even if correctional officers must be held overtime or called in from off duty. No such sense of obligation applies to the rehabilitation function.

      2. custodial staff only do custody. They guard; they don't help, advise, counsel, treat, or express any interest in the inmate as a human being. To them he is just a number, and all they are interested in is the numbers adding up to the right total.

Contemporary prisons have explored different approaches to getting the custodial staff and the staff providing rehabilitation, recreation, and other programs to work more effectively together. One approach pioneered in the federal prison system and now used in one form or another in many state systems is called **unit team management**. This approach breaks the prison up into quasi-autonomous parts, usually based around residential quarters. All the staff working in the unit report to one administrator. The idea is to break down barriers between specialists and get staff to take a broader role with inmates. Some correctional officers take well to this concept; many, schooled in the narrowest possible definition of their function, want no part of it. Custody and treatment remain more often adversaries than allies.

SELF TEST

Multiple Choice

1. Most prison wardens today would identify the principal objective in operating their prison as:
    a. rehabilitation
    b. secure custody
    c. deterrence
    d. retribution
    e. humanitarianism

2. Which of the following types of personal searches would be considered most invasive or intensive?
    a. frisk search
    b. metal detector
    c. strip search
    d. pat down
    e. body cavity search

3. Four of the following are important hispanic gangs in the Texas prison system. Which one is NOT?
    a. Texas Syndicate
    b. Raza Unida
    c. Aryan Brotherhood
    d. Mexikanemi
    e. Hermanos de Pistoleros Latinos

4. The turnover rate among correctional officers has averaged about _____ percent in recent years.
    a. 2
    b. 7
    c. 12
    d. 20
    e. 36

5. The principal purpose associated with use of the sally port is:
    a. to maintain a secure perimeter at all times
    b. to separate mentally ill offenders from the general population
    c. to train new guards
    d. to isolate gang members
    e. to search large areas, such as dormitories or cellblocks

6. A new approach, tried in the federal system and some state prisons, breaks large prisons down into smaller operating sections and tries to get all staff, regardless of specialization, to work cooperatively together. This approach is called:
    a. compartmentalization
    b. chain of command
    c. theory X
    d. unit team management
    e. vertical control

7. The "blue flu" is most closely associated with:
    a. inmate suicides
    b. perimeter security
    c. labor relations
    d. protective custody
    e. elderly inmates

8. To say that inmates are "infantilized" is to say that:
    a. guards get too close to inmates
    b. the prison offers too many programs
    c. prisoners spend too much time alone
    d. the prison treats inmates like children
    e. prisoners who fail to respond to treatment ought to stay in prison

9. California's recent technological application, intended to save personnel costs while maintaining perimeter security, focuses on the use of:
    a. robots patrolling with lasers
    b. highly sensitive radar
    c. electrified fences
    d. motion detectors
    e. escape-activated exploding neck collars on inmates

10. The requirement for preservice training of new correctional officers in the states is in the range of about how many total hours, on the average?
    a. fewer than 40
    b. 80 to 100
    c. 120 to 160
    d. 200 to 240
    e. 400 to 480

True or False

_____ 11. Custody has always been dominated by treatment in prison.

_____ 12. An inmate in maximum custody could not qualify to be a trusty.

_____ 13. Correctional officers are generally not allowed by law the right to strike as part of any labor union job action.

_____ 14. Most prison authorities would agree that prison gangs are declining in importance within the inmate social system.

_____ 15. Inmates who have abused drugs before coming to prison are generally less likely to violate prison rules than inmates who did not abuse drugs.

_____ 16. Until after World War II, the prison guard was usually an uneducated minority male from a poor urban neighborhood.

_____ 17. Allen and Simonsen suggest that security and custody have traditionally been the weakest parts of the correctional institution's operation.

_____ 18. One of the characteristics of bureaucracy is that the process is more important than the individual.

_____ 19. Correctional officer turnover rates dropped at one time but then increased again during the decade of the 1990s.

_____ 20. Medium custody and minimum custody prisons have exactly the same perimeter security; it is their internal security that is very different.

Fill In the Blanks

21. The level of immediate control exercised over offenders within correctional institutions is called _____.

22. The primary reason given for California's use of electrified fences is _____.

23. The old saying goes: "A prison is designed to be as strong as _____."

24. In the discussion of who should take command of the prison during a prison riot, the preferred choice seems to be _____.

25. Allen and Simonsen describe the prison management problem of a continuing adversarial relationship between custody and _____.

26. The practice of uniformed correctional officers taking sick leave en masse to back up their labor demands is called _____.

27. The authors describe two recent developments that have made custody's job of managing the inmate social system more difficult; these problems are _____ and _____.

28. The most important white prison gang in American prisons is the _____.

29. The most important task for which the custody staff is responsible is _____.

30. Of maximum, medium, and minimum security prisons, the greatest number of escapes occur from _____ security.

117

Matching

_____ 31. What might happen to you if you were suspected of "keestering" drugs.

_____ 32. The idea that prisons seek to completely dominate every facet of an inmate's existence.

_____ 33. The chief custodial officer in the old-style penitentiary.

_____ 34. A more general search of an area, such as a cellblock or a dormitory.

_____ 35. A custodial response that involves keeping inmates confined in their cells for extended periods of time.

_____ 36. A job action by public employees who are not allowed to strike.

_____ 37. The type of report that would be filed when a correctional officer had a physical confrontation with an inmate.

_____ 38. The rule-structured environment of the contemporary prison.

_____ 39. The environment an inmate would be assigned to if he were not under any type of special control measures.

_____ 40. The idea that inmates work their way down the levels of custody until they earn at least partial freedom again.

a. bureaucratic control
b. custody
c. supermax custody
d. maximum custody
e. close custody
f. medium custody
g. minimum custody
h. general population
i. graduated release
j. "the Captain"
k. "screw"
l. correctional officer
m. turnover rate
n. bureaucratic-legal order
o. unionization
p. blue flu
q. total institutions
r. prisonization
s. prison gangs

t. lockdowns
u. the count
v. sally port
w. prison rules
x. preservice training
y. inservice training
z. contraband
aa. frisk search
bb. strip search
cc. "keester"
dd. body cavity search
ee. shakedown
ff. escape
gg. electrified fence
hh. paramilitary model
ii. minimum critical staffing
jj. unit team management
kk. "use of force"

Discussion

41. How does the inmate social system work to undermine the efforts of the custody staff?

42. How do the principles of bureaucratic control apply within the prison setting?

43. Why was (and is today) the position of the deputy warden for custody so powerful?

44. What are the main custodial devices and techniques used to maintain security in a maximum custody prison?

45. What evidence can you cite of the prevalence of the "paramilitary model" in prison operations?

46. How is the makeup of the correctional officer work force different today from what it was half a century or longer ago?

CHAPTER THIRTEEN

Management and Treatment

CHAPTER OBJECTIVES

As a formal, complex organization, the prison presents unique management concerns, particularly in its efforts to balance the competing interests of custody and treatment. Uniformed correctional officers are the prison's most visible staff, but many other people not in uniform are need to perform the rehabilitative, administrative, and specialized functions necessary to the operation of a large prison today. A prison is like a small town: Every function or service that must be provided in a small town must be provided in prison also. After reading the material in this chapter, you should be familiar with:

1. The important themes of correctional management.
2. the problems of managing custody and treatment in prison.
3. prison health care and medical services.
4. religious services in prison.
5. prison academic education and job training programs.
6. important non-custody staff positions in a typical prison.
7. the functions of behavioral science professionals in prison.
8. the application of the reintegration model in prison programming.

KEY TERMS AND CONCEPTS

Sanford Bates
"model muddle"
treatment services
backfilling
autocracy
hierarchical management
George J. Beto
"control model"
gradualism approach
isolationism and withdrawal
James V. Bennett
"individualized treatment"
"special programs"
medical services
sick call
goldbrickers
hepatitis A and B
multidrug-resistant tuberculosis
plastic surgery

penitence
correctional chaplaincy
facility manager
food service manager
health system administrator
industrial specialist
medical officer
ombudsman
recreation specialist
teacher
functionally illiterate
Howard Gill
learning disabled
GED
Project Newgate
furlough
vocational training
prison industries
Prison Industries Enhancement Act (1979)

psychologist   caseworker
psychiatrist   counselor
sociologist   reintegration model
social worker

CHAPTER SUMMARY

The Treatment Model: Alive or Dead?

Correctional administration has come a long way from the days of the early penitentiary. The reformers who met to found the National Prison Congress in Cincinnati in 1870, remember, had to vote on a proposal to agree that "reformation and not vindictive suffering" should be the purpose of penal confinement. It took the lifetime efforts of such correctional administrators as **Sanford Bates**, the man who is called the father of modern penology for his work as director of the Federal Bureau of Prisons and other professional achievements covering half a century, to move prisons from the punitive to the rehabilitative era. The way has not always been clear. A "**model muddle**" has persisted for more than half a century, since the decline of the industrial prison, in regard to prison management. What is the prison supposed to do? How does the manager get the most out of the institution's staff? How democratic can prisons be in allowing participation by both staff and inmates? While custody must be maintained at a reasonable level, what can be done to enhance the effectiveness of treatment services within the prison setting?

We often use "treatment" and "rehabilitation" as synonymous terms. In the narrow definition, **treatment services**--such as counselling, casework, and therapy--are offered by the professional staff to change the behavior of prison inmates. Treatment is one part of rehabilitation, along with academic education, vocational training, recreation, religion, outside visitors, and inmate self-help activities. In its broadest definition, rehabilitation can be anything positive that happens to an inmate in prison, even if neither the institution nor the inmate knows what it is or how important it is at the time. There has been a kind of skepticism about the effectiveness of rehabilitation in the correctional setting for more than two decades. "What works?" Robert Martinson and his colleagues asked in 1974. "Nothing works," they replied, or at least, "Nothing works consistently enough to apply it across the board with any reasonable expectation of success."

We say that institutions gave up on treatment, but in fact treatment had always been incidental to secure custody in prison. Treatment got what was left after custody, administration, and work programs took their share of the budget. This typically amounted to no more than five percent to ten percent of the institution's budget, which is hardly a firm commitment to change. And even though we say we have given up on treatment, the portion of the budget devoted to rehabilitative services is greater in most prisons today than it was two decades ago. The medical model, as the most extreme form for the application of treatment, may be dead; correctional administrators' hopes for the possibility of changing criminal behavior into law-abiding behavior are far from dead. They are still seeking the right avenues for treatment, even if they do not talk about it as much as they once did.

Treatment is still custody's weak sister. Secure custody gets more resources and staff than all other functions added together. "Minimal critical staffing" must be maintained at all times. You cannot shut down the guard towers that provide perimeter security just because you do not have enough guards or because there is a flu epidemic. You call in off-duty guards or extend the hours of guards already on duty (the term is "**backfilling**") to fill the essential positions, pay them overtime, and take the money out of treatment services. The inmates will never miss the transactional analysis sessions they did not have, or the extra computer classes, or the job skills training for pre-release inmates. "You have to keep them in prison," the warden can point out, or nothing else matters. And the quickest way for him to get fired is to let some of them escape; no prison warden has ever been fired for failing to rehabilitate inmates. Indeed, after two centuries of locking up felons to serve prison terms, no one has a good idea as to whether or not prison wardens *can* rehabilitate inmates.

121

The domain of the prison warden of a century ago was described as an **autocracy**, meaning he ruled his institution with the authoritarian personal style of a dictator. He was not responsible to the courts or the public and was barely responsible to the politicians who put him in office. The autocratic management style has yielded to the more bureaucratic style of today, in which the prison is administered from a centralized state corrections bureaucracy. Prison wardens today are usually products of the system, people who have moved around from one institution to another and have no particular ties to any institution. Their personalities and philosophies do not mean as much as they did at an earlier time. The centralized bureaucracy defines important policies, procedures, and practices; the state legislature and the governor's office provide political guidance; and the courts provide you with customers and tell you how you must treat them in confinement.

The contemporary prison is characterized by **hierarchical management**. The formal organizational structure has managers at the top, supervisors in the middle, and operating staff at the bottom. Management is more broad based and diffuse, involving more specialists in different areas. The warden is more likely to see himself as a CEO, working with his management team in the traditional warden's role while also dealing actively with a host of outside forces, rather than as a general commanding an army of privates, some of whom are prison inmates and some of whom are prison guards, in isolation from the outside world, as would have been the case in the nineteenth century autocracy.

Allen and Simonsen suggest that correctional management continues to be dominated by three pervasive themes:

1. focus on the individual offender. Instead of looking at the community, the family, employment, or other parts of the world outside prison, managers try to make changes in the offender only, and within the prison rather than through community-based programs. This is probably because the offender is much more under their control, and it is easier, more convenient, and requires much less imagination to do so. It is also safer, reducing the risk of an offender in the community committing a crime.

2. a **gradualism approach** to change. Managers keep doing what they have always done, or when they do change they go in for fads because everybody else is doing so, not because anyone can say that the new is any better than the old. Then they fail to test and research effectiveness, continuing with what they have until the next fad comes along. They fail to direct change, instead letting other forces external to the prison direct them. They are more acted upon than actors.

3. **isolationism and withdrawal**. Managers keep low profiles. They seldom speak out on issues; rarely, except in the legislative forum, do they attempt to shape public policy. Correctional managers today are college-educated professionals. Why don't they write more, speak up more, and attempt to influence public policy more than they do? The public profile of most correctional administrators resembles the posture of the soldier crossing the battlefield with the enemy shooting at him. He is as low to the ground as he can be, his face is buried in the dirt, and he is inching along not sure where he is going. He only wishes everyone would stop shooting at him.

There are correctional administrators who have become both well respected by their peers and well regarded publicly as leaders of correctional reform. **George J. Beto**, the director of the Texas Department of Corrections in the 1960s and early 1970s, was one such figure. Beto developed the "**control model**" of corrections, emphasizing work, discipline, and education in a rigorously controlled prison setting. Although many elements of his model were later dismantled in the *Ruiz v. Estelle* federal lawsuit against the Texas prison system, his influence is still felt in many state systems today. **James V. Bennett**, who headed the Federal Bureau of Prisons from the 1930s through the early 1960s, is another such figure. Bennett advocated "**individualized treatment**" of inmates, an idea which if actualized would mean that each prisoner would have his or her own personalized treatment regimen to guide the process of change that is supposed to take place in confinement. He built the federal prison system into a model that the states often borrowed from in trying to improve their own systems. Corrections today would benefit from having more leaders like these men and fewer bureaucrats who "just follow orders."

Correctional administrators are still struggling with the same problems they have always faced, aggravated by contemporary problems such as overcrowding, gangs, longer sentences, and violently unstable younger inmates. They are probably much better at managing their staff today; improved working conditions and more professional standards have made corrections a much better place to work. But they remain uncertain about what to do with inmates. Allen and Simonsen once used the analogy of driving a two-horse team--the Shetland pony of treatment on the right and the Clydesdale of custody on the left. It is hard to keep them moving in the same direction. It is hard to convince the Shetland pony that he is really important, when so much of the public and the political system would have you shoot him dead and leave his body in the ditch. Correctional administrators want to believe in change, and surveys indicate that they are far more understanding of criminals (and far more cognizant of the futility of much of what goes on in their own prisons at present) than one might expect, but in the current climate it is not hard to understand why many of them would want to throw up their hands and ask, "Why bother?" Give the Clydesdale his head and let him run.

The Three Traditional Basic Services

Prisons of all security levels, even maximum security in which custody is most emphasized, provide inmates with many services and activities beyond simply being locked up. Politicians and people on the street sometimes grumble about services provided inmates. Why are convicts entitled to these "**special programs**?" they ask, with images of "convict coddling" and "country club prisons" fresh in their minds. "They have it better in prison than they did on the street," they might add. Correctional managers have four ready responses:

1. Convicts are not on the street any longer. When they give up their freedom, the state assumes the responsibility for their welfare and safety.

2. Prisons are obligated to maintain constitutional living conditions. To do otherwise would invite costly lawsuits and court intervention.

3. Prisons at one time did not provide many of these services and activities, at least not at present levels. Inmates spent all their free time trying to exploit each other and escape. Giving prisoners more positive activities reduces their involvement in misconduct and makes the institution easier to manage.

4. The special programs may actually make inmates better human beings. Isn't it worth spending a little more if criminality is reduced as a result?

The level and quality of prison services to inmates varies greatly from one state to another, depending on the philosophy of corrections officials and how much the state is willing to spend to "help criminals." Some states have a tradition of doing a lot; others provide only minimal services. There are three basic services--medical, religious, and education and training--and a wide variety of staff positions allocated to provide these and other necessary and optional services. The custodial staff still dominate in numbers and, as Allen and Simonsen suggest, in their influence on inmates, but many inmates have been helped and redirected by a prison teacher, a counselor, a psychologist, a vocational instructor, or a chaplain. There is no formula that prescribes exactly how one person reaches another; in the prison environment anyone, even the food service manager in the dining hall, may be the one responsible for starting an inmate down the road away from a criminal lifestyle.

All prisons must provide **medical services** to inmates. This has become an increasingly expensive obligation, with the sicker inmates of today. More inmates are substance abusers, more are elderly, more are mentally ill, and more come in with serious infectious diseases--HIV, **hepatitis A and B**, rubella, and tuberculosis, including **multi-drug resistant tuberculosis** (MDR-TB) among inmates with other ailments. The close living quarters of prisons, the unhealthy lifestyles of its inmates, and the no-care attitudes of many inmates who feel they have little to gain by refraining from drugs and sex in prison make prisons a fertile ground for the spread of disease.

Prison medical services are often criticized as deficient. Poor medical care is an issue in many lawsuits. The medical staff is often underpaid and transitory. The equipment and treatments are often out of date. Many prison hospitals are little more than infirmaries; serious illnesses and injuries must be dealt with in real hospitals off the prison grounds. It is still inconvenient in many prisons for inmates to get to **sick call**; getting two aspirin can take half a day in some prisons. Prisoners make their own medical care worse by faking illnesses and injuries to get out of work or to get to lay up in a hospital bed. These **goldbrickers** take up time that would be better spent treating patients with real problems. A number of state corrections departments have already enacted policies requiring inmates to pay minimal fees each time they get medical care, just as we would have to pay in the outside world. They hope this will cut down on imaginary complaints. Some prison hospitals do provide first-class medical care. They do surgery, including **plastic surgery** for physical disfigurements, and they provide care for HIV and AIDS, cancer, heart disease, and the other major illnesses that afflict contemporary prisoners in abundance. How costly is prison medical care? Texas spends almost half a *billion* dollars a year, one of every five dollars spent on prisoners, on inmate health care.

Religion is a very important prison activity. Some inmates fake it, to get to go to church and hang out with their buddies. Others, who never took the time to seek out religion when they were running the streets, find that prison religious programs change the whole direction of their lives. Many prisons have thriving religious communities, from Black Muslims to Eastern religions to every variety of Protestantism, Catholicism, and Judaism. Free-thinking prisoners are always inventing new religions and then demanding that prison authorities let them practice them (sometimes asking for such supplies as plastic inflatable dolls, altars, incense and candles, all of which authorities deny). Inmates direct many of their own religious activities, because it is hard to get free people to come into prison to work with inmate groups. The **correctional chaplaincy** has been a staple of the institution for 200 years, since the Walnut Street Jail was created to apply Quaker principles of **penitence**. Some prison chaplains are dedicated, highly regarded men and women who have a special calling to work with prisoners; others are viewed as uninspired hacks who are little more than snitches for security.

The chaplain is one of many specialized careers required by prisons that people on the street rarely think of. People are aware of guards, and administrators, and maybe the psychologists who work in treatment, but they fail to think of many other positions necessary for the day-to-day operation of the prison. These would include such positions as:

facility manager. The person responsible for maintaining the prison's buildings and grounds. The director of the physical plant.

food service manager. The person responsible for procuring food supplies and supervising the kitchen and dining facilities. Meal preparation is very important to inmates. This position is usually filled by a registered dietician.

health system administrator. The manager of the institution's health care and medical programs. Usually he or she is an administrator, not a physician.

industrial specialist. The person who supervises the inmates working in a prison industry. Generally this is someone who has special training or work experience in the specific work supervised.

medical officer. A doctor licensed to practice medicine in the state, either a general practitioner or a specialist.

ombudsman. A person who receives and investigates inmate (and sometimes staff) complaints. Only a few states have this position, though most have some type of grievance officer or investigator who looks into complaints.

recreation specialist. A specialist in physical or other forms of recreational activities. Because most prisoners are young men, recreational programs are very important in prison.

teacher. A person certified in education. Prisons need teachers with certifications from lower elementary through high school.

Howard Gill, a Massachusetts correctional administrator, founded the Institute for Correctional Administration at the American University in Washington, D.C. This school and several others now provide specialized management training for prison administrators in many fields.

The role of the academic teachers and the vocational training instructors is particularly important. Education does not cure crime, but recidivism studies have found that better educated ex-offenders are less likely to return to prison. Likewise, an inmate with no employment record and no job skills is more likely to recidivate than someone who can get and hold a good job.

Allen and Simonsen say that teachers are the most numerous of the treatment staff, though this may not be true in all institutions, some of which may have more counselors or caseworkers than teachers. It is not easy to teach in prison, where the students often have long records of failure at both school and work. About two-thirds of prison inmates lack a high school diploma. Many are **functionally illiterate**; a good number (ranging from 7 to 25 percent in different studies) are **learning disabled**. But some inmates make remarkable progress in making up for their educational deficiencies. Most prisons offer adult basic education, literacy, and **GED** classes to move an inmate toward obtaining the equivalent of a high school diploma. A number of prisons have formed relationships with nearby colleges to provide college courses behind the walls; **Project Newgate** was the prototype of a prison college education program, starting in prison and then taking the offender out into the community to attend classes on campus. Some states continue to allow their inmates to go out on educational **furloughs** to get vocational training or college courses, though in the present political climate furloughs are used much more cautiously than they once were (and than they could be again).

Vocational training is more important in many prisons than academic education. Some prisons have so many types of job training for inmates that they resemble technical schools behind bars. One of the problems with giving inmates job training has been that since the decline of the industrial prison in the 1930s, real work for prisoners has been limited. **Prison industries** in the federal system and in most state systems concentrate on making products to be consumed by other units of government--such as state offices and institutions. If prisoners cannot do "real work," if they can only be trained and given busy work to do that does not make use of their skills, it is difficult to get them to see the connection between training and employment. Congress passed the **Prison Industries Enhancement Act** in 1979, to encourage greater private sector involvement with state penal industries. About twenty states have subsequently authorized private business to establish different types of business operations within prisons. The number of inmates participating in real world work (and earning real world wages) is very small; the prison remains a mostly untapped labor force.

Behavioral Science Professionals in the Field of Corrections

The delivery of treatment services in the more narrow sense may involve the participation of several kinds of professionals from the behavioral sciences. These would include:

psychologists, who do testing and measurement of inmates, construct personality profiles and provide counseling.

psychiatrists, who are few in number and not highly regarded in prisons. Their long-term therapies are often seen as being out of place in a secure custody environment. They do more diagnosis than treatment in most prisons.

sociologists, who do more research and monitor the effectiveness of treatment programs, rather than treating offenders directly.

social workers, typically called **caseworkers**, whose tasks include assessing needs, assigning and conducting programs, and evaluating progress.

counselors, who are sometimes known as classification officers or by other titles within the prison job structure. This is a kind of generic job title for a person who often lacks the specific higher education in the behavioral sciences the other professionals possess. Counselors and other trained therapists do apply a number of treatment modalities--such as reality therapy, transactional analysis, behavior modification, and guided group interaction--in prison, but counseling in prison implies a more common sense approach as opposed to a more rigorously therapeutic treatment regimen.

The greatest debate among treatment professionals over the past two decades or more is whether treatment, in the broadest sense, is either possible or desirable within the prison setting. The institutional model keeps large numbers of inmates locked up in secure institutions; treatment programs are built into the custodial routine. Many behavioral scientists would much prefer to see a reemphasis on the reintegration model, which sends offenders out into the community for treatment programs. They quarrel with the prison administrators of today who say they are following the **reintegration model**, but strictly within prison walls. That is not reintegration, they say; it is just a slicker version of the old institutional model, and prisoners can tell the difference. Treatment within prison is more likely to appear incidental to custody;

125

treatment in the community is more likely to feel like the real thing. If the intent is to keep prisoners isolated and focused on the prison experience, we should continue as is; if we want them to look beyond the boundaries of the prison, we should explore every possibility of contact with the outside world. Treatment within prison can probably be improved, but it will always be under the domination of custody. Treatment in the community is much closer to how we want the offender to live for the rest of his life.

SELF TEST

Multiple Choice

1. The old-style prison warden was said to run his prison by which model?
    a. technocracy
    b. autocracy
    c. democracy
    d. plurality
    e. plutocracy

2. This correctional leader spent most of his career as head of the Federal Bureau of Prisons; he advocated "individualized treatment" for rehabilitation of offenders.
    a. James V. Bennett
    b. Walter Reckless
    c. Frederick Taylor
    d. Robert Stroud
    e. Louis Wainwright

3. In a typical prison, how much of the operating budget would be devoted to treatment services?
    a. less than 10%
    b. about 20%
    c. about 30 to 35%
    d. exactly 40%
    e. more than 50%

4. "Backfilling" has to do with:
    a. hiring a relative or friend to fill an empty position
    b. holding an officer overtime to man a position that must be filled
    c. increasing the level of vigilance to deal with an anticipated problem
    d. cutting back on custodial positions because of budget shortages
    e. reverting to a more authoritative management style to regain control of a prison

5. Which one of the following diseases is probably least important to the contemporary prison?
    a. hepatitis
    b. rubella
    c. tuberculosis
    d. HIV
    e. smallpox

6. Which one of the following services to prison inmates is probably most recent in origin?
    a. psychological counseling
    b. medical care
    c. academic education
    d. vocational education
    e. religious services

7. The leading cause of death among Texas prison inmates in 1994 was:
   a. cancer
   b. a flu epidemic
   c. AIDS
   d. heart disease
   e. classroom boredom

8. Which of these early purposes of imprisonment was associated with religious visitation?
   a. incapacitation
   b. economic productivity
   c. deterrence
   d. retribution
   e. penitence

9. One of the recent problems associated with tuberculosis in prison is that it:
   a. has been linked to mental illness
   b. has developed strains resistant to the usual drug treatment
   c. spreads through the sewer system
   d. has gotten completely out of control in juvenile institutions
   e. has required state prisons to set up separate prison hospitals just for TB patients

10. The Federal Bureau of Prisons established a mandatory education program a number of years ago; what level of literacy does this program set as the standard for federal inmates?
    a. third grade
    b. eighth grade
    c. tenth grade
    d. General Education Development (GED) certificate
    e. associate degree from college

11. Project Newgate was considered a pioneer program in promoting _____ in prison.
    a. spiritual development
    b. college education
    c. plastic surgery
    d. marital harmony
    e. political consciousness

12. Allen and Simonsen suggest that the behavioral scientists held in the least regard by the custodial staff are the:
    a. caseworkers
    b. psychologists
    c. sociologists
    d. counselors
    e. psychiatrists

13. The institutional model of programming is often said to be in conflict with the:
    a. deterrence model
    b. logical consequences model
    c. control model
    d. reintegration model
    e. revisionist model

14. The prison official whose function deals with receiving and investigating inmate complaints would be called an _____ in several states.
     a. omnivore
     b. oblation
     c. ombudsman
     d. overlord
     e. omnibus

True or False

_____ 15. Allen and Simonsen argue that custody and treatment both thrive in a bureaucratic system.

_____ 16. The authors criticize prison managers for lacking the willingness to innovate and experiment with change in their organizations.

_____ 17. Classification of new inmates is used far more for the benefit of treatment than it is for custody.

_____ 18. Prison administrators have generally been very open and accessible individuals who have not minded representing their institutions in the public eye.

_____ 19. The shift to determinate sentencing, which reduces the ability of the prison to release prisoners early, has brought about a sharp decline in inmate participation in prison programs.

_____ 20. The prison population is generally healthier than the population outside prison.

_____ 21. Prison ministries are among the most highly sought after assignments for chaplains in the outside world.

_____ 22. Research indicates that prison inmates with college degrees have a higher recidivism rate than those lacking a high school diploma.

_____ 23. Most of the Texas prison system's budget for inmate health care is spent treating inmates who have substance abuse problems.

_____ 24. Most prisons have trouble hiring and retaining competent medical officers.

_____ 25. Chaplains were banned from early penitentiaries because they were thought to inspire too much hope in prisoners.

_____ 26. The portion of inmates who are illiterate or learning disabled is greater than that found in the population outside prison.

_____ 27. It is presently against federal law for a private business to use prison labor in any way.

_____ 28. With the decline of rehabilitation, most states no longer allow inmates to take part in any programs that might make them better-suited to life in the outside world.

Fill In the Blanks

29. Sanford Bates and James V. Bennett are both associated with the _____ prison system.

30. George Beto applied the _____ model in Texas prisons, emphasizing work, education, and discipline.

128

31. Allen and Simonsen call the present day uncertainty of the correctional manager over which management style to apply to his or her institution the _____.

32. In explaining why prison administrators concentrate on programs with incarcerated inmates behind prison walls, Richard Cloward points out that _____ tends to be the weakest part of the correctional process.

33. The Kairos program uses volunteers to promote _____ in prison.

34. The institute that Howard Gill founded at the American University was primarily intended to provide professional training for _____.

35. The most virulent and treatment-resistant strain of tuberculosis is known as _____-TB.

36. You would describe PNN at the Marion Correctional Institution (MCI) as an inmate _____.

37. The tuberculin skin test is used to test for the disease of _____.

38. With the passage of restrictive federal laws, prison work programs went into decline during the decade of _____.

39. Psychiatrists who work in prison often suggest that long-term treatment does not work well in the prison setting; instead of treatment, they often concentrate on _____.

40. The most common term for the professionally trained social worker in prison is _____.

41. Allen and Simonsen suggest that in the routine of prison life, the most pleasant (and legal) activity for the inmate day in and day out is _____.

42. The single most influential agent of change in prison, according to the authors, is _____.

Matching

_____ 43. The head of the Texas prison system for over a decade; he applied the "control model" to Texas prisons.

_____ 44. A general term for the counseling and therapy-related programs of a prison.

_____ 45. The Bureau of Prisons director who is called "the father of modern penology."

_____ 46. The term Allen and Simonsen apply to prison managers' view of change.

_____ 47. The idea that each offender ought to have programs tailored to meet his or her own needs.

_____ 48. A job title for a free person who works in prison industries.

_____ 49. The staff member responsible for the operation of the prison dining hall.

_____ 50. A graduate behavioral scientist who would do testing, measurement, and treatment.

_____ 51. The term for an inmate who fakes an illness or injury to get out of work.

_____ 52. The term for a person who functions at or below the third grade educationally.

_____ 53. What the public calls any treatment service provided to prison inmates.

_____ 54. The time for inmates to put in an appearance if they want to be examined by medical staff.

_____ 55. The model that focuses on working with prisoners in community-based programs.

_____ 56. The specialist who would oversee the prison's intramural athletic program.

a. Sanford Bates
b. "model muddle"
c. treatment services
d. backfilling
e. autocracy
f. hierarchical management
g. George J. Beto
h. "control model"
i. gradualism approach
j. isolationism and withdrawal
k. James V. Bennett
l. "individualized treatment"
m. "special programs"
n. medical services
o. sick call
p. goldbrickers
q. hepatitis A and B
r. multidrug-resistant tuberculosis
s. plastic surgery
t. psychologist
u. psychiatrist
v. sociologist
w. social worker

x. penitence
y. correctional chaplaincy
z. facility manager
aa. food service manager
bb. health system administrator
cc. industrial specialist
dd. medical officer
ee. ombudsman
ff. recreation specialist
gg. teacher
hh. functionally illiterate
ii. Howard Gill
jj. learning disabled
kk. GED
ll. Project Newgate
mm. furlough
nn. vocational training
oo. prison industries
pp. Prison Industries Enhancement Act (1979)
qq. caseworker
rr. counselor
ss. reintegration model

Discussion

57. What major criticisms do Allen and Simonsen direct at correctional managers?

58. Why is custody so much more important than treatment?

59. Someone explained the passive approach of many prison managers by saying "they have to take whatever is dumped on them." What does this statement mean?

60. If you were the prison's health system administrator, what important problems would you expect to have to deal with in your work?

61. Why do ministers from the outside world often not want to work in prison?

62. What are the advantages of expanding prison industries and including more private sector investment in prisons?

63. Briefly explain what graduate-trained behavioral scientists do inside prisons.

64. Contrast the institutional and reintegration models.

65. Explain the effects of the Americans with Disabilities Act (ADA) on correctional institutions.

CHAPTER FOURTEEN

Female Inmates

CHAPTER OBJECTIVES

Women have historically made up a small percentage of imprisoned offenders, but in recent years their rate of imprisonment has increased sharply. As the number of women in prison continues to go up, prison officials have been obliged to pay greater attention to the management of women offenders as a group different from men. After reading the material in this chapter, you should be familiar with:
1. the crimes women commit.
2. how the criminal justice system views women offenders.
3. the impact of the "war on drugs" on women.
4. the characteristics of women in jail and prison.
5. the typical problems of women in prison.
6. the role of co-correctional facilities.

KEY TERMS AND CONCEPTS

arrests by gender
preferential treatment
"traditional" female crimes
victimless crimes
careers in prostitution
Indiana Reformatory Institute
Alderson
paternalistic attitude of judges
differential treatment
Mary Belle Harris
women's liberation movement
the underclass

abused women
Elizabeth Gurney Fry
co-correctional institutions
pregnant inmates
family cohesion
"forgotten" inmates
single-sex experience
psychological deprivations
sexual abuse
physical abuse
reintegration
vengeful equity

CHAPTER SUMMARY

Female Crime and Incarceration Rates Climbing

Women now make up between six and seven percent of the total prison population, which seems like a comparatively inconsequential part of a much larger problem. But a quarter-century ago, women made up just over four percent of felony prisoners. Patterns of **arrests by gender** and the incarceration rate of women have changed dramatically in this short period of time to cause such a rapid increase. Women actually make up just over ten percent of all prisoners entering prisons each year, but because their terms are generally shorter and the number of men already there so much greater, their representation in the total population of imprisoned offenders remains somewhat smaller.

Among the FBI's index crimes, women are arrested in much greater numbers for property crimes, particularly larceny/theft, than for violent crimes. Women make up exactly a third of all arrestees for larceny. But their arrests for the other index crimes, except homicide, are increasing also. Research suggests that the criminal justice system is less inclined to give women offenders **preferential treatment** today than it was a generation or two ago. If the system did practice "chivalry," the term Otto Pollak used in *The Criminality of Women* to describe how the male-dominated system treated women, it seems less chivalrous now as women broaden their criminal careers beyond the **"traditional" female crimes**.

Cesare Lombroso said the only crime to which women were well suited was prostitution, because it was passive and required little skill. The early criminal justice system seemed to spend a lot of time trying to correct prostitutes and make them into moral, law-abiding wives and mothers. We do not know if this worked or not; we suspect not. The early women's prisons, which were only separate wings of larger men's prisons, were full of women who were whores, thieves, and consorts of criminal men. Many correctional reformers of the 1800s, such as the English Quaker **Elizabeth Gurney Fry**, advocated dealing with these women in special facilities, run for and in some cases by women (though usually under the direction of men). The more progressive states began to establish separate prisons for women by the end of the 1800s.

The first all-female prison was the **Indiana Reformatory Institute**, which opened in 1873 and applied Zebulon Brockway's reform methods. The first federal prison for women, at **Alderson**, West Virginia, opened in 1927. The woman called the first female warden (though other women held other titles as heads of other early women's prisons), **Mary Belle Harris**, was its head. These and other prisons set the tone of women's corrections--the idea that women prisoners were immoral beings, unduly influenced by men, who needed to be reformed but did not present much of a physical threat to safety and security. Women offenders were capable of evil, but they were not really dangerous, professional criminals.

Prostitution remains an important criminal offense today, though not a felony for which the offender is put in prison. But many practitioners of prostitution get in trouble for other crimes--for crimes of violence related to their work, for drug-related offenses, and for other crimes related to their hustling lifestyles. As one of the service-related or **victimless crimes**, prostitution remains at the center of an unsavory, often dangerous lifestyle. **Careers in prostitution** run the "professional" gamut, from the oldest to the newest, from the streetcorner hooker who might perform oral sex ten or twenty times a night, to the crack whore who has unprotected sex for a rock or two of crack cocaine, to the "pretty woman" courtesan who might have a six figure income, at least for awhile.

A Differential Justice System for Women?

Many scholars of the criminology of women believe that women once received preferential treatment-- translated as "leniency"--within the legal system. There are several reasons cited for this favorable treatment:

    1. the non-violent nature of women's crimes, except for murder, which when committed by females usually involved family members or loved ones as victims.

    2. the lack of serious prior criminal histories among most women offenders.

    3. the presence of a man to put the blame on.

    4. the condition, still very important today, of motherhood; about 75% to 80% of women in jail and prison are mothers, the great majority of these with minor children still living with them.

    5. the role of males with conventional middle-class values as the prime decision-makers in criminal justice--as police, prosecutors, judges, and prison officials. The **paternalistic attitude of judges** toward women is often cited, though you can just as easily point out that judges are also paternalistic toward juveniles, drunks, and sometimes even male felons.

Differential treatment did not always mean better treatment, particularly once a woman actually ended up in prison. Women's prisons might be smaller, less restrictive, and less secure, but they were also typically more demeaning to women offenders and less inclined to offer support services and rehabilitation programs.

Liberation theory, which is based on analysis of the impact of the **women's liberation movement** on society, suggests that women are not as likely to be given preferential treatment or differential treatment today; they are more likely to be viewed as the criminal equals of men, in a system where women are moving more into important decision-making roles as well. Laws that treat all offenders equally, particularly drug laws, have greatly reduced the likelihood that women, even the mothers of small children, will get undeservedly favorable treatment by the system.

The War on Drugs Creates Female Casualties, Too

Despite all these professions of equal treatment, the plain truth is that the percentages of women in prison would not have changed significantly over the past two decades were it not for the war on drugs. The war on drugs has been fought on many fronts, but the pitched battles have been fought against the urban **underclass**, mostly blacks and hispanics, who use crack cocaine. Large numbers of drug users who have dealt and consumed crack cocaine have found their way into America's prisons over the past fifteen years. Drug abuse is at the very heart of the upsurge in women's imprisonment today.

Females in Jail

Although jails hold more minor offenders who do not go to prison, the profiles of women jail inmates and prison inmates are not dramatically different. Women in jail are likely to be young minorities, never married but with minor children living with them. They came from crimogenic families, in which other close family members had been confined. Almost half had experienced either **sexual abuse** or **physical abuse** in their lives before incarceration. Most used drugs, especially crack. Almost as many abused alcohol. The pattern of abuse, of what other people did to them, of what they did to other people, and of what they did to their own bodies, marks them for life. Jails and prisons are full of **abused females**.

Females in Prison

Women in prison stand convicted of more serious crimes, so there is a greater incidence of both violence and recidivism in their background, and a much greater likelihood that they are in prison for a drug crime. Otherwise, their lives before imprisonment were similar to the lives of jail inmates. We see in both jails and prisons large numbers of poor women, struggling to raise their children, troubled with personal problems--drug and alcohol abuse, sexual and physical victimization, and unstable relationships with men--undereducated and underemployed, hustling sex, hustling drugs, and stealing to make a living. The women who end up in prison are hardly liberated, and the lives they led on the streets were far from glamorous.

As the number of women in prison has increased so rapidly, from about 10,000 25 years ago to more than 80,000 in 1998, the number of women's prisons has increased quickly as well. The 1980s was the biggest single decade in the history of building prisons for women; 34 new prisons for women were built in this decade. Many of the new prisons are designed with more maximum security features to house a "deeper-end," more long-term and hard-core population. There is still a perception in corrections that women's prisons are nicer than men's prisons, but the women in prison are still routinely described as harder to manage and more difficult to deal with day-to-day than men in prison. Correctional officials do not mean that the women are more violent or escape prone, but they say women complain too much, get involved in too many petty disputes, and do not adapt as well to prison routines. The women inmates, who almost universally are addressed as "ladies," for their part complain that they are treated like children and written up for petty violations that would be ignored in a men's prison.

There is no doubt that incarceration is a different experience for women. About a fourth of women are either pregnant or have infants when they arrive in prison. They cannot keep their children with them. **Pregnant inmates**, whom Allen and Simonsen suggest should be placed in halfway houses, have to give their children to someone--a family member (very rarely the father) or the state--within a few days after giving birth.

About eighty percent of women in prison are mothers, so it is no surprise that women prisoners report that separation from their children and family outside ranks as the greatest pain of imprisonment. Women's prisons are often located far away from the urban population centers the women come from, and most family members lack the resources for convenient travel. Visiting is often limited or restricted, with little opportunity for prisoners to meet privately with their children, their mothers, and their sisters. The security environment of prison also discourages many mothers from wanting their children to visit. Who wants to see her four-year-old "assume the position," hands on wall, while a security officer frisks him? Some prisons are much more open to visiting than others, and new programs allowing mothers to spend more time with their children are always being established, but much more needs to be done to promote **family cohesion** as a prison policy rather than just a collection of incidental programs.

The graying of American prisons is beginning to show its effects in women's prisons. More long-termers and habitual offenders are aging in prison, and more middle-aged and older women are coming in convicted of homicide and attempted homicide offenses. Allen and Simonsen call these women **"forgotten" inmates**; they tend to be isolated from the outside world and also ignored within the prison system because they are so few in number.

The Co-correctional Institution

The life of prison inmates in the United States is designed around the **single-sex experience**. Prisoners looking for any kind of sexual intimacy with another person are compelled toward homosexuality. There are no other choices. Most researchers who have studied prison sexual behavior believe that the incidence of homosexuality, particularly voluntary, stable relationships based on love and affection, is much greater in women's prisons than in men's. Women inmates themselves often suggest that women are more emotional and need that other person to feel close to. Homosexuality in a men's prison may be one thing; homosexuality in a women's prison may be something entirely different, reflecting **psychological deprivations** based on women's needs to have both physical and emotional ties to other persons.

This does not mean that women's prisons are rampant with homosexuality. Prison homosexuality is rarely a prolonged, full-scale sexual encounter. In the women's prison it is more likely to be note-writing, discreet touching, hand-holding (though this is now a write-up in many women's prisons), and maybe a hurried kiss when security is not looking. The lurid sexual encounters between crazed lesbians in cut-offs and halter tops happen only in those "B" movies one finds in the Action/Adventure video section.

One often-proposed way of combatting the single-sex prison environment is the **co-correctional institution**, sometimes called the co-educational prison. John Smykla defines co-corrections as a confinement facility where men and women inmates have daily opportunities for interaction. This is intended to promote a more normal social environment and reduce predatory homosexuality, even at the risk of promoting increased heterosexual activity. No co-correctional facility allows inmates to engage in heterosexual sex, but then no one-sex prison allows inmates to engage in homosexuality. Only about three percent of American prisons are co-correctional. Most are small, most house more men than women, and most of them feature special programs that the general inmate population in other prisons does not have access to. For the time being, co-correctional institutions remain more of a curiosity than a harbinger of change. Most states have no co-correctional facilities.

Intermediate Punishments for Females

When you look at the population of a women's prison, you see large numbers of women who are repeat property or drug offenders and a comparatively small population of violent criminals, very few of whom are predatory criminals who have victimized strangers. As intermediate sanctions are pushed for male offenders, they should be pushed even more aggressively for females. Women who are more disadvantaged and abused than a serious criminal threat ought to be dealt with by means of community-based correctional alternatives stressing **reintegration**, Allen and Simonsen recommend, or confined in the lower security co-

correctional facilities that could encourage more contact with family members outside. Few women belong in prison, but in these times of **"vengeful equity,"** where men and women stand equal before the law, their numbers continue to increase.

SELF TEST

Multiple Choice

1. In terms of total arrests, for which of the following index crimes are the fewest number of women arrested?
> a. robbery
> b. burglary
> c. aggravated assault
> d. murder and manslaughter
> e. motor vehicle theft

2. The first separate prison for women opened in this state in 1873:
> a. Massachusetts
> b. Ohio
> c. Illinois
> d. Pennsylvania
> e. Indiana

3. About what percentage of women in prison are mothers?
> a. 11-12%
> b. 20-22%
> c. 35-38%
> d. 54-58%
> e. 75-80%

4. The most prevalent "traditional" female crime of the 1800s was probably:
> a. burglary
> b. prostitution
> c. infanticide
> d. arson
> e. robbery

5. Which women prisoners do Allen and Simonsen call "forgotten" inmates?
> a. abused women
> b. older women
> c. the mentally ill
> d. white-collar offenders
> e. the members of Charles Manson's family

6. Four of the following are advantages commonly cited for co-corrections facilities; which one is NOT?
> a. creates a more normal environment
> b. reduces predatory homosexuality
> c. the public is highly in favor of it
> d. allows better use of scarce prison space
> e. provides better training programs for the women inmates

7. The greatest number of prisons for women were built in which decade?
    a. 1850-1860
    b. 1910-1920
    c. 1930-1940
    d. 1960-1970
    e. 1980-1990

8. In terms of the inmate subculture, the psychological deprivations of women's prisons are most strongly associated with which topic?
    a. escape attempts
    b. suicide
    c. homosexual behavior
    d. gang membership
    e. television viewing habits

9. When judges are described as having "paternalistic" attitudes toward women offenders, it means the judges treat the women like:
    a. sex objects
    b. children
    c. mad dogs
    d. illegal aliens
    e. the mentally ill

10. The largest number of arrests of women are for which of the following crimes?
    a. forgery
    b. vandalism
    c. embezzlement
    d. larceny/theft
    e. burglary

True or False

_____ 11. Women offenders agree that separation from their male partners is the worst part of doing prison time.

_____ 12. Both the arrest rate and the incarceration rate of women are going up faster than comparable rates for men.

_____ 13. There are more women in prison for prostitution than for any other single crime.

_____ 14. Among women in prison for drug offenses, the largest number are there for using or dealing crack cocaine.

_____ 15. About half of women in jail or prison report being victims of either sexual abuse or physical abuse (or both) before incarceration.

_____ 16. Allen and Simonsen suggest that women offenders need to be completely isolated from the outside world to get the maximum benefit from imprisonment.

_____ 17. The number of women correctional administrators heading institutions is declining as prison management becomes more conservative.

_____ 18. Allen and Simonsen suggest that pregnant women offenders should be placed in halfway houses to serve their sentences.

137

_____ 19. Women inmates generally have access to more numerous and varied rehabilitation programs in prison than men do.

_____ 20. According to the idea of chivalry or preferential treatment, men always got more lenient punishments than women because judges tended to view women as being the cause of men's criminal behavior.

Fill In the Blanks

21. Most of the increase in the number of women in prison over the past fifteen years is due to the increased incarceration of _____ offenders.

22. Women make up about _____ percent of the total prison population.

23. Allen and Simonsen suggest that women who need to be kept locked up should be confined in _____ facilities.

24. What criminal offense is called "the oldest profession"? _____

25. Blanche LaDu, Helen Corruthers, and Bobbie Huskey are women who have what in common? _____

26. The "drug of choice" of the urban underclass is _____.

27. Mary Belle Harris is often credited with being the first female _____.

28. The national organization with chapters in several states promoting closer contacts between women prisoners and their daughters is _____.

29. Allen and Simonsen suggest that women inmates' abuse by men makes them more likely to engage in _____ behavior in prison.

30. The major impact of pursuing a policy of "reintegration" in regard to women offenders would be that more women would be confined in _____.

Matching

_____ 31. The first federal prison for women.

_____ 32. This Quaker woman was an early advocate of separate prisons for women.

_____ 33. Some researchers believe this social movement has had significant impact on women's criminality, whereas others argue it has missed women criminals almost entirely.

_____ 34. The term for the urban poor who make up the greatest percentage of women in prison.

_____ 35. In terms of policy changes, the greatest need of women's prisons, according to Allen and Simonsen.

_____ 36. Meda Chesney-Lind's term for the concept that female prisons are being modeled directly on male prisons.

_____ 37. The statistics you would look at if you were trying to compare males and females taken into custody for certain crimes.

_____ 38. The inmates to whom child care is of the most urgent concern.

_____ 39. The vocational starting place for many female criminal histories.

_____ 40. The term used for vice offenses such as prostitution that are unlikely to be reported to the police.

a. arrests by gender
b. preferential treatment
c. "traditional" female crimes
d. victimless crimes
e. careers in prostitution
f. Indiana Reformatory Institute
g. Alderson
h. paternalistic attitude of judges
i. differential treatment
j. Mary Belle Harris
k. women's liberation movement
l. the underclass

m. abused women
n. Elizabeth Gurney Fry
o. co-correctional institutions
p. pregnant inmates
q. family cohesion
r. "forgotten" inmates
s. single-sex experience
t. psychological deprivations
u. sexual abuse
v. physical abuse
w. reintegration
x. vengeful equity

Discussion

41. What crimes would you find most numerous among women in prison?

42. What was the criminal justice system's traditional view of women criminals?

43. Some observers have characterized the "war on drugs" as a "war on women." What do they mean?

44. Give a brief profile of a typical woman in prison.

45. If you were an inmate, what would be the advantages of being in a co-correctional facility?

46. What would most women inmates identify as the most serious problems they face while imprisoned?

CHAPTER FIFTEEN

Male Offenders

CHAPTER OBJECTIVES

Since the early 1800s, imprisonment has been used to punish offenders convicted of serious crimes. Each year in America, more than half a million people enter prison to experience the most severe control a society can exercise over its members without killing them. After reading the material in this chapter, you should be familiar with:

1. the effect of the baby boom on prison population.
2. the background of male prison inmates.
3. prisonization and the inmate subculture.
4. sexual behavior among men in prison.
5. the aging of the prison population.

KEY TERMS AND CONCEPTS

bastion-like prisons
court commitments
commitment lag
"Iron Law of Prison Commitments"
baby boom
racial and ethnic issues
"designer" drugs
functionally illiterate
institutional work assignment
prisonization
deprivation

the inmate code
stand-up guy
anticipatory socialization
population at risk
age at risk
homosexual attacks
polarization
conjugal or family visits
elderly inmates
geriatric centers
warehousing

CHAPTER SUMMARY

Overview

Beginning in the early 1800s, America built a huge network of state prisons to hold convicted felons. Today over 1,500 prisons, still mostly state operated, hold well over a million prisoners in custody. Over 100,000 people are confined in the old maximum security institutions that Allen and Simonsen call **"bastion-like prisons,"** for their medieval castle appearance. Such institutions practice **"warehousing"** of inmates--storing them without making them better (and perhaps too often making them worse or more criminal)--to temporarily protect the public. The prison population continues to increase at a rate of between five and ten percent per year, as it has for more than two decades.

Going to prison is a hard, life-altering experience for the men and women sentenced to "felony time." Everyone who enters prison experiences "prisonization," in Donald Clemmer's term, but the experience depends on what kind of prison the offender is sent to, how he is classified, where he lives and works within the prison, and many other circumstances, some of which he brings with him when he comes in-- such as a gang affiliation or family support--and others waiting for him on arrival--such as enemies waiting to victimize him or rehabilitation programs that might change the direction of his life.

No one can predict with certainty what the outcome of imprisonment will be, in its effect on the offender, and there is ample indication that a large segment of the American public does not really care what happens to offenders in prison: They only want as many people as possible locked up for as long as possible. Politicians have been only too happy to oblige in recent years, passing new "get tough" laws in every legislative session. Despite the development of intermediate sanctions, new **court commitments** to prison continue to fill up all available spaces.

The Kevin Costner character in "Field of Dreams" was told, "If you build it, they will come." He tore up his cornfield to make a baseball field, and his long-dead heroes did return to play on it. The "**Iron Law of Prison Commitments**" says, "If you build the prison, the prisoners will come." Most state prisons systems remain at capacity, even as they build new prisons, contract with private prisons, and deal with a backlog of state prisoners held in county jails. It is almost impossible to shut down an existing prison, because there is no place to put the inmates. The courts fill up new prisons as soon as they open.

The post-World War II "**baby boom**" produced a huge population bulge, children born from the late 1940s to about 1960. Because of the built-in "**commitment lag**"--meaning that younger, first-time or second-time felony offenders often are not sent to prison until they are in their twenties--explosive prison growth really began after 1980. The combination of abundant numbers of young people, important sociocultural changes in American society, the public's continuing fear of criminal victimization, and legal and policy changes, particularly in regard to drug offenses, have combined to propel America to unprecedented imprisonment rates. With an "echo boom"--the children of baby boomers--projected to hit the prison system at the end of the century, there is no end in sight. Prisons remain one of America's prime growth industries.

Prison Populations Continue To Soar

Driven by our determination to wage war on crime by locking up criminals, prisons continue to seek new "clients." Most of the prison's clientele are men; between six and seven percent are women. Most are young, poor, and underemployed; about 65% are black or hispanic. It is very difficult to discuss the politics of imprisonment without confronting issues of class, race, and ethnicity among prisoner populations. The "War on Drugs," for instance, is much more punitive on users of crack cocaine, who are predominately minorities, than it is on users of powder cocaine, predominately whites. Most prisoners come from the large urban underclass that makes up what is called the "**population at risk**." One element of this population often highlighted is the "**age at risk**," the span between 18 and 29 years of age when a young man is likely to start picking up felony convictions.

Prisoners suffer from a broad range of social disabilities. Many come from unstable and abusive families. A much higher percentage of prisoners than non-prisoners have alcohol and drug abuse problems. About a third of male prisoners report alcohol use at the time of their imprisonment offense; another third report drug use at the time of the offense. Use of hard drugs--heroin (which has recently enjoyed a resurgence of popularity in New York City and elsewhere), cocaine, and the "**designer**" **drugs**--is much higher among prisoners than the general population. Most prisoners have not graduated from high school; a good portion are **functionally illiterate**. Many prisoners have personality or "attitude" problems that made it difficult for them to get along with people. Many have personality disorders fitting the description of anti-social personalties (what used to be called sociopaths). They have problems staying attached to people in the free world, and then they get put into the even more extremely filtered world of prison--where all their neighbors are convicted felons with the same kind of convoluted background.

Prisonization Plays a Big Role

Donald Clemmer, in his 1940 work, *The Prison Community*, used the term "**prisonization**" to describe the inmate's adaptation to the subculture of the penitentiary. New inmates, or those who identify with conventional non-criminal values, were in for a severe culture shock in the old days. Prisons were cut off from the outside world. Life inside many prisons was dominated by a strong inmate culture in which guards allowed inmates to have control over other inmates as long as security was maintained. Professional criminals ran the old subculture to their benefit. Prisoners were introduced to prison slang (or argot); they learned words like "fish," "pruno," "shank," "hack," and "snitch," describing elements of the prison experience. They learned the rules of **the inmate code**: "Don't be a rat." "Do your own time." "Be a man." "Don't talk to the guards." The model of conduct was the "**stand-up guy**" or "right guy," or in some prisons, the "real man." The subculture reflected the inmates' response to the **deprivations** and restrictions of the maximum security prison; it represented the prisoners' efforts to defeat the system's controls and maximize their own independence and pleasure (and often their influence over other inmates) within the environment of the maximum security prison.

The values of the old inmate code do not mean as much in contemporary prisons. Most prisons are not maximum security; inmates live more comfortable, privileged lives in medium and minimum security institutions. In the "big house," the old penitentiary, old convicts say the young criminals of today are more violent, less respectful of authority, more personality disordered, and more likely to be drug and alcohol abusers. The inmate population is more fragmented into gangs and small groups and more divided over **racial and ethnic issues**. Security is better, and many large prisons are broken up into smaller operating units, which disrupts the influence of the subculture. Most prisoners have an **institutional work assignment**--often a menial job of some sort--to occupy their time, they have recreational and rehabilitation programs, and in their free time they have clubs and other activities to keep them occupied. Prisoners of today are much more in contact with the outside world, if they choose to be and if anyone out there is listening. Some researchers have suggested that a combination of shorter prison terms and even more contact with the outside society would further diminish the influence of prisonization on contemporary prisoners. These researchers talk of "**anticipatory socialization**" and the need to keep inmates focused on their return to society, instead of focusing on their adaptation to an artificial society with values contrary to those needed to avoid a life of crime after release.

Rape in All-Male Prisons

Except in those few states that allow conjugal visiting, sex of any kind is forbidden in American prisons--no consensual homosexuality, no sex between inmates and guards; the inmate is not even allowed to have sex with himself. If the inmate is caught engaging in any kind of sexual act, disciplinary action will be taken. The popular belief is that prohibition of sexual activity turns lusty young men into sex-starved beasts who go around raping each other with alarming frequency. While **homosexual attacks**, including gang rapes, do take place in jails and prisons, predatory assaults do not happen as often as many outsiders believe. The motivation for prison sex is more likely to be exploitation or domination, a way of expressing one person's control over another, rather than frustration or sexual pathology. Sex is used as a tool in prison just as it may be used as a tool among people in the free world; the only difference is that in practically all prisons both the user and the usee are of the same sex. In the prison of today, with greater **polarization** of inmates into competing groups based on race, ethnicity, gang, or neighborhood affiliation, coercive sex becomes just one more weapon in the war for internal domination, one more expression of the machismo so highly valued among young urban inmates.

Conjugal or family visits and furloughs have been suggested as the best ways to counter sexual violence in the monosexual prison, but these are not very popular ideas with the public at present. If inmates have heterosexual sex, babies are almost sure to result, and these babies will almost surely grow up to become criminals themselves. Another tenet of American prison life is that prisoners are supposed to be suffering pains of deprivation, not having fun. Remember penitence? So for the foreseeable future sex is out: Prisoners can check their sex lives, like their street clothes, when they enter the prison gate.

The Graying of America's Male Prisoners

One prison population trend of important long-term impact is the increase in the number of older inmates. In prison the emerging definition of an older inmate is anyone over 50. In Florida and several other states, older prisoners make up the fastest growing part of the prison population. Older prisoners get to be old in prison in three main ways. Some come as younger men and stay as lifers or long-term inmates. Some are habitual offenders who get hit with a final long stretch (as in "three strikes and you're out") in middle age. And some come to prison late in life, usually for crimes of violence or sex offenses. However they may get there, older prisoners present particular problems for prison officials. Medical care is much more expensive, they have trouble mixing with the young urban gangsters of today, and their needs--nutrition, recreation, programs, and mental health--are different. Many state prisons have already established **geriatric centers** for **elderly inmates**. These centers are more often like minimum security nursing homes, but they are necessary to satisfy the legal requirements that these prisoners be kept in confinement (and diminished options for early or medical release). The percentage of inmates over age 50 is expected to continue to increase to about 10% by early in the twenty-first century.

SELF TEST

Multiple Choice

1. Allen and Simonsen use the term "bastionlike prisons" to mean prisons that resemble:
   a. country clubs
   b. farms
   c. medical hospitals
   d. prisoner of war camps
   e. medieval fortresses

2. When male prison inmates are drug tested, the greatest percentage test positive for which drug:
   a. marijuana
   b. cocaine
   c. heroin
   d. LSD
   e. methamphetamine

3. Four of the following fit the old inmate code; which one does NOT?
   a. "Do your own time."
   b. "Don't be a rat."
   c. "Be friendly to the guards."
   d. "Don't exploit other inmates."
   e. "Be a man."

4. About what percentage of prison inmates today are black and hispanic?
   a. 17%
   b. 30%
   c. 48%
   d. 65%
   e. 83%

5. The "Iron Law of Prison Commitments" is most directly related to which subject?
   a. violent crime
   b. prison space
   c. mental health issues
   d. misconduct by inmates
   e. conjugal visiting

6. What kind of inmates would a prison "geriatric center" most likely be intended for?
   a. sexual psychopaths
   b. women inmates
   c. elderly inmates
   d. HIV/AIDS inmates
   e. mentally ill inmates

7. Four of the following are standard words of prison vocabulary. Which one is NOT?
   a. quark
   b. hack
   c. shank
   d. snitch
   e. fish

8. Behavioral scientists suggest that prisoners at the end of their term are more interested in trying to learn how to live successfully in the society they are about to rejoin. We call this idea:
   a. brainwashing
   b. transactional analysis
   c. milieu therapy
   d. anticipatory socialization
   e. pathological thinking

9. "Population at risk" refers to an age range that is most at risk for imprisonment; this age range is:
   a. 15-19
   b. 55-64
   c. 18-29
   d. 30-39
   e. 36-48

10. In the old inmate subculture, if another inmate called you "a stand-up guy," he would be suggesting that you were:
   a. the aggressive partner in a homosexual relationship
   b. someone who had sold out to the guards
   c. a target of another inmate's animosity
   d. someone who was only out for his own welfare
   e. a man who practiced the principles of the code

True or False

_____ 11. The use of imprisonment in America today is at an all-time high.

_____ 12. There are more black inmates in prison than there are either whites or hispanics.

_____ 13. About 80 percent of prison inmates are men.

_____ 14. In 1997, most inmates who died in prison died from natural causes.

_____ 15. Researchers suggest that most inmates involved in homosexual attacks in prison were already deviant homosexuals before they came to prison.

_____ 16. Prison inmates on the whole are slightly better educated than the general population outside prison.

_____ 17. Almost all states allow some inmates, usually trusties, to participate in heterosexual sexual activities through a formal conjugal visiting program.

_____ 18. The majority of American prison inmates have no job assignment while they are serving their prison sentence.

_____ 19. Donald Clemmer used "prisonization" to refer primarily to the negative, mean-spirited acts of prison guards toward weaker prison inmates.

_____ 20. The percentage of older inmates in prison is declining as prisons try to clear out beds to take in more violent young criminals.

Fill In the Blanks

21. After drug offenses, the second largest category of male inmates are in prison for the crime of _____.

22. About _____ percent of all prison inmates are men.

23. If you could get some sugar, some water, some brewer's yeast, some raisins and other fruits, and a crock to let this mixture ferment in (an unused commode will do all right in a pinch), you could make the homemade alcohol inmates call _____.

24. "Brown shirt," "duck," and "hack" are all slang terms referring to _____.

25. About _____ of every 100 state prisoners were HIV positive in 1996.

26. Anthony Scacco's research suggested that conjugal visiting within prisons and _____, which allow inmates to go home to have sexual relations with their spouses, would both help reduce the incidence of prison homosexuality.

27. Allen and Simonsen suggest that the pre-prison drug abuse habits of inmates have changed recently to include the consumption of more powerful, behavior-altering substances they call _____.

28. When Allen and Simonsen refer to "The Second Great Prohibition Experiment," they are referring to _____.

29. Allen and Simonsen suggest that the imprisonment rate is not a function of the crime rate; rather, they call it a(n) _____ to a heightened fear of crime.

30. The authors suggest that a prison environment based on _____ encourages inmates to work through the subculture to satisfy their status, sex, and material needs.

Matching

_____ 31. The standards of prisoner conduct in the old inmate subculture.

_____ 32. The term that implies a prison policy of simply keeping prisoners locked up and doing nothing to change their behavior.

_____ 33. The term suggesting that the inmate subculture derives from the inmates' efforts to replace those aspects of outside life denied them by the prison.

_____ 34. The model of inmate conduct under the old inmate code.

_____ 35. The practice of allowing inmates to have heterosexual physical relations while in prison.

_____ 36. The educational level of a large part of the prison population.

_____ 37. Clemmer's term for the inmate's adaptation to the subculture of the penitentiary.

_____ 38. The principle that the court system will sentence more people to prison to fill up any existing empty beds.

_____ 39. The high post-World War II birth rate was responsible for this phenomenon that resulted in unusually large numbers of young people in the American population in the 1960s and 1970s.

_____ 40. Allen and Simonsen's term for the physically imposing prison castles of the 1800s.

a. bastion-like prisons
b. court commitments
c. commitment lag
d. "Iron Law of Prison Commitments"
e. baby boom
f. racial and ethnic issues
g. "designer" drugs
h. functionally illiterate
i. institutional work assignment
j. prisonization
k. deprivation
l. the inmate code
m. stand-up guy
n. anticipatory socialization
o. population at risk
p. age at risk
q. homosexual attacks
r. polarization
s. conjugal or family visits
t. elderly inmates
u. geriatric centers
v. warehousing

Discussion

41. How does the "baby boom" relate to the increase in prison populations?

42. How is the pre-prison background of prisoners markedly different from the background of non-prisoners?

43. How does "prisonization" take place?

44. What has happened to the old inmate code?

45. What measures does Anthony Scacco suggest to reduce prison homosexuality?

46. What problems do elderly inmates present for prison officials?

CHAPTER SIXTEEN

Juvenile Offenders

CHAPTER OBJECTIVES

A century ago the first formal juvenile courts were established to stress treatment and rehabilitation of youthful offenders rather than punishment. Over time an entirely separate justice system has developed to intervene with delinquents and in certain circumstances other non-criminal children and adolescents also. After reading the material in this chapter, you should be familiar with:

1. the common law origins of juvenile courts.
2. the extent of juvenile crime and violence.
3. violent victimization of juveniles.
4. legal categories within the juvenile court.
5. the legal rights of juveniles.
6. institutions for juvenile offenders.

KEY TERMS AND CONCEPTS

common law
parens patriae
ward
chancery court
juvenile delinquency
OJJDP
super predator
statutory exclusion
waiver
direct filing
juvenile gangs
crack cocaine
Edwin Sutherland
differential association
juvenile
delinquent juvenile
status offender
incorrigible juvenile
PINS

dependent
neglected
intake
petition
training school
treatment
"crime schools"
Kent v. United States
In re Gault
Juvenile Justice and Delinquency Prevention
    Act (1974)
decarceration
deinstitutionalization
decriminalization
Jerome Miller
custody philosophy
diversion
detention
vertical prosecution

CHAPTER SUMMARY

Where Does the Juvenile Fit In?

For a very long time juvenile offenders were dealt with by the same courts and under the same terms as adult offenders: Age made no legal difference in processing or punishing offenders, except whatever human feelings a judge might have for an offender of tender years. The origins of American juvenile law can be traced to English **common law**, which divided children into three categories depending on the issue of whether they knew right from wrong. The youngest age of adult responsibility was seven. As the common law developed, a special civil court called the **chancery court** was created. One of its functions was to provide for the welfare of minor children, in particular those left orphaned or abandoned. The doctrine of *parens patriae*, meaning "the state as parent," gave the king, as the father of the country, authority to manage the affairs of dependent children through the courts. Such a child was called a **ward** of the state. Thus the concept of state intervention in the lives of children was established long ago, though it was not until the 1800s that modern behavioral scientists defined the concept of **juvenile delinquency**; reformers argued that youthful offenders should be handled by a separate court following civil procedures far different from the adult criminal court. The modern juvenile court represents a merger of the old authority of the chancery court and more contemporary ideas about causes of behavior.

The Juvenile Crime Problem

Today we take the existence of the juvenile court for granted: If you are a juvenile--meaning that you are under the age of adult criminal responsibility, which in the majority of states is 18--you will be dealt with by a separate system that processes only juveniles, under special rules and procedures. The only exceptions would be those persons legally juveniles who are waived or transferred to the adult courts for prosecution, usually either as habitual offenders or as defendants charged with the most serious violent crimes.

The juvenile justice system of today is often criticized as being ineffective in dealing with a growing problem of juvenile violence. The Office of Juvenile Justice and Delinquency Prevention (**OJJDP**), in the federal Department of Justice, along with FBI and court statistics and other juvenile crime research, suggests that juvenile crime, especially violent crime, has increased steadily at a time when adult crime is stable or declining (though in the last five years juvenile crime has declined also). Present estimates are that about one in six boys and one in twelve girls will be referred to the juvenile court before their eighteenth birthday. In 1994 one-third of arrests for the index crimes and one-sixth of arrests for the index violent crimes were of persons under 18. The arrest rate, which is the likelihood that a person of a certain age will be taken into custody, actually peaks out at age seventeen now and declines substantially over the next few years into the mid-twenties, where it declines even further. Our crime problem is increasingly a juvenile problem.

The perception that today's juveniles are meaner than those of even a few years ago has led to calls to "get tougher" on juvenile crimes, with the usual results--more court referrals, longer sentences, more juveniles behind bars, and more juveniles subject to transfer to adult court. Many urban jurisdictions now use the **vertical prosecution** approach, in which one prosecutor handles a case all the way through, to make sure that hard-cord juvenile offenders do not "slip through the cracks." We use such terms as "predator" and "**super predator**," usually referring to a violent, inner-city minority youth who is also a gang member, to define our fear of juvenile criminality. More violent and habitual offenders are being sent to the adult criminal court. This process, generally called **waiver**, transfer, or certification, is sometimes made mandatory by **statutory exclusion** of some underage criminals from the juvenile court; prosecutors in several states have **direct filing** authority to charge juveniles as adults. Still, only a small percentage of juveniles, less than two percent at present, are sent to adult court, and these are most often those whom court officials find to be "beyond rehabilitation," meaning they have been through the system several times and show little sign of changing. Most juvenile offenders today remain in the juvenile court.

Juvenile Violence: A Growing Problem

Juveniles not only commit violent crimes; they are also victims of violent crime at higher rates than are adults. Juvenile violence is often associated with gangs which now exist in many inner city and suburban areas. The victims of violence are often members of other gangs, or people who get in the way of inter-gang conflict. Much juvenile violence takes place at school; many schools in violent neighborhoods have become high-security fortresses in an effort to control violence by students and non-students on school property. As **juvenile gangs** have become more involved in drug trafficking, particularly with **crack cocaine**, they move into a more violent world of rip-offs, retaliation, and riddance of the opposition, namely other intrusive drug dealers.

The greater accessibility of weapons to juveniles and the enhanced cultural support for the use of deadly force to resolve disputes make life in the poorest parts of many large cities much like living in a war zone of some third world country. **Edwin Sutherland's** influential 1930s social learning theory of criminality, **differential association**, suggested that juveniles learn criminality from their peers and reject the more conventional values of middle-class society. The youngsters of today's urban underclass have been exposed to so much violence in their environment--being around such a high concentration of both offenders and victims their entire lives--that violence for them is just a fact of life. What values will they teach their own children?

Categories of Juvenile Offenders

The juvenile court was designed to apply civil law procedures to the lives of young persons who required state intervention. "**Juvenile**" comes from the Latin *juvenis*, meaning young, and it applies to children under the age of adult majority. The role of the state, through the juvenile court, was to provide protection or salvation, which developed over time into the contemporary idea of rehabilitation. We think of the juvenile court as handling criminals, but in fact a sizeable number of juvenile court cases deal with juveniles not charged with crimes.

A **delinquent juvenile** is a minor who has committed a crime for which an adult could be arrested. Technically a juvenile is not a delinquent until he has been to court and in a hearing before a judge has been "adjudicated delinquent." Delinquency is in this sense a legal label. In the broader social sense of delinquency, we call young people delinquent who engage in all sorts of inappropriate behavior, whether it is criminal or not. Delinquents are one category of young people processed through the juvenile court.

Another category is made up of what are called "**status offenders**," who have engaged in acts that are specifically wrong for underage youth but not against the law for adults. Such acts typically include running away, curfew violations, truancy and school misconduct, disobeying or threatening parents, sexual promiscuity (emphasized much more for girls than boys), and underage drinking. Status offenders may be referred to in the statutes as "**incorrigible juveniles**." In the terminology of the juvenile court, they are often identified as **PINS**, Persons In Need of Supervision, or CHINS or CINS, Children In Need of Supervision, or MINS, Minors In Need of Supervision. Some states have broadened this concept to FINS, Families In Need of Services, to recognize that the status offender's problem is usually part of a larger family context. The whole family often needs intervention, rather than just one problem child.

The third category of children subject to juvenile court intervention is made up of what the Uniform Juvenile Court Act--a legal model drawn up by the American Bar Association in the juvenile court reform era of the 1960s--calls "deprived, neglected, or dependent children." These children have not done anything wrong, or at least they are not in court because they have. Their problems lie with their parents' failure to provide for them. These children are usually termed either "**neglected**," meaning their parents are at fault for not taking proper care of them, or "**dependent**," meaning that the parents, through no fault of their own (such as sickness or mental illness or extreme poverty), have failed to provide a proper home environment. Children in either category can end up wards of the state, under *parens patriae*.

The juvenile court system uses different terminology and operates (at least in theory) under a premise different from the adult criminal court. Juveniles brought into the system are screened through a process called "intake." The majority of all juveniles taken into police custody are released or handled through other informal alternatives at this point; the more serious or chronic offenders will have a petition filed. The **petition** is the legal document that specifies the basis for juvenile court action. The juvenile who goes to court gets two hearings, one called "adjudication," which proves guilt, and the other "disposition," which determines the proper sentencing alternative--most often some form of probation. The most severe penalty that can be applied to a juvenile is a sentence to a **training school**, the nineteenth-century term for a juvenile prison. A training school or training institute was intended to apply the modern principles of training, education, and discipline necessary to turn the misbehaving young person into a righteous, productive adult citizen. The training schools for juveniles were like the reformatories for young adult offenders: they reflected the positive belief that **treatment** programs in an institutional setting could change behavior for the better. Not all people believe this today, but we keep acting as if we still believe.

Juvenile Rights: The Landmark Cases

The juvenile court was founded on the hope of rehabilitation. It was intended to help, embracing a broad range of young people, more non-criminals than criminals at first, but gradually mixing large numbers of each indiscriminately, within its loving arms. Acting through the kindly, paternal figure of the juvenile court judge, who represented the authority and discipline so obviously missing from the young person's life, the court was to push the juvenile along into the institutional or non-custodial setting where he or she could get the assistance needed for the problem behavior.

What happened over time was that juvenile justice became the most neglected part of the criminal justice system. It was the worst-funded and least-supported. It operated outside the visible adult system, and few people really knew how the juvenile courts operated. The legal process in the juvenile court was highly informal, lacking any relation to due process, and the power of juvenile court judges to impose sanctions absolute, as long as they remained within statutory age limits. A murderer could be put on probation, whereas a habitual runaway could be locked up until he turned 18 or 21. Criminals and non-criminals were dealt with as if they had similar problems and needs and were equally deserving of confinement. A generation ago, you could go to a secure juvenile training school in most states and find large numbers of status offenders and neglected children, as well as the mentally retarded, handicapped, orphans and abandoned children, and any other juvenile for whom the state lacked placement, confined with delinquents who had committed serious crimes. This mix gave rise to the frequently stated notion that what were intended to be "reform schools" became **"crime schools"** which made their young residents much worse. The recidivism rates of training schools, which were much higher than the rates for adult prisons, tended to support this notion.

In the 1960s and 1970s the courts, the federal government, and many state governments began to address the problems a half-century of neglect had created in the juvenile courts. The first two in a series of important United States Supreme Court decisions, *Kent v. United States*(1966) and *In re Gault*(1967), addressed the legal rights of juveniles. *Kent* was an important background case, although in substance it dealt only with the issue of waiving juveniles to adult courts for trial, in that it reviewed the history of second-rate juvenile court operations. The *Gault* case was much more important, applying adult standards of due process to what had previously been a very informal legal environment. With *Gault*, juveniles got the right to counsel, to notice of charges, to an adversarial proceeding, and to the privilege against self-incrimination that had been lacking previously. Other cases over the next decade further clarified the juvenile's legal rights.

In 1974, Congress passed the **Juvenile Justice and Delinquency Prevention Act**. This important piece of legislation had great impact on the states, requiring several important changes of direction in juvenile justice if the states wished to continue receiving federal crime control money:

    1. non-criminal status offenders, and other non-criminals, were not supposed to be mixed with criminal delinquents in secure custodial settings.

2. juveniles were not supposed to be mixed with adult offenders in jails and prisons.

3. a policy of **decarceration**, often called **deinstitutionalization** in its specific application to non-criminal juveniles, which involved reducing the number of young people held in secure custody, was to result in larger numbers of young people being dealt with through community-based alternatives rather than in secure settings.

4. **decriminalization** of deviant behavior was to result in the removal of non-criminals from the juvenile court and particularly from secure institutions such as detention homes and training schools. Criminals should be dealt with formally, according to the emerging concepts of juvenile due process, but non-criminals should be handled informally outside the system as much as possible.

Officials at the state level and in many local jurisdictions tried to go even further. **Jerome Miller** in Massachusetts closed his state's juvenile training schools in the early 1970s, trying to work with almost all delinquents, including violent offenders, in community-based programs. Miller rejected the **custody philosophy**, which suggests that some juvenile offenders on a scale of seriousness must always be locked up. He believed that for rehabilitation secure custody did far more harm than good.

Other jurisdictions pushed diversion programs designed to take lesser offenders and non-criminals out of the process early on. Seeking to avoid the effects of labelling, **diversion** allows the offender to avoid a conviction by participating in a program providing treatment, community service, or some other alternative disposition. Diversion programs in local courts continue to siphon off a good percentage of young people who a few years ago would have been passed along to formal adjudication in the juvenile court. Diversion programs are sometimes accused of "net-widening," that is, of bringing more minor offenders into the system (because an individual who fails in diversion is usually sent back to the formal system for routine processing), but these alternatives remain very popular with local officials who are often very discouraged by the results of more formal juvenile court processing.

Today's Approach to Juvenile Institutions

The two main secure institutions of juvenile justice remain the detention center or detention home and the training school--sometimes called the industrial school, reform school, training institute, or other names. **Detention** care is provided in a smaller, secure, locally operated facility. It is a jail for juveniles, holding pre-adjudicated and pre-dispositional delinquents and those awaiting transfer to state custody. Many detention homes are in the same situation as county jails. Inmates destined for state custody have backed up in local facilities, because of overcrowding in the state institutions. Then the mix of pre-court and sentenced juveniles in the detention center creates other tensions, especially when overcrowding becomes a problem here, too.

Over 60,000 juveniles are now confined in state training schools, with a lesser number in detention centers, and the numbers in both kinds of facilities are increasing steadily. Juvenile criminals are more violent and more chronic. More of them are being sentenced to secure custody and for longer periods of time. The new juvenile training schools being built now often resemble real prisons, rather than the high school campuses they were once modelled after. There is more maximum security and more guards. They remain far more expensive than adult prisons because of their education and treatment programming. Training schools remain committed to providing treatment for juveniles, even in the face of extensive research that shows it is mostly ineffective as measured by recidivism. No one wants to write a teenager off as being beyond redemption or change, even if he or she has committed a serious crime.

The premise of juvenile justice is that no child should be consigned to a wasted life before he reaches adulthood; the people who work in this system continue to advocate the goal of rehabilitation even though they fail far more often than they succeed. Sometimes success is defined in different terms: Sure he's still a criminal, but maybe he's not quite as violent as he was before, or maybe he can read a little better. Maybe he won't change now, but maybe he will change earlier than he would have otherwise. The people who work in juvenile justice are often their own worst critics. Considering the clientele society gives them to work with, they say, failure comes with the territory. But most still believe that our system of juvenile justice works better with young people than the alternative, often discussed today, of abolishing the juvenile court and simply treating all juveniles as adults, including punishing them with adult sentences. That was the old way of dealing with juveniles, before the 1800s, and it failed to deter or prevent the emergence of juvenile delinquency as a serious social problem.

Today's juvenile courts are more punitive than previously, and more juveniles are being sent to adult courts for trials, but most juveniles continue to be handled by a system committed to two principles:

     1. helping is more purposeful than locking people up.

     2. hoping for change is better than punishing failure. Most juveniles will outgrow their criminal behavior before they become adults. The ones who are punished least are the ones most likely to avoid adult criminality.

SELF TEST

Multiple Choice

1. If your mother was a crack-head prostitute who ran the street and left you, at ten years old, alone in your apartment for days at a time, you might be brought into juvenile court as a(n):
   - a. delinquent
   - b. status offender
   - c. neglected child
   - d. emancipated child
   - e. incorrigible juvenile

2. The Latin phrase meaning "the state as parent," used as the basis of the authority of the juvenile court, is:
   - a. *vox populi*
   - b. *non compos mentis*
   - c. *sub judice*
   - d. *particeps criminis*
   - e. *parens patriae*

3. *In re Gault* is said to provide for:
   - a. more professional juvenile probation officers
   - b. due process in the juvenile courts
   - c. forbidding the execution of anyone who is still legally a juvenile
   - d. expanded crime prevention in poorer urban areas
   - e. broader police powers to search for weapons on the street

4. Which one of the following would NOT be a juvenile status offense?
   - a. running away
   - b. curfew violation
   - c. possession of a concealed weapon
   - d. truancy
   - e. ungovernability

5. Edwin Sutherland's sociological theory used an equation calculating definitions favorable to criminality divided by definitions favorable to law-abiding behavior. The name of his theory was:
   - a. sociobiology
   - b. conflict theory
   - c. concentric zone
   - d. differential association
   - e. routine activities theory

6. Recent estimates are that about one in every _____ boys will appear in juvenile court sometime before their eighteenth birthday.
     a. 2
     b. 4
     c. 6
     d. 10
     e. 20

7. A policy of "decarceration," if followed seriously over a period of years, would result in the population of juveniles in confinement:
     a. going down
     b. remaining stable
     c. being made up more of habitual offenders
     d. containing more violent and property offenders but fewer drug offenders
     e. increasing rapidly

8. A critical decision is made early in the juvenile justice process that determines whether the juvenile will be discharged at once or sent on to court; this point is called:
     a. aftercare
     b. recidivism
     c. waiver
     d. intake
     e. monitoring

9. The serious crime for which more juveniles than adults are arrested is:
     a. arson
     b. burglary
     c. drug possession
     d. forcible rape
     e. simple assault

10. The most common age at which a person committing a new crime would no longer be under the jurisdiction of the juvenile court is:
     a. 14
     b. 16
     c. 18
     d. 19
     e. 21

True or False

_____ 11. One of the principles of the common law was that persons under 18 could not be punished in the criminal court for violating the law.

_____ 12. The arrest rate of juveniles for violent crimes went up from the early 1980s through 1994, then began to decline.

_____ 13. The first juvenile court was established in London in 1783.

_____ 14. The law provides that any juvenile who commits a felony can be locked up in an adult jail and mixed with adult offenders.

_____ 15. The Juvenile Justice and Delinquency Prevention Act of 1974 encouraged a policy of locking up more juveniles to control serious crime.

_____ 16. Detention care is primarily intended for those juveniles who could not be held in secure confinement if they were adjudicated delinquent.

_____ 17. All states allow juveniles to be transferred for trial in the adult criminal court under certain circumstances.

_____ 18. Teenagers are victims of violent crimes at rates higher than adults are.

_____ 19. A diversion program for juveniles is like shock probation for adults--a short stay in a secure facility before being placed on formal probation in the community.

_____ 20. In the juvenile court, a "juvenile delinquent" is any child whose behavior fails to conform to the expectations of the police or other social institutions.

Fill In the Blanks

21. The English common law court that was given jurisdiction over "unattached" children was the _____.

22. The first United States Supreme Court decision of the 1960s that directly challenged the traditional authority of the juvenile court was _____.

23. The policy which would remove non-criminal deviant behavior from juvenile court jurisdiction is called _____.

24. The legal category of anti-social acts committed by minors is _____.

25. Recent statistics indicate that crime peaks out at age _____.

26. The two most noticeable differences between juvenile trials and adult trials are that juveniles have no right to _____ and no right to _____.

27. The violent crime for which juveniles are arrested most, as a part of all offenders arrested for that crime, is _____, 30 percent of the total of all arrests for this crime in 1997.

28. The minimum age (at the time of the crime) for which a juvenile can get a death sentence in the United States today is _____.

29. According to Allen and Simonsen, in the 1970s the traditional educational focus of juvenile institutions expanded to make more room for the component of _____.

30. The most important piece of federal legislation, in terms of changing the direction of the juvenile justice system, was the _____.

Matching

_____ 31. Under common law, a child who was placed under government control by the chancery court.

_____ 32. The legal document used to process the child through the juvenile court.

_____ 33. The Massachusetts juvenile commissioner who closed down his state's juvenile training schools in the 1970s.

_____ 34. The idea that training schools turn juveniles into hardened criminals.

_____ 35. The general term for a program that takes a juvenile out of the formal system before his court hearing.

_____ 36. The purpose, at least in theory, of the modern juvenile court.

_____ 37. Where a juvenile would be held pre-court instead of being held in jail.

_____ 38. The federal office with general authority for juvenile justice and delinquency prevention.

_____ 39. The term for a minor who commits an offense that would be a crime if it was committed by an adult.

_____ 40. The term used for the violent, menacing juvenile offender who is associated with the poor, gang-infested inner city neighborhood.

a. common law
b. *parens patriae*
c. ward
d. chancery court
e. juvenile delinquency
f. OJJDP
g. super predator
h. statutory exclusion
i. waiver
j. direct filing
k. juvenile gangs
l. crack cocaine
m. Edwin Sutherland
n. differential association
o. juvenile
p. delinquent juvenile
q. status offender
r. incorrigible juvenile
s. PINS

t. dependent
u. neglected
v. intake
w. petition
x. training school
y. treatment
z. "crime schools"
aa. *Kent v. United States*
bb. *In re Gault*
cc. Juvenile Justice and Delinquency Prevention Act (1974)
dd. decarceration
ee. deinstitutionalization
ff. decriminalization
gg. Jerome Miller
hh. custody philosophy
ii. diversion
jj. detention
kk. vertical prosecution

Discussion

41. Briefly explain the origin and meaning of the concept of *parens patriae*.

42. How has the legal system responded to the common perception that violence by juveniles is getting worse?

43. How have juvenile gangs contributed to the worsening problem of juvenile violence?

44. List the main so-called "due process" provisions of the *Gault* decision.

45. What are some kinds of behavior that might cause a juvenile to be petitioned to court as a status offender?

46. How are juvenile training schools different from adult prisons?

CHAPTER SEVENTEEN

Special Category Offenders

CHAPTER OBJECTIVES

We have already seen that men and women in prison have many problems--few of them were very successful at anything, including criminality, before they came to prison. But many prisoners, because of physical, mental, behavioral, or background disadvantages, are further isolated from the prison mainstream. They are often called "special needs" or "special category" offenders who require extra care within the prison population. After reading the material in this chapter, you should be familiar with the issues about each of these categories of prison inmates:
1. the mentally ill offender.
2. the mentally retarded or developmentally challenged offender.
3. the sex offender.
4. the HIV/AIDS inmate.
5. the geriatric inmate.

KEY TERMS AND CONCEPTS

mentally disturbed
asylum
Community Mental Health Act
deinstitutionalize
transinstitutionalization
not guilty by reason of insanity (NGRI)
incompetent to stand trial
criminally insane
guilty but mentally ill (GBMI)
insanity defense
predict potential dangerousness
developmentally challenged
mentally retarded
Ruiz v. Estelle
sodomy

sex offenses
sex offender
child abuser
child molester
buggery
depo provera
HIV infection
AIDS
antiviral drugs
elderly inmates
geriatric prisoner
three strikes laws
assisted-living prison
right to treatment

CHAPTER SUMMARY

The Mentally Disordered Offender

The mentally ill or **mentally disturbed** have been dealt with in an institutional setting since the late middle ages, when the **asylum** first appeared in Europe. Committing the seriously mentally ill to the asylum became a standard practice of modern society. State-operated asylums grew plentiful and huge, many of them larger than modern penitentiaries. Beginning in the 1960s, the state mental hospital's role in providing long-term confinement for large numbers of marginally mentally ill patients came into serious question. In the 1970s, the **Community Mental Health Act** adopted in the states accomplished a major change. Only the non-functioning and dangerous (to themselves or others) inmates were to remain hospitalized. The others were to be **deinstitutionalized**--returned to the community and treated through clinics on an out-patient basis.

What was wrong with this scenario? It certainly sounded good, and it was protective of the rights of the confined. But it turned loose on the streets many thousands of mentally dysfunctional former patients--people who weren't directly dangerous but who were also not very productive and not playing by other people's conventional rules. Many of them are today's homeless people, marching the streets to their different drum. And many of them, in the process called "**transinstitutionalization**," have left the asylum for the jail and prison. Left on their own, they keep messing up enough to stay in trouble with the law. The population of mentally ill inmates in corrections increased as the population of the asylum declined.

Mentally Ill Inmates

It is estimated that about fifteen percent of prisoners have severe or significant psychiatric disabilities. Although the prison is not required to provide treatment in the sense of rehabilitation programming to make the inmate better, it is required to provide medical care, including treatment for serious emotional illness. Thus the jail and prison have gotten more and more into the delivery of mental health services. Every large correctional facility has to make some provision for treating the large numbers of mentally ill inmates coming its way.

The Criminally Insane

Insanity is a legal term for a mental condition. Insanity as a legal defense is of fairly recent origin. Before a couple of hundred years ago, it really did not matter if the offender was mentally disordered. He still got the same punishment that a right-thinking offender got. Today the states use several different definitions, but all of them center around the person's ability to know right from wrong and behave accordingly. The **insanity defense** is used infrequently, generally in less than one percent of criminal cases. When it is, the defendant must typically have a fairly well-documented history of mental disorders for it to be used successfully. The defendant enters a plea of "**not guilty by reason of insanity (NGRI)**" and then must prove that he did not know right from wrong at the time of the crime. Some defendants do not deny they were sane at the time of the crime but argue that they have subsequently gone insane--they are "**incompetent to stand trial**," typically because they do not understand the proceedings against them and cannot aid their lawyer in the defense.

Criminally insane people may end up in prison mental wards if they become severely mentally disordered after conviction; or they end up in secure confinement within mental hospitals if they are found incompetent to stand trial or if they are found not guilty by reason of insanity. Their discharge becomes a medical decision, subject to the court's approval. Someone who was incompetent and regains competency after treatment can then be tried on the original criminal charges. So sometimes it is better to stay incompetent as long as possible and wait for everything to die down.

In the 1980s, after John Earl Hinckley was found not guilty by reason of insanity for shooting President Ronald Reagan, several states abolished the insanity defense and created the optional verdict of **"guilty but mentally ill (GBMI)."** Offenders get an ordinary sentence but serve it in a mental hospital or a prison mental ward--if space is available. They are convicts first and patients second.

The question psychiatrists are often called upon to answer is: "Will this person commit another crime if he or she is released after treatment?" Psychiatrists cannot **predict potential dangerousness** with any degree of certainty. There is evidence that insane offenders after discharge have a lower recidivism rate than sane offenders, but the public in large measure looks upon insane offenders as either dangerous persons or con artists and at the insanity defense as a way of beating the system.

The Developmentally Challenged Offender

In a different category from the mentally disordered offender is the offender who is **mentally retarded** or **developmentally challenged**, determined by an IQ score of 69 or below. Five to ten percent of the offenders in a typical state prison population test in this category; some might be above it one time and below it the next. Many of them seem normal in a brief conversation, and they are fully accountable legally for their actions, yet they are often seriously handicapped in the prison environment. They have trouble learning and following the rules, they do not adapt well socially, they are often exploited or victimized by other inmates, and they often do not do well in prison programs because of their intellectual impairment (which affects parole consideration and the likelihood of early release).

The state of Texas, which found in the landmark case of *Ruiz v. Estelle* that about ten to fifteen percent of its inmate population was retarded, said these inmates were more likely to be injured and more likely to be found guilty of disciplinary infractions. Most experts today do not believe that the mentally retarded are significantly more likely to engage in criminal behavior because of their limited mental capacity, but they do recognize that the mentally retarded offender is doubly disadvantaged in prison. He has trouble conforming to the strict rules, and his fellow inmates too often take advantage of his limitations. Such inmates often end up in protective custody.

Sex Offenses and Sex Offenders

Broadly defined, a **sex offense** can be any criminal act of a sexual nature. On one end of the scale is the violent offense of forcible rape; on the other end are such minor crimes as window peeping, indecent exposure, and prostitution. In between are lesser sexual assaults, child molestation, incest, and offenses in the "crimes against nature" category rarely prosecuted today--sodomy, buggery, and bestiality. **Sodomy** refers to any sex act other than conventional penis-to-vagina sex between a man and a woman. **Buggery** refers to anal sex between a man and another man, a woman, or an animal. And bestiality refers to sex between a human and an animal (regardless of whether the animal is an adult and consents of its own free will). There are many other older sex offenses, such as fornication and adultery, that are rarely prosecuted any longer, unless you happen to be a member of the armed forces where such acts remain court martial offenses.

Sex offenses may be heterosexual or homosexual, they may be violent or consensual (as in carnal knowledge or statutory rape where one participant is under age), they may involve strangers or people in the same family, they may be one time events or they may involve the same people in relationships that go on for years (as in family incest), they may involve offenders who are otherwise apparently normal (like athletes or fraternity boys), or who are so twisted and perverted that their whole lives are wrapped around their criminal acts (like the serial rapists or sex fiends of lore).

A **sex offender** is by definition anyone convicted of a sex offense. What imprisoned sex offenders have in common is that most are men and most are there for heterosexual acts. There is a popular perception that sex offenders are stigmatized within the inmate subculture. While it is true that child molesters and other offenders convicted of sex crimes against family members may be looked down on as being slimy and weird, these offenders are probably less likely to be systematically victimized today than they once were. The hierarchy is not as rigid and the stigma not as strong; among today's inmates, there is more of an "anything goes" attitude.

Comparatively few sex offenders are in institutions designed specifically for treating their behavioral problems; comparatively few sex offenders are taking part in any regular treatment program. Of the ones who are in treatment, Allen and Simonsen suggest that the great majority fall into one of these five categories of offenses:
1. rape, attempted rape, assault with intent to rape, and the like.
2. child molestation.
3. incest.
4. exhibitionism and voyeurism.
5. miscellaneous offenses (breaking and entering, arson, and the like) in cases in which there is a sexual motivation.

Participants are primarily young men who have a history of involvement in a variety of offenses of a sexual nature. Many of them may be seeking self-understanding or enlightenment, and many may be seeking ratification of treatment--the proof they need that they have been "cured" so they can get out of prison faster. Treatment modalities often involve a combination of topics, including sex education, social skills, anger management, and avoiding risks. Some treatment programs also involve the participation of victims of sex crimes to discuss their feelings with offenders.

Offenders who sexually victimize children are not very popular at the moment. **Child abusers**, who physically abuse children, are dealt with more severely now than they were a generation ago; **child molesters** have fared even worse under the law of late. "Megan's Law" and other sex-offender notification laws have spread across the states. These statutes generally require convicted child molesters to notify law enforcement authorities and often nearby neighbors of their criminal history. Several states have passed laws giving prisons the authority to keep dangerous sex offenders locked up even after their prison term expires, in effect holding them in extended quarantine as if they were mentally ill. Other states have experimented with castration, either voluntary physical castration or chemical castration through the use of the drug **depo provera** to kill the offender's sex drive. The other inmates may not care as much now what you are in prison for, but society does. The incidence of recidivism among people who sexually victimize children is high enough that the public wants such people identified and isolated.

HIV and AIDS in Prison

The rate of **HIV infection** in prison is estimated to be six to seven times higher than in the general population, primarily because prisons contain such a high concentration of intravenous drug users. Just over two percent of the present prison population are known to be HIV positive; about a quarter of these men and women have **AIDS**. Generally the higher the number of drug offenders in prison, the greater the number of HIV inmates. In New York state prisons, about one in six inmates is estimated to be HIV positive. The figures for female inmates are even higher than for males, with Hispanic females having the highest rate of infection of any prison population group. Once HIV male inmates enter prison, the spread of infection through homosexual contact becomes a real concern. Many state prisons have education programs about HIV and AIDS, warning inmates of the dangers of prison sex. These programs often fall on deaf ears. Most jails and prisons refuse to take the more practical course of giving inmates condoms for sex or bleach for needles used to inject drugs, because that would constitute *de facto* recognition that inmates in the prison are having sex and using drugs. Some states test incoming inmates for HIV and some do not; court decisions have approved both policies. In all states HIV status is a confidential medical condition, unless the inmate chooses to tell others about it. Most states do not segregate HIV inmates merely because they are infected; if and when they develop AIDS, they are then typically segregated because of the more extensive and controlled medical care required. Healthy inmates often take out their hostilities on HIV inmates in general population; they do not want the sick inmates in their environment.

HIV and AIDS are particular problems in correctional facilities because of the cost of treatment, the danger to staff, and the danger to other inmates. AIDS has become a leading cause of prisoner deaths in recent years. But other infectious diseases also thrive in prison--hepatitis, rubella, and tuberculosis. The prison's clientele--young men who have abused drugs and alcohol and not received good medical care--are prime candidates for disease. The incidence of tuberculosis--including multi-drug resistant strains in people with weakened immune systems--in jails and prisons has increased markedly in recent years. Correctional facilities now spend far more time treating sick inmates than they once did. The **antiviral drugs** and the new protease inhibitors used to treat HIV and AIDS are expensive medications. The level of medical care required to treat the later stages of AIDS is prohibitively expensive.

Prisons are rarely accused of providing exceptionally good medical care. When prisoners are seriously ill, they are always in fear of dying because the prison will try to use the cheapest, most marginal treatment available. The prisoner's **"right to treatment"** is viewed by prison administrators (and the courts) as secondary to the other purposes of imprisonment. Prisoners put it another way: "Prison hospitals save money, not lives." They know a serious illness in prison is often a death sentence.

Geriatric Inmates: The Graying of American Prisons

We have already looked at issues relating to the aging of men and women in prison. In a few more years, about one in ten inmates will be over fifty. Prisons will have to deal with spiralling health care costs and with issues relating to inmate interaction, housing, and work assignments. Many states are already building new prisons--usually minimum security--for **elderly inmates**. And because many of these inmates are ineligible for release under the more punitive **three strikes laws** and no-parole laws adopted in recent years, many of them, though healthy now, are facing the definite prospect of dying in prison. Older inmates are often forgotten about by people in the free world. The **geriatric prisoner**--frail, ill, disoriented--is often a truly pathetic person, obviously presenting no danger to the public but still confined in an **assisted-living prison**, destined to die behind bars.

SELF TEST

Multiple Choice

1. What institution is described as a long-time dumping ground for the mentally disordered?
    a. the hospice
    b. the prison hospital
    c. the asylum
    d. the jail
    e. the community mental health clinic

2. Yesterday's ambulatory, non-criminal mental patient is today's:
    a. hopeless lunatic
    b. political official
    c. homeless person
    d. drug addict
    e. cult member

3. Four of the following statements about developmentally challenged offenders are true, according to Santamour and West; which one is NOT?
    a. They get paroled later.
    b. The follow the rules much better.
    c. They are less likely to take part in rehabilitation programs.
    d. The‚ are often harassed by other inmates.
    e. They have trouble adjusting to prison routines.

4. During the period of "denial and neglect," from roughly 1921 to 1960, theorists argued about whether _____ predisposed one to commit criminal acts.
   a. excess body hair
   b. mental retardation
   c. lack of education
   d. extra male chromosomes
   e. homosexuality

5. The greatest number of sex offenders in treatment programs are:
   a. young men
   b. mentally retarded
   c. homosexual women
   d. people who have sexually abused animals
   e. juveniles confined in training schools

6. What is the drug depo provera used in treating?
   a. mental retardation
   b. AIDS
   c. Alzheimer's
   d. schizophrenia
   e. compulsive sex offenders

7. It is estimated that about _____ percent of prisoners have severe or significant psychiatric disabilities.
   a. 1
   b. 4
   c. 15
   d. 27
   e. 80

8. The new insanity verdict of the 1980s, which several states used to replace the "not guilty by reason of insanity" verdict, was:
   a. "diminished capacity"
   b. "exceptional personality"
   c. "totally deranged"
   d. "guilty but mentally ill"
   e. "crazy but culpable"

9. The higher rate of HIV infection in prison, in comparison to the outside world, is most related to:
   a. drug usage
   b. homosexuality
   c. prostitution
   d. poor nutrition
   e. child abuse

10. If you were discussing "transinstitutionalization," you would be suggesting that the mentally impaired had been removed from mental hospitals and put into:
   a. private homes
   b. work camps
   c. suspended animation
   d. shock therapy
   e. jails and prisons

True or False

_____ 11. The basic purpose of the Community Mental Health Act was to remove more homeless people from the street by confining them in jails for treatment.

_____ 12. Most inmates who come to prison HIV positive are male homosexuals.

_____ 13. The number of elderly inmates in prison, as a percentage of the total population, is in decline as prisons try to make room for younger, more violent offenders.

_____ 14. Once someone is found incompetent to stand trial, he or she can never again be tried for that crime, even if his or her mental state improves, under the rule of double jeopardy.

_____ 15. A person with an IQ of 69 or below is generally acknowledged to be retarded.

_____ 16. There are probably more men in prison for heterosexual forcible rape than for any other sex offense.

_____ 17. Female inmates are much less likely to be HIV positive than male inmates are.

_____ 18. By early in the twenty-first century, about one in three prisoners will be age fifty or older.

_____ 19. The case of _Ruiz v. Estelle_, which dealt with the issue of medical care provided to Texas prison inmates, found that less than one percent of these inmates were mentally retarded.

_____ 20. Psychiatrists have developed a battery of tests that allow them to predict with a high degree of accuracy which mentally ill persons will be dangerous after release from confinement.

Fill In the Blanks

21. Allen and Simonsen call asylums or mental hospitals a(n) _____, because for a long time they operated out of the sight and concern of society.

22. A defendant found "not guilty by reason of insanity" would ordinarily be found in a(n) _____ within a few days to a few weeks after the trial.

23. Allen and Simonsen estimate that of those defendants using the insanity defense at trial, only about one in _____ is found to be "not guilty by reason of insanity."

24. Judge Justice, in his findings in the Texas prison lawsuit of _Ruiz v. Estelle_, observed that the mentally retarded have two major disadvantages. They did not do well in disciplinary hearings, and they were more likely to be _____.

25. In Minnesota, the largest single category of prisoners are in prison for _____ offenses.

26. You would characterize Ahtanum View as a(n) _____ prison.

27. Besides HIV and rubella, the two other major communicable diseases considered serious threats in correctional facilities today are _____ and _____.

28. Celus, the Roman scholar, proposed that "hunger, chains, and fetters" should be used to chastise the _____ person who did or said anything wrong.

29. If you had sexual relations with a person under the age of puberty, you would probably pick up the label of _____.

30. Of AIDS, suicide, and homicide, the one responsible for the most prison deaths each year is _____.

Matching

_____ 31. The social institution developed to house the mentally disordered.

_____ 32. A transvestite male prostitute who made his living performing oral sex on other men could be convicted of this crime.

_____ 33. The term for those older prisoners who are specifically debilitated and in need of greater care.

_____ 34. The term for the effort to take harmless patients out of mental hospitals and put them back into the community.

_____ 35. The term for someone who was sane at the time of the crime but becomes insane before trial.

_____ 36. The slightly more politically correct term for retarded.

_____ 37. Any offender convicted of a crime involving the performance of a sexual act.

_____ 38. The term for AZT and other chemical substances used in combatting HIV infection.

_____ 39. A new legal judgment that developed in the 1980s; its effect is to put insane defendants in prison serving sentences while they receive treatment.

_____ 40. The process of transferring mental patients from hospitals to the street to prison.

a. mentally disturbed
b. asylum
c. Community Mental Health Act
d. deinstitutionalize
e. transinstitutionalization
f. not guilty by reason of insanity (NGRI)
g. incompetent to stand trial
h. criminally insane
i. guilty but mentally ill (GBMI)
j. insanity defense
k. predict potential dangerousness
l. developmentally challenged
m. mentally retarded
n. *Ruiz v. Estelle*
o. sodomy

p. sex offenses
q. sex offender
r. child abuser
s. child molester
t. buggery
u. depo provera
v. HIV infection
w. AIDS
x. antiviral drugs
y. elderly inmates
z. geriatric prisoner
aa. three strikes laws
bb. assisted-living prison
cc. right to treatment

Discussion

41. Explain what happened to cause more mentally ill persons to wind up in correctional facilities.

42. Contrast the verdicts of "not guilty by reason of insanity" and "guilty but mentally ill."

43. What problems is the developmentally challenged offender likely to experience in prison?

44. What are the different types of sex offenders you would find in greatest numbers in prison treatment programs?

45. What problems does the increasing number of HIV positive inmates present to the prison administration?

46. How significant in number and impact are the special category offenders? Which category do you think probably has the greatest effect on the operation of the prison?

CHAPTER EIGHTEEN

Inmate and Ex-Offender Rights

CHAPTER OBJECTIVES

The convicted felon in confinement exists in a legal world much different from that of free people outside prison. Prisoners give up many rights upon conviction, and the rights they retain are constrained by the nature of confinement. The loss of citizenship rights is not limited to felons serving prison terms. Anyone convicted of a felony, including those persons who never go to prison, may lose any number of citizenship rights and face other restrictions due to the criminal conviction. After reading the material in this chapter, you should be familiar with:

1. the historical legal status of the convicted felon.
2. principal issues in prison litigation, including contact with the outside world, religion, access to the courts, and medical care.
3. inmate lawsuits challenging conditions of confinement.
4. social changes affecting the legal rights of prisoners.
5. different approaches to reforming prison conditions.
6. the collateral consequences of a conviction.
7. the civil rights commonly denied felons.
8. procedures for registering ex-offenders.
9. methods of erasing criminal records and restoring offenders' rights.

KEY TERMS AND CONCEPTS

convicted offender

final guilty verdict

civil death

"hands off" policy

family ties

conjugal visit

home furlough

"clear and present danger"

compelling state need

contraband

certain literature

established religion

Black Muslims

Ex parte Hull

jailhouse lawyers

Estelle v. Gamble

deliberate indifference

Section 1983

tort

grievance board

ombudsman

court master

ex-con

ex-offender

collateral consequences

social stigma

"marked man"

self-esteem

transitional period

occupational disability statutes

firearms disabilities

employment restrictions

annulment

"vest-pocket" record

registration of criminals

"yellow card"

CHAPTER SUMMARY

The Status of the Convicted Offender

At one time there would have been no need for this chapter. A convicted felon had no legal status and no legal rights. Under common law an English felon was put in the position of an outlaw. He was no longer a member of society; thus he lost the rights of citizenship, becoming the equivalent of what the later Soviet system would call a "non-person." When the **final guilty verdict** was pronounced, the **convicted offender** became a dead man in the eyes of the law. The legal concept was called **"civil death,"** meaning that the felon no longer had the civil rights of other persons. Whatever happened to him after conviction, including death, was legally fitting. This legal status, or lack of legal status, attached to the convicted felon continued for a very long time, well into the days of the penitentiary. An 1871 Virginia court decision, *Ruffin v. Commonwealth*, declared the convicted felon to be "a slave of penal servitude to the State ... for the time being, the slave of the State." By this time ex-convicts were no longer considered civilly dead, but they lost many rights upon conviction that they did not automatically regain; they had to pursue executive clemency, through the governor's pardon power, to get these lost rights back.

While they were in custody, the law still viewed them as dead men. If anything happened to them, if they died from poor treatment, if they were harmed by another inmate, or if they were killed by a guard, no explanation was necessary. A prisoner in confinement had no legal rights, and the state was not liable for any misadventure that befell a felon in prison. The courts left prison operations alone, maintaining that court officials lacked the expertise to tell prison officials how to run their institutions. The concept, called the **"hands off" policy**, allowed prison wardens to run their institutions with absolute legal impunity. Prison officials were not accountable in either state or federal courts for their actions or for conditions within their institutions.

Incidental court decisions as early as the 1940s began to crack the shell of hands off, but it was not broken completely open until the 1960s. The due process revolution led by the Warren Court, named for the Chief Justice of the U.S. Supreme Court at the time, reached into prisons to provide prisoners with expanded legal rights, including the right to collect damages for injuries or harm done, and far greater access to the courts--both state and federal courts.

The legal standing of prison inmates today is much different from what it was before the 1960s. *Wolff v. McDonnell* (1974), an important U.S. Supreme Court decision providing for due process in prison disciplinary proceedings, said that the prisoner "is not wholly stripped of constitutional protections. . . . He may not be deprived of life, liberty or property without due process of law." This obviously puts the prisoner in a very different environment. He loses those rights necessary to confinement but he retains access to the courts to determine if he is being punished in a constitutional manner.

What are the rights of a convicted felon in confinement? Much of the litigation coming out of prison deals with recurring issues, including:
1. visiting, both ordinary family visits and conjugal visiting
2. mail and correspondence
3. searches and contraband
4. established religion
5. access to courts and counsel
6. medical treatment and care

In the deprived world of prison, prisoners would like to extend their rights as far as possible. Rights impose obligations on prison authorities. What prisoners would like to be called "rights," prison authorities would like to call "privileges" which must be earned and which can be taken away if the prisoner misbehaves. At one time the direction of the major court decisions seemed to be moving toward rights, but in recent years more conservative federal and state courts have sided more with privileges, giving prison officials more discretion to limit and take away. The courts' basic premise now is that as long as a prison rule or policy makes sense and can be justified by prison officials, it is likely constitutional. So two states can have policies completely opposed to each other, such as testing and not testing incoming inmates for HIV, and the courts allow *both* policies to stand, as long as the reasons for the policies are sensible.

Community Ties

One of the defining qualities of imprisonment is separation from the outside world. Most prisoners are unattached young men, but even those who have **family ties** face severe limits on the frequency, duration, and type of contact allowed in visiting. Many prisons (and even more jails) still enforce rules on non-contact visits, and in many institutions the display of any kind of personal affection is a write-up. Sex is absolutely forbidden, except in the six states that allow **conjugal visits** for at least a portion of the inmate population, usually trusties or medium security inmates who are married and have good conduct records. Allen and Simonsen suggest that the use of **home furloughs** could do much to restore family ties, but alternatives that allow prison inmates to wander around loose for three days or a week at a time are suspect at the moment.

Mail and Contraband

Prisons control not only the flow of people but also the movement of property into the institution. Mail can be opened and inspected but is generally not censored any longer, absent what is called a **"clear and present danger"** to security or a **compelling state need** to censor the mail of an individual inmate. Prisons limit the amount of property a prisoner can have in his possession, for obvious space reasons, and they control the types and numbers of property items allowed--one small radio, two blankets, six pairs of shoes, and so on. Anything not allowed--which could be weapons or drugs or escape tools but could also be sugar-free gum or liquid paper--is **contraband**, subject to seizure and disciplinary action. Prisoners have no real Fourth Amendment freedom from unreasonable searches and seizures; the need for security overpowers the Fourth Amendment in prison. Much recent litigation has concerned **certain literature** that comes to prisoners through the mails, especially magazines focusing on sex, drugs, terrorism, weapons, and other harmful things that prisoners should not be thinking about. Although court decisions generally allow prisons the authority to censor incoming publications, some prisons do so and some do not. Practices within states vary considerably.

Religious Rights in Prison

Religion is very important to many prisoners, the center of their prison life. Some of the most important early prisoners' rights cases back in the 1960s dealt with the right of inmates to practice an **established religion**, in these cases the **Black Muslim** faith. The prisons saw the Muslims as an adversarial political group; the courts ruled that prisoners had to be allowed to practice their faith and not be punished for doing so. Other religious groups have been involved in prison litigation, and prisoners are always inventing new religions to see what the courts will allow them to do.

Access to Court and Counsel

To win any of the legal rights they enjoy today, prisoners had to have access to the courts to file their lawsuits. *Ex Parte Hull*, a 1940 Supreme Court case, established that state prisoners have a right to file *habeas corpus* petitions (asking the court to determine if they are being held legally) in the federal courts.

This avenue was not used much until the 1960s, because the courts were not listening much prior to that time; it continues to be used a lot today, even though the courts are not listening as much now as they were a few years ago. Inmates do have much greater access to prison law libraries and to the assistance of **jailhouse lawyers**--politely called inmate counsels or counsel substitutes--but these rights are not unlimited, and prisoners generally do not have the right to have counsel appointed to represent them in prison litigation.

The Right to Medical Treatment and Care

Many prison lawsuits concern prison medical care, either the general quality of care provided the inmate population or the specific treatment an inmate received for an illness or injury. Many of these lawsuits find their way into federal court under Title 42, Section 1983, of the U.S. Code. A **Section 1983** suit gives the federal courts authority to hold local or state officials, such as prison guards and wardens, liable for damages if the public officers deprived the plaintiff (in these cases a prisoner) of his civil rights. It might be bad medical care, but, instead of malpractice, to a prisoner it is a civil rights violation. The current general standard in medical care litigation under Section 1983 is **"deliberate indifference,"** which is derived from a landmark Texas case, *Estelle v. Gamble* (1976). Prison officials must be shown to have been deliberately indifferent to the medical needs of the inmate for the inmate to collect damages. The exact meaning of deliberate indifference has been modified by succeeding court decisions over the past twenty years, and the plaintiff now bears quite a burden to prove his case.

Inmates also file **tort** suits for damages in state courts. It may often be easier to prove their allegations in state courts than in federal courts, but many state prison inmates do not place much faith in their own state court systems, which after all put them where they are. Most inmates believe the federal courts will give them a fairer shake, and the chances of winning are so slim in either setting it does not make a whole lot of difference.

Inmates' Lawsuits

Even though prisoners rarely win they continue filing lawsuits in massive numbers. A few of these suits are serious and valid; most are termed "frivolous," meaning without substance. The Prison Litigation Reform Act, passed by Congress in 1996, is intended to cut down on prison litigation in the federal courts by making it more difficult for inmates to get issues to court and keep them there. But prisoners are resourceful and have lots of time on their hands; they keep searching for new themes and for new wrinkles on old themes. Most lawsuits in federal court are filed either under the Eighth and Fourteenth Amendments--"cruel and unusual punishment" and "equal protection" and "due process" in the states--or under the Section 1983 civil rights provisions. Suits may be filed by individual inmates, alleging harm to them directly, or they may be class action suits attacking conditions (such as cigarette smoking) on behalf of the entire inmate population.

Even if much of it is a waste of time and energy, prison litigation has been responsible for many improvements in prison living conditions over the past thirty years. Reforms have been accomplished particularly through the federal courts, which have often placed individual prisons or entire prison systems (especially in the South) under court order to improve conditions. The courts often appoint experts called **court masters** to see that the correctional facilities comply with the orders of the court.

In the last few years many state corrections departments have looked at new ways to resolve inmate complaints about prison conditions short of litigation. These are internal devices which put the inmate in the position of complaining about prison conditions to the people running the prison. Are they really listening? In many cases, yes, because it is easier and cheaper to resolve complaints internally rather than fight the issues out at length in the courts. Several different methods are used. Most states have an internal complaint process, often called an administrative remedy procedure, to resolve minor complaints without filing lawsuits. In several states internal **grievance boards** are used to look into inmate complaints.

Several states have appointed a prison **ombudsman**, based on a Scandinavian official, whose job it is to accept and investigate inmate (and staff) complaints and recommend corrective action. Finally, as dispute resolution comes of age, several states are using outside mediators to resolve disputes between prisoners and prisons.

All of these mechanisms have been used successfully and hold much promise for the future, but prisoners still remain committed to challenging the system through the courts. They have not yet seen that their own excesses from the past, filing trivial suits as "recreational litigation," and the more conservative turn of the courts have undermined support for extending prisoners' rights any further. Prisoners' rights is not a completely dead issue, and no one is suggesting that we return to the "hands-off" era, but no one outside of prison really seems highly interested in expanding inmates' rights as a legal priority for now. Prisoners need to be more content with what they have and work to make themselves better instead of attacking the system, the litigation experts are saying. Otherwise they run the risk of further alienating the public, the political officials, and, most important, the judges whose support they really need.

Collateral Consequences of a Conviction

One of the traditions left over from civil death is the felon's loss of civil rights, even after discharge from prison or supervision and carrying over beyond the end of his sentence. These civil rights, such as voting, holding public office, marital and parental rights, serving on a jury, and possessing firearms, are often lost to the convicted felon until he goes through the formal procedure to get them restored. The **ex-offender**, often labelled an **ex-con** if he or she has been imprisoned, must also comply with administrative and legal restrictions, such as registration or notification of authorities, and employment licensing; he must also deal with the **social stigma** of being a felon. These are the **collateral consequences** of a felony conviction. Even with an estimated 50 million persons who have been arrested at least once in their lives, 14 million or more with felony convictions and more than five million presently under some form of correctional supervision (about two percent of the population), the ex-felon is still a "**marked man**" as he moves through decent society. Allen and Simonsen describe him as a "social and economic cripple" with low **self-esteem**. A gap separates him from the rest of society. In the **transitional period** between discharge from custody and reestablishing his or her place in the world, the ex-offender's status as an outcast with legally diminished status can have important attitudinal and behavioral effects.

The civil rights lost vary greatly from one state to another. Some are very restrictive, such as Mississippi, others, such as North Carolina and Washington, much less so. Felons in eleven states face disenfranchisement, the loss of the right to vote. In more than half the states, a felony conviction is automatic grounds for divorce. About a third of the states bar felons from holding public office, and about the same number bar felons from holding public employment. Convicted felons almost universally face **firearms disabilities** preventing them from lawfully owning or possessing firearms.

Many offenders probably could not care less about some of the common civil rights they have lost. What they need and want, more than anything else, is a job. Ex-offenders face **employment restrictions**, including **occupational disability statutes** that bar them from licenses in certain trades and professions. When they go in to apply for many jobs, the standard line on the employment application throws them into a quandary: "Have you ever been convicted of a felony?" In some states the application may ask the broader question about arrests, not just convictions. If ex-offenders answer yes, truthfully, their employer may turn them down as criminals (although the official reason would be that they were not right for the job). If they say no, they run the risk of being fired later for falsifying the employment application. Which option would you choose?

The Problem with a Record

The offender's criminal record does not go away by itself; generally the offender must pursue legal action at his own initiative to clear his record. The most sweeping--and least available--method of wiping out a record is through what is called **annulment**. The National Council on Crime and Delinquency, in its Model Act for Annulment of Conviction of Crime, states that the effect of an annulment is to restore all lost civil rights and to cancel the record of conviction and disposition. The responsibility for annulment would lie with the court which convicted the offender. The judge would issue the annulment order to assist in rehabilitation, when it was consistent with the public welfare.

Little support exists for the practice of annulment at present; the trend seems to be in the other direction, toward maintaining better records on convicted criminals and using the records to impose greater control over ex-offenders. Many courts used to maintain what are called **"vest-pocket" records** of criminal offenses, particularly minor offenses, meaning that the records were maintained locally for the information of the local courts, but not sent forward into the central repository at the state level. With the computer networks of today, it has become much more difficult to keep records out of the system.

Centralized data banks are often used as sources of information in those states that require **registration of criminals**. Registration of certain classes of criminals, particularly sex offenders, is becoming more common in the United States today. In Europe, where citizens have often been required to carry identity papers, former prisoners were once required to carry a **"yellow card"** showing that they had been in custody previously. When asked for their identification, they had to show their yellow card to the police, which probably did not do a lot for their credibility as law-abiding citizens. They carried the yellow card for life.

Sex offenders are acquiring their own yellow cards in the United States today. They are often required to register with law enforcement agencies and notify neighbors of their presence in the neighborhood. The state of Washington, which has been cited as a state that imposed few civil rights restrictions on ex-offenders, enacted a new **Community Protection Act** in 1990. Sex offenders are required to register with local police, who maintain a **sex-offender file** and can notify the community if they choose to. Police do not consider most sex offenders to be sexual predators who prey on strangers. Most sex offenders, including the child molesters who appear to be the focus of most sex-offender registration laws, do not victimize strangers. Their victims are acquaintances, friends, and relatives. But sex offenders are the center of so much negative attention (as in the murder of seven-year-old Megan Kanka by convicted sex offender Jesse Timmendequas in New Jersey in 1994, the crime that gave us **Megan's Law** and generated the national trend toward sex offender registration) that people have not yet asked if the registration laws will have any real effect in reducing sex crimes.

Restoring Offenders' Rights

The most conventional way for an offender to get lost civil rights restored is through the **executive clemency** process, under the authority of the governor or president. What the offender needs is a **pardon**. In some states certain classes of offenders whose terms have expired may be entitled to so-called automatic pardons, where no discretionary board action is needed. In other states, offenders must petition the state pardon board and appear in person to ask for a pardon--either full or conditional--to get those rights restored. The governor remains in charge of clemency, though in some states the pardon board has the authority to make decisions without his approval being necessary.

Even if a pardon is granted to the ex-offender, restoring the lost civil rights, the offender still has a criminal record. To get rid of the record, the ex-offender must get an **expungement** order signed by the court in which the offender was sentenced. This order would result in the destruction of the criminal history record related to the instant case. Both manual and computer files at all levels--local, state, and federal--should be purged of all information related to the defendant's involvement in the case. A similar process, called **"erasure of record,"** is used for juvenile court records, which by law are supposed to be sealed and not mixed with or carried over to the offender's adult criminal records. If the ex-offender follows both tracks--pardon and expungement--legally available in his state, he can get his lost rights back and his record wiped clean. The only limitations may be that he must wait some period of time past the expiration of his sentence to apply for either action, that each disposition on his record must be attacked separately, and that repeat offenders may not be eligible to apply. In truth, many ex-offenders, who are not known for their attention to bureaucratic detail, view these processes as so much mumbo jumbo. They never bother to apply. Ex-offenders are no longer civilly dead, but it still is not easy to make a fresh start.

The public image of the felon released from prison has been shaped not only by legal tradition but also by the media, in particular the crime movies of an earlier era. We think of the tough-talking, amoral ex-con, dedicated to a life of crime, pursuing the company of others living like himself in the criminal underworld, and anxious to resume the criminal activities interrupted by a prison term. In the real world it is not so simple. Many offenders released from prison want to "go straight" and avoid further run-ins with the law. Half of them may end up back in prison, but this statistic also means that half don't. Ex-offenders have families and friends; they need a place to live, a job, and productive ways to spend their time. It is not easy to leave prison, particularly if you have been away several years, and jump right back into mainstream society--not as an "ex-con."

SELF TEST

Multiple Choice

1. Title 42, Section 1983, of the U.S. Code is a statute specifically about:
    a. civil rights
    b. the death penalty
    c. the powers of prison officials
    d. disabled persons
    e. freedom of religious practice

2. The concept of "clear and present danger," in the prison context, is most related to:
    a. communicable diseases
    b. prison gangs
    c. threats to prison security
    d. terrorist groups
    e. knowledge gained from books in the prison library

3. The "hands-off" policy was finally abandoned during what decade?
    a. the 1790s
    b. the 1850s
    c. the 1930s
    d. the 1960s
    e. the 1980s

4. The purpose of the Prison Litigation Reform Act (1996) was to:
    a. provide more lawyers for inmates who want to file lawsuits
    b. require all lawsuits to be filed in a special federal court
    c. provide federal funds for prison libraries
    d. make the Bill of Rights applicable to the states
    e. reduce the number of prisoner suits filed in federal court

5. Which one of the following items would most likely be contraband in most prisons?
    a. toothpaste
    b. running shoes
    c. money
    d. a Bic razor
    e. a pencil

6. Several of the first important freedom of religion cases from the 1960s dealt with which of these religious groups?
   a. Quakers
   b. Pentecostals
   c. Wiccans
   d. Black Muslims
   e. Seventh Day Adventists

7. An important standard of prison medical care was established in the Texas case of *Estelle v. Gamble* in 1976; this standard was:
   a. "imminent danger"
   b. "benign neglect"
   c. "civil death"
   d. "deliberate indifference"
   e. "constructive contamination"

8. The principal role of the ombudsman in corrections would be to:
   a. act as the warden's counsel in lawsuits
   b. investigate complaints
   c. supervise medical services
   d. act as a liaison to the news media
   e. monitor the prison for the federal courts

9. The concept of collateral consequences generally has to do with:
   a. lack of participation in prison rehabilitation programs
   b. loss of civil rights upon conviction of a crime
   c. harassment by the police because of a criminal record
   d. lack of education and family support among ex-offenders
   e. the friends the ex-offender is not supposed to see after his release

10. In the application of the term "marked man" to an ex-offender, I am suggesting that:
    a. he is blessed with the opportunity to start over
    b. he is a different man from when he went to prison
    c. society looks at him differently because of his record
    d. no one has to be damaged for life just because he has a felony record
    e. many offenders use the prison experience to better themselves

11. The term for a judicial proceeding that cancels out the ex-offender's arrest and conviction on a particular charge is:
    a. allocution
    b. annulment
    c. autonomy
    d. aggravation
    e. amalgamation

12. Four of the following rights are among those commonly denied ex-offenders; which one is NOT?
    a. the right to hold public office
    b. the right to appointed counsel if indigent
    c. the right to public employment in their home state
    d. the right to serve on a jury
    e. the right to possess a firearm

13. The use of the term "predator" as it applies to sex offenders means someone who:
    a. is mentally ill
    b. preys on strangers
    c. was sexually abused as a child
    d. is serving a life term
    e. only abuses little boys

14. If you were looking at the President's use of his clemency powers, you would say that Presidents of the 1990s have been _____, in comparison to Presidents of the 1980s.
    a. very generous
    b. easier on white-collar criminals and harder on everyone else
    c. very kind to drug offenders only
    d. more stingy
    e. highly susceptible to political influence

15. According to Allen and Simonsen, the principal impact of stigma on the offender is its effects on:
    a. self-esteem
    b. education
    c. legal representation
    d. the parole board
    e. political rhetoric

True or False

_____ 16. At one time under common law, a convicted felon was considered civilly dead.

_____ 17. The "hands-off" policy basically meant that the governor did not want to know anything about how state prisons were being run.

_____ 18. The courts have generally ruled that all prisoners except those in lockdown are entitled to unrestricted and unsupervised access to visitors.

_____ 19. Ohio has a strict policy of reading all incoming and outgoing mail and blacking out all the dirty words and criticisms of the prison (which sometimes does not leave much to read).

_____ 20. State prisoners have always had access to the federal courts through the "freedom of petition" clause in the First Amendment to the Bill of Rights.

_____ 21. One of the rights prisoners lose is the right to file a lawsuit for damages in state court.

_____ 22. Long ago a convicted felon's wife was declared a widow and was eligible to remarry immediately after her husband's conviction.

_____ 23. Strict controls over visiting and outside contacts probably turn prisoners' attention inward and make them more dependent on the inmate subculture.

_____ 24. To get a pardon in California, one of the general requirements is that the offender must have led a crime-free life for ten years after discharge from parole.

_____ 25. Any convicted felon, whether in custody or not, faces the loss of his civil rights as provided under state law.

_____ 26. The governor is the legal official who gives the order for an expungement to take place.

_____ 27. The offenders targeted most frequently by recent registration laws are drug dealers.

_____ 28. A conditional pardon not only restores lost rights, but it also wipes out the record of the offense.

_____ 29. The authors suggest that ex-offenders' search for self-esteem promotes socialization with non-criminals who welcome them and encourage them to adopt law-abiding ways.

_____ 30. Branding was an early form of registration of criminals.

Fill In the Blanks

31. If you were called a _____ under the Prison Reform Litigation Act (1996), it would be because you had filed several frivolous lawsuits in the past.

32. The standard of medical services prisoners are supposed to receive, according to the federal First Circuit Court of Appeals, is "_____ medical care."

33. A(n) _____ is an independent arbiter brought in to resolve a dispute between an inmate and prison officials.

34. Inmates in about half a dozen states are allowed to have a special type of family visit which allows for sexual relations; this practice is called _____.

35. Prison officials called the Black Muslims a political or radical group; the courts said they were a _____ group.

36. The justification for prison officials to open and inspect mail is that they are looking for _____.

37. Allen and Simonsen estimate that about _____ million people are under some form of correctional supervision at present, almost all of whom will one day be "ex-offenders."

38. The civil right that is almost universally denied to convicted felons is _____.

39. The President's power to grant executive clemency is specifically authorized in what legal document? _____

40. Washington's Community Protection Act appears to focus on _____ offenders.

41. The idea of collateral consequences, or civil rights lost upon felony conviction, is derived from the old common law practice of _____.

42. The authors describe _____ as "the ultimate rehabilitation."

43. Either annulment or expungement would have to be authorized by what legal official? _____

44. The public image of the ex-offender is perpetuated in the movie image of the _____.

45. The focus of a Section 1983 lawsuit is on the inmate's _____.

Matching

_____ 46. The legal case that established the right of state prisoners to have access to the federal courts.

_____ 47. An independent expert appointed by the federal court to monitor compliance with a court order.

_____ 48. The term for any item the prisoner is not supposed to have in his possession.

_____ 49. The most widespread form of legal assistance available to most prison inmates.

_____ 50. What suffers most when the inmate's visiting privileges and outside contacts are unduly restricted.

_____ 51. The concept that the felon forfeited all legal rights upon conviction.

_____ 52. The form of contraband that pornography, bomb-making manuals, and drug magazines would be classified as, if the prison wanted to keep them out.

_____ 53. The term for a civil wrong that would serve as the basis for a lawsuit.

_____ 54. The practice of maintaining criminal history records in a local court without submitting them to a central records repository.

_____ 55. The most influential recent statute leading to the registration of sex offenders.

_____ 56. A broad legal action that wipes out the conviction and restores lost rights; it effectively erases the court record.

_____ 57. The critical time period after release from prison when the offender often needs help reintegrating into society.

_____ 58. Either full or conditional; this act restores lost civil rights.

_____ 59. The general term for the long-term civil disabilities attached to a felony conviction.

_____ 60. The European practice that required ex-offenders to carry a specific type of identity card.

a. convicted offender
b. final guilty verdict
c. civil death
d. "hands off" policy
e. family ties
f. conjugal visit
g. home furlough
h. "clear and present danger"
i. compelling state need
j. contraband
k. certain literature
l. established religion
m. Black Muslims
n. *Ex parte Hull*
o. jailhouse lawyers
p. *Estelle v. Gamble*
q. deliberate indifference
r. Section 1983
s. sex offender file
t. expungement
u. erasure of record
v. pardon

w. tort
x. grievance board
y. ombudsman
z. court master
aa. ex-con
bb. ex-offender
cc. collateral consequences
dd. social stigma
ee. "marked man"
ff. self-esteem
gg. transitional period
hh. occupational disability statutes
ii. firearms disabilities
jj. employment restrictions
kk. annulment
ll. "vest-pocket" record
mm. registration of criminals
nn. "yellow card"
oo. Megan's Law
pp. Community Protection Act
qq. executive clemency

Discussion

73. What was the legal status of a convicted felon under common law?

74. How do prisons control the prisoner's contacts with the outside world?

75. What standard of medical care is the prison required to provide?

76. What does Section 1983 mean to a prison litigant?

77. What are several alternatives open to the prison in trying to resolve prisoner complaints without filing lawsuits?

78. How has the attitude of the courts toward prisoner suits changed in recent years?

79. Why is there any such thing as collateral consequences attached to a felony conviction?

80. Contrast the effects of pardon and expungement.

81. What effect on employment does a felony record have?

82. What did Washington state's Community Protection Act provide about ex-offenders?

83. How important do you think "stigma" is, as a problem faced by ex-offenders?

84. A federal law is passed restoring all lost civil rights to ex-offenders upon expiration of their sentence. Is this good or bad? Explain.

CHAPTER NINETEEN

The Death Penalty-- The Ultimate Right

CHAPTER OBJECTIVES

This year in America about 300 criminal defendants will be found guilty of capital murder and sentenced to death. A much smaller number, perhaps about 100, will be executed. Because of appeals and legal delays, more than 3,600 men and women sentenced to death have accumulated on death rows across America awaiting execution. Properly speaking, they are awaiting not correction but eradication; but because they are held in prison and the execution is performed by corrections officials, capital punishment is considered a correctional function. After reading the material in this chapter, you should be familiar with:

1. methods used to impose the death penalty.
2. how the death penalty is carried out in the United States today.
3. legal principles related to the use of the death penalty.
4. important legal cases in the recent history of the death penalty.
5. arguments for and against the death penalty.
6. the practical impact of capital punishment on the legal system.

KEY TERMS AND CONCEPTS

capital punishment
execution
lethal injection
death row
capital crimes
arbitrary punishment
malice aforethought
intent to kill
Eighth Amendment
cruel and unusual punishment
Furman v. Georgia
Gregg v. Georgia

bifurcated trial
aggravating circumstances
mitigating circumstances
proportionality
appellate review
deterrent
life certain (no parole)
gatekeeper function
equability
equity
tradition of retribution

CHAPTER SUMMARY

Origins of the Death Penalty

Since ancient times society has reserved for its most severe crimes its most severe penalty--the penalty of death. In some early societies the execution itself was a simple communal act, most often carried out by stoning. In other societies offenders were simply cast out of society to die as outlaws. Executions were generally held in public; indeed, the theory of the execution was that everyone was supposed to watch. How else could it have the desired deterrent effect? As modern societies developed, the death penalty, which had always been used sparingly, was used more often. Ordinary criminals might be hung or decapitated. More important criminals, such as political dissidents or religious heretics, were often tortured and burned. The physical pain that could be inflicted as part of the execution was limited only by the imagination of the executioner. Dozens of different methods were used in different places at different times. In the twentieth century the death penalty has been used much less often; most of the European countries no longer use a death penalty, even with the worst offenders. But in America the death penalty is still going strong.

The Death Penalty in America: A Long Trip, a Bumpy Road

Of the Western democracies only the United States regularly imposes **capital punishment** on ordinary criminal offenders. In colonial times executions were carried out in public at the local level, most often by hanging. In the latter 1800s state governments began to take over the imposition of capital punishment, and the **execution** itself, the end result, was moved indoors, to be carried out in private inside the jail or prison. The death penalty trial itself remains a highly visible public event, but the execution, often done in the middle of the night in the most isolated part of the prison, has become so remote from public experience that few people have any idea what it is like to see another person deliberately put to death. The last officially open public execution in America (not counting unofficial lynchings) took place before a crowd of 20,000 in Owensboro, Kentucky, in 1936. After that we got too civilized to make a public spectacle out of killing a criminal. There have been any number of proposals to televise executions live, and several criminals have volunteered, but thus far the courts have refused to allow an execution to be broadcast live or taped for playback later. We can only read about executions, not watch them.

Better Ways To Die?

As other nations have rethought their traditional notions about killing criminals in the twentieth century, we in the United States have concentrated instead on improving our technology. Hanging was too slow and gruesome. Shooting was too violent (although the firing squad remains on the books in three states, including Utah, where Gary Gilmore was shot to death in 1977, resuming executions in America after a ten-year layoff). The guillotine was a peculiarly French institution. What we needed was something more efficient, and sanitary, and . . . modern. What we got, in turn, was the electric chair, the gas chamber, and, starting in 1982 in Texas, **lethal injection**.

The electric chair was first used in New York in 1890. It became the principal means of executing criminals in this century as the states gradually phased out hanging. Several states, starting with Nevada in 1924, switched to the gas chamber, using cyanide gas as the lethal element. But the search for a more completely painless (and thus more politically palatable) means for ending the criminal's life finally brought us to the lethal injection table. Most of the people being executed today are lethally injected; more than three-quarters of the 38 states with death penalty laws on the books provide for lethal injection as one of the options. The injection itself is through an IV; three chemicals in sequence provide an anesthetic, stop respiration, and stop the heart. It is like, in the words of one advocate, "putting a dog to sleep." That it is a human being and not a dog seems to be beside the point.

Today in America there is only one **capital crime**--first-degree or capital murder. Although several states have death penalty laws on the books for other crimes, no one has been executed for a crime other than the highest degree of murder since the 1960s. Inmates who are sentenced to death are housed in the part of prison called "**death row**." In many states it may be only a few cells. Texas has so many people on death row that it has a whole prison, the Ellis Unit, to house the several hundred people awaiting execution in the most prolific death-penalty state in the country. More executions are carried out in Huntsville, Texas, than anyplace else in the world. The inmates being executed today, unless they are volunteers who have waived appeals to speed up the process, have typically been on death row for eight to ten years or longer, up to 25 years, before they are finally executed.

The execution protocol followed today combines years of suspended animation, in which the inmate is held under careful guard, most often in isolation to prevent anything from happening to him, with a few final hours of mechanical ritual. The inmate waits in his cell for years while legal maneuvers swirl around him. When he loses all his legal battles (almost half the defendants originally sentenced to death win their battles and avoid execution through one avenue or another), a final execution date is set. The last few hours of the ritual we know more about--being moved to a holding cell near the death chamber, the last meal, the last visit with family and friends, the last word from attorneys that the courts or the governor will not intervene, the last walk into the chamber, the last opportunity to speak, the last look at the invited official witnesses, and finally the last breath before the chemicals or the electricity hit you. The states that do a lot of executions have gotten very good at it. The only remarkable execution any longer is the one where something goes wrong, when the execution team can't find a vein for the IV, or when the inmate's head bursts into flame from a shorted-out electrode. Now *that's* news.

The Eighth Amendment and the Death Penalty

From colonial times until about World War II, the death penalty was pretty much taken for granted in America. Most states had the death penalty and used it frequently. There might be a few odd states in the North, like Wisconsin, which has not carried out a legal execution since 1830, with no death penalty, but the enthusiasm of the Southern states for executing people for capital crimes more than made up for these weak sisters. Watt Espy, the leading national historian of executions, has documented more than 19,000 legal executions since colonial times, the majority of them taking place in the South.

Although only first-degree murder is a capital offense today, before the 1960s, there were several, including aggravated rape (which as a death penalty offense in the South was almost totally a crime of black men raping white women), armed robbery, kidnapping, treason, and other felony offenses. Under common law, any felony crime was potentially a death penalty offense, at the discretion of the judge. It took a while to narrow down the list to the most serious crimes and, finally, only the one most serious form of homicide. First-degree murder is defined in various ways from one state to another. Sometimes premeditation, or **malice aforethought**, is an element of the crime; sometimes it is not. **Intent to kill** is a general requirement. The most common circumstance resulting in a death sentence today is a felony murder--a homicide committed during an armed robbery, rape, kidnapping, or other listed crime against the person.

Opposition to the death penalty began to mount after World War II. The grounds of attack were several. The death penalty was called an **arbitrary punishment**, in that only a small percentage of the offenders who committed a capital crime actually got a death sentence, especially for the non-homicide crimes. Even for murder, only about one in 60 homicides today results in a death sentence. The death penalty was criticized as racially discriminatory. Of the men executed for aggravated rape, 89% were black, the victims white almost to the same degree. Ample evidence suggests that today the race of the victim is critical to a death verdict. About 85% of all death sentences are returned in cases with white victims. Cases involving blacks or hispanics or lower-class whites as victims are much less likely to result in a death verdict.

The most general objection to the death penalty was that it violated the **Eighth Amendment's** prohibition against "**cruel and unusual punishment**." The number of executions slowed to a trickle in the 1960s and stopped altogether after 1967 as the courts waited for a definitive U.S. Supreme Court ruling on the constitutionality of the death penalty. The ruling finally came in *Furman v. Georgia* (1972). The Supreme Court struck down the death penalty as cruel and unusual punishment, but it did not say the death penalty was inappropriate to a civilized society. It said only that the death penalty as it was then being used was arbitrary, unfair, and capricious. The Supreme Court attacked the manner rather than the penalty itself.

The result was that the states immediately rewrote their death penalty laws to try to come up with statutes that would withstand Supreme Court scrutiny. Georgia, which lost the first time, won the second. In *Gregg v. Georgia* (1976), the Supreme Court allowed Georgia's death penalty statutes to stand, in effect defining a legal process to impose the death penalty that other states could follow as well. Gregg created the process for imposing death sentences we continue to follow today, over twenty years later. To impose a death sentence, *Gregg* established the following legal procedures:

1. a narrow definition of the crime. Not just "murder," but, more specifically "a murder while committing another felony against the person" or "the murder of a police officer."

2. a **bifurcated trial**. A trial split into separate guilt and penalty phases.

3. a penalty phase in which both **aggravating circumstances** (which make the crime worse, such as the defendant's prior criminal record or victim impact evidence) and **mitigating circumstances** (which make the defendant look better, such as his age or how he might have been affected by child abuse) are considered.

4. an automatic appeal, including **appellate review** of the issue of **proportionality**, or how other parts of the state have dealt with similar offenses.

Since *Gregg*, about 6,000 people have been given death sentences. Just above 10% have been executed so far, though the rate is picking up as old cases run out of appeals. About 40% have had their convictions or sentences overturned, have died, or have had their sentences commuted. The rest, which make up the statistical majority, are still on death row, waiting to see what happens next.

The Controversy Continues

Can we devise a process that fairly selects those offenders who truly deserve to be executed? Even if we can, should we use the power of the state to punish these few offenders so harshly? Does it make a big difference, or any difference at all, if we do execute a few dozen criminals each year? Controversies about the use of the death penalty continue. Most Americans support the death penalty for some crimes, in the range of 75 to 80%. Politicians argue that capital punishment is a **deterrent** to violent crime, but its critics charge it is pure and simple retribution, nothing more. Opponents suggest that a true **"life certain"** or **no parole** life sentence would be just as much a deterrent, would be more humane, and would actually be less costly, primarily because of the reduction in legal expenses associated with the appeals. Proponents reply that some people deserve it, and the way to reduce costs is to speed up the process by reducing appeals, which would also enhance the deterrent effect associated with swift punishment. We should execute more, not fewer, criminals, do it as soon as possible after the trial, and make executions mandatory public events, like beheadings in Saudi Arabia. Why not put executions on prime time television? We could start off with one a week, and then make it one a day in prime time if it catches on. "Live, from Death Row!" (which is actually the title of a book by a notorious death row inmate in Pennsylvania).

Legal critics of the death penalty point out that many of the arbitrary and highly variable practices criticized by the Supreme Court in *Furman* are still a part of the process today. Prosecutors exercising their **gatekeeper function** have unchecked discretion in deciding which offenders who meet the legal definition of first-degree murder will go on trial for their lives. Juries vary greatly from one place to another in the likelihood that they will impose a death sentence. Competence of counsel is an important issue. Appellate courts in some states are far more likely to strike down death sentences than courts in other states. The race and class of both victims and offenders (and jurors as well) are important variables. We are supposed to be following procedures that provide for **equability**, or uniformity, and **equity**, or impartiality, but in fact our system, by allowing each state to set its own standards for these criteria, ensures neither.

The entire process much resembles an old-fashioned crapshoot, in which elements of chance combine with a **tradition of retribution** to ensure that someone pays for murder. It may not always be the offender who deserves it most, but someone *will* pay. It may not even matter that the worst murderers are not always the ones who are executed. To a society terrified of violent crime and determined to get even with violent criminals, it matters only that *some* murderers be executed. Some critics see the whole capital punishment controversy in symbolic terms. We reserve the right to randomly select a few scapegoats from a vast pool of murderers and put them to death--just to show we have not lost our will in the war on criminal violence.

Their deaths have no real impact on crime; they only show that we still mean business. We like capital punishment because it is tough, direct, and easy to understand. In the search for simple solutions to crime, the death penalty leads the way.

SELF TEST

Multiple Choice

1. An offense for which the death penalty can be imposed is called a:
    a. heinous act
    b. crime against humanity
    c. malice aforethought
    d. *mala prohibita*
    e. capital crime

2. The case upon which the current practice of imposing the death penalty in America is based is:
    a. *Bundy v. Florida*
    b. *Kaiser v. New York*
    c. *Gregg v. Georgia*
    d. *Spartacus v. Caesar*
    e. *Chessman v. California*

3. About how many federal crimes provide for death as a possible penalty?
    a. 2
    b. 7
    c. 15
    d. 60
    e. 203

4. What phrase from the Eighth Amendment is often used in court cases against the death penalty?
    a. "the inevitability of error"
    b. "a vengeful public"
    c. "arbitrary judgment"
    d. "cruel and unusual punishment"
    e. "reasonable means to protect"

5. This Utah double-murderer led the way into the new era of capital punishment by demanding to be put to death in 1977; his last words were, "Let's do it."
    a. William Wallace
    b. Billy Bob Black
    c. Gary Gilmore
    d. Danny Dewitt
    e. Sirhan Sirhan

6. Which state has carried out more than twice as many executions as its next closest rival over the past 20 years?
    a. Texas
    b. California
    c. New York
    d. Illinois
    e. Florida

7. If you believed in the death penalty as a deterrent, you would be most in favor of:
   a. more use of clemency to commute death sentences to life imprisonment
   b. allowing death row inmates every possible appeal in their cases
   c. holding executions in public once again
   d. using a review panel to ensure that only the most deserving murderers get death
   e. not allowing any media coverage of an execution

8. In referring to the gatekeeper function of the prosecutor, we would most likely mean that:
   a. prosecutors influence the flow of death penalty cases by deciding which cases to try as capital
   b. most prosecutors are really liberals who oppose the death penalty
   c. the prosecutor has to prove the offender guilty twice to get a death sentence
   d. prosecutors are usually unduly influenced by the wishes of the victim's family
   e. prosecutors try to get jurors in favor of death on the jury

9. One of the concepts that must be considered in appellate review of a death sentence is whether the crime is similar to others in which people have gotten death sentences; this concept is called:
   a. status quo
   b. proportionality
   c. utilitarianism
   d. affinity
   e. punishment by analogy

10. Which one of the following means of execution was never used in the United States?
   a. firing squad
   b. gas chamber
   c. electric chair
   d. hanging
   e. guillotine

True or False

_____ 11. The race of the victim appears to be more important to the death penalty than the race of the offender.

_____ 12. *Furman v. Georgia* (1972) abolished the death penalty briefly but allowed inmates on death row to continue on the path toward execution.

_____ 13. The courts have approved the televising of executions, but so far no stations or networks have wanted to broadcast an execution live.

_____ 14. Executions were still being carried out in public in the United States in the 1930s.

_____ 15. The most commonly used method of execution in the United States today is lethal injection.

_____ 16. Outside the South, there are more states without the death penalty than with.

_____ 17. William Kemmler is famed as the inventor of the electric chair.

_____ 18. An offender must be at least 18 (at the time of the crime) to get a death sentence.

_____ 19. Between 75 and 80 percent of Americans express general support for the death penalty.

_____ 20. Economic studies show that it is far more costly to imprison someone for life than to give him or her a death sentence and follow through to execution.

Fill In the Blanks

21. The last _____ took place in Owensboro, Kentucky, on August 14, 1936.

22. Allen and Simonsen suggest that America's most innovative contribution to the methods of execution was the invention of the _____.

23. At last count, _____ states had a death penalty statute on the books.

24. An important early anti-death penalty case was a Louisiana case in which a defendant named _____ survived the first attempt to electrocute him. He argued that it would be "cruel and unusual punishment" to try again. The court disagreed, and the second time he was properly executed.

25. The *Gregg* and *Furman* cases both originated in the state of _____.

26. One of ᴛᴇ most publicized executions in the 20th century was that of Bruno Hauptman. The infamous crime he was convicted of was _____.

27. The region of the country that has been responsible for the great majority of recent executions is _____.

28. Let's assume that you were driving drunk and killed a small boy in a traffic accident. When you were convicted of murder, the jury gave you a death sentence because of your bad driving record and your unremorseful attitude. The state supreme court should overturn your death sentence as being violative of the principle of _____.

29. Of whites, blacks, and hispanics, the group of which the greatest number have been executed since capital punishment resumed in 1977 is _____.

30. Women make up about _____ percent of the death row population in America.

Matching

_____ 31. The term for offenses that carry the death penalty as a possible punishment.

_____ 32. The Supreme Court case which approved the death penalty procedures used today.

_____ 33. A condition that makes the crime worse.

_____ 34. Every death-sentenced defendant is entitled to one of these before he or she can be put to death.

_____ 35. The legal custom that Allen and Simonsen suggest drives the death penalty in America today.

_____ 36. The effect the death penalty accomplishes if it keeps other people from committing similar crimes.

_____ 37. Where death-sentenced inmates are held to await execution.

_____ 38. The Constitutional phrase most often used in attacking the death penalty.

_____ 39. The objection to the death penalty based on the small percentage of offenders on whom it is imposed.

_____ 40. This concept recognizes the prosecutor's key role in starting the offender on the road to the death house.

a. capital punishment
b. execution
c. lethal injection
d. death row
e. capital crimes
f. arbitrary punishment
g. malice aforethought
h. intent to kill
i. Eighth Amendment
j. cruel and unusual punishment
k. *Furman v. Georgia*
l. *Gregg v. Georgia*
m. bifurcated trial
n. aggravating circumstances
o. mitigating circumstances
p. proportionality
q. appellate review
r. deterrent
s. life certain (no parole)
t. gatekeeper function
u. equability
v. equity
w. tradition of retribution

Discussion

41. What methods have been used to execute criminals in America over the last century?

42. Briefly discuss the trends in the frequency of executions in the twentieth century.

43. What are the main arguments for the death penalty?

44. If you were making a "cruel and unusual punishment" argument against the death penalty, what grounds would you cite?

45. How does the death penalty affect the corrections system?

46. Give a compelling argument that executions should be televised.

CHAPTER TWENTY

Parole

CHAPTER OBJECTIVES

Created in the 1800s as an early out from imprisonment for a few deserving prisoners, parole has become the most common way for inmates to leave American prisons. After reading the material in this chapter, you should be familiar with:

1. the early development of parole.
2. the different types of parole boards in the states.
3. the process prisoners go through to be selected for parole.
4. the parole revocation process.
5. the growth of shock parole and boot camp parole programs.
6. the forms of executive clemency.

KEY TERMS AND CONCEPTS

released on parole	Alexander Maconochie
parole	mark system
truth in sentencing	Walter Crofton
"max out"	ticket-of-leave
executive clemency	Irish system
pardon	"convict bogey"
amnesty	reintegration center
reprieve	parole violation
commutation	technical violation
parole board	*Morrissey v. Brewer* (1971)
consolidated board	front end solutions
jamming time	shock parole
good time	shock incarceration
earned time	shock probation
parole agreement	boot camp
"flopped"	"just deserts" model
mandatory release	determinate sentencing
discretionary release	victim participation

CHAPTER SUMMARY

Pardon and Parole: Two Ways Out of Prison

Most offenders leaving prison are **released on parole**, which is a conditional release under supervision. The term **"parole"** is attributed to an American physician, Dr. S.G. Howe, of 1840s Boston, but the historical predecessors of parole are the **mark system** and **ticket-of-leave**, developed by Captain **Alexander**

Maconochie on the British penal colony at Norfolk Island, off the east coast of Australia, and the **Irish System** of parole supervision and revocation of the ticket-of-leave, developed by **Sir Walter Crofton** in 1850s Ireland. These practices established the idea that convicts--through hard work and good behavior--ought to be able to earn early release from imprisonment.

Many people confuse parole with pardon, which is actually one form of **executive clemency**. In earlier times the king or ruler often intervened to moderate sentences or prevent them from being imposed, as in a case of capital punishment. Today this traditional executive authority is called clemency. The authority resides in the office of the President of the United States and the governors of the states. Through a legally defined process, often involving preliminary screening done by a pardon board, an executive may intervene in the legal process in several different ways:

    1. **pardon**, which was originally used to set aside wrongful convictions; it is now more often used to restore lost civil disqualifications, such as the right to vote or own firearms. Today we expect the appellate courts, rather than the governor's office, to overturn wrongful convictions and set innocent people free.

    2. **amnesty**, which is a blanket freedom from criminal prosecution given to a group of offenders, such as those Americans who fled the country to avoid serving in the military during the Vietnam War. Amnesty may be granted before people are charged, or it may be used to set free offenders who are in prison. Amnesty is obviously often set in a political context; someone characterized it as the government's way of saying, "I'm sorry."

    3. **reprieve**, which is a stay, usually short term, from the imposition of a sentence. We think of reprieves particularly in regard to executions, when the offender in the prison movie waits for a last-minute call from the governor's office (that in real life never came).

    4. **commutation**, which is the shortening of a sentence by executive order. Commutations remain very important to sentenced offenders in many states that make abundant use of life sentences and other very long prison terms. If the executive finds the offender deserving, the commutation is an early out (if the sentence is commuted to time served) or an early parole date for the imprisoned offender.

In the present era of "get tough on criminals," many governors are reluctant to use their clemency powers for fear of being called soft on crime. No politician wants to be haunted later by his opponent's criticism that he was "too nice to criminals." Clemency options, except for the restoration of lost rights, do not matter nearly as much as they used to.

If a prisoner does not get clemency or parole, his options are limited. He can escape, which is highly improbable with the improved security of maximum and medium security prisons today. He can die, which an increasing number of older, sick, and life-term inmates do. He can "**max out**," which means to serve his entire sentence. He can be released on probation, in those states that have **shock probation** or split sentence options. In a few states a very small number of offenders, usually old or sick inmates, might qualify for special release options, such as medical furloughs. Or he might serve his term, less time off his sentence for good behavior. **Good time** can be either automatic or earned for specific work or accomplishments, or it can be both. Some states use terms such as "**earned time**" or "gain time" or "enhanced good time" to mean extra good time earned through program participation, as opposed to regular good time which accrues by simply avoiding prison misconduct.

The good-time release date is now generally called **mandatory release**. In most states inmates on mandatory release are still considered on parole, even though they were not released through the authority of a parole board. They are supervised by a parole officer and held accountable to the conditions of parole until their sentence expires or active supervision is terminated. Mandatory releasees are usually counted in the same statistics with parolees, because their legal status is the same even though they did not get the approval of the board to be released on parole. About a third of prisoners released today are on mandatory release, almost as many as were released through parole board action.

Parole Administration

Parole has become much more formalized and bureaucratized since the days of Maconochie and Crofton. Today the parole decision is typically made by a multi-member **parole board** and parole is carried out by a parole officer, who in most states supervises probationers as well. Parole board members are usually political appointees who may or may not have a professional criminal justice background. Different models of parole boards have been used over the years. Parole was once commonly granted by the institution in which the offender was imprisoned. Later, parole authority was placed in an entirely independent board outside the corrections system. Today the parole board most often functions within the state department of corrections but is not affiliated with any particular institution; this **consolidated board** is supposed to be independently professional.

Several states have abolished parole or restricted eligibility requirements in recent years. They do this by making some offenses no parole, by placing limits on the eligibility of repeat offenders, or by requiring offenders to serve more time before they are eligible for a hearing. Parole boards also say "no" much more often. Limits on parole have increased the importance of mandatory release.

At one time, before parole was broadly available, inmates served what is called "**jamming time**," meaning every day of their sentence. The liberal use of good time soon reduced the actual time served, although inmates who lost their good time might still be required to serve their entire sentence. Once parole became an accepted practice in all corrections systems, inmates became accustomed to going through the parole selection process. Parole is a form of **discretionary release**. It can be a highly arbitrary decision, based on the personalities and prejudices of parole board members. Parole is not a right, and no appeal can be made from a denial, which inmates call being "**flopped**." The standards for parole release vary widely from state to state; even within the same state a change of governors can bring a vastly different outlook to the board. Parole can also be used as a "safety valve" mechanism; parole rates can be increased when prison overcrowding occurs. About half the states have adopted parole guidelines to give some structure to the parole decision.

The inmate released on parole becomes another example of the "**convict bogey**." Although both the probationer and the parolee are convicted felons, the parolee is viewed with greater fear. He has been to prison. The stigma is greater, as is skepticism about reform. Parole supervision tends to be much closer than probation supervision. The conditions of parole on the **parole agreement** are not much different from the conditions of probation. They are just enforced more strictly, so that **parole violation** rates are much higher, sometimes double the violation rates of probationers. **Technical violations**, for alcohol or drug use, failing to work, pay restitution, send in reports, or keep in contact with parole officers, increase as supervision is tightened. Some states deal with technical parole violations by simply returning large numbers of violators to prison to serve more of their original sentences. Ohio uses parole **reintegration centers**, where technical violators who may be having adjustment problems can get help in lieu of being sent back. In all states, parolees are entitled to a formal hearing, under *Morrissey v. Brewer* (1971), before their liberty is revoked. Despite the greater attention being paid to technical violations, slightly more than half of all parolees nationwide complete their paroles without being revoked.

Innovations in Parole Supervision

Ohio, which pioneered shock probation, was also an early sponsor of **shock parole**. First-time offenders would serve six months in prison and then be put on early parole. The program was intended to accomplish the objective of specific deterrence. This idea has been incorporated into **shock incarceration** or **boot camp** programs found in most states today. Boot camp parole programs generally subject young adult offenders to a rigorous short-term confinement followed by intensive parole supervision. The prison regimen features strenuous physical activities and military-style discipline, often with supporting components of education, responsibility, and substance abuse counseling. Shock incarceration at this point does not appear to be particularly effective in reducing recidivism among young adult offenders, and many question its usefulness as a **"front end solution,"** pointing out the net-widening effects of putting lesser offenders behind bars. The shock programs do process offenders more quickly, save some of the costs of longer-term confinement, and avoid some effects of prisonization on younger inmates.

Emerging Issues in Parole

Although parole is under attack from several directions and has undergone many changes over the past three decades, it remains a critical part of the modern corrections system. Even the states that have "abolished" parole--through adoption of **determinate sentencing** or **"just deserts"** sentencing models that limit or eliminate discretionary release--typically find some way to supervise offenders after their release from prison. The federal system, which abolished discretionary parole release more than a decade ago and moved to the 85% good time rule, as part of its **truth in sentencing** law, still adds on a period of supervision, called supervised release, after the offender gets out of prison. Even without parole, the offender is still on parole. Parole accomplishes both the surveillance function and the helping function, although the emphasis in practice differs greatly from one parole officer to another and from one jurisdiction to another. Questions about the authority of parole boards, screening guidelines and eligibility for parole, the nature of parole supervision in the community, and the effectiveness of short-term parole programs keep parole stirred in controversy. As **victim participation** in the parole process has increased, parole boards, already more politically conservative, have become even more cautious about paroling violent offenders. Parole operates in a very definite political context, and in these times any program that turns convicts loose on a fearful society had better be both watchful and prepared to explain its mistakes.

SELF TEST

Multiple Choice

1. *Morrissey v. Brewer* is a landmark case most directly related to which subject?
    a. parole revocation
    b. appointment of parole board members
    c. use of parole guidelines
    d. compensation to crime victims for injuries caused by parolees
    e. denial of parole

2. The authority of the parole board is called:
    a. exemplary sanction
    b. discretionary release
    c. administrative direction
    d. exceptional intervention
    e. regulatory dominion

3. Which one of the following has nothing to do with the programs of Maconochie and Crofton that preceded modern parole?
    a. mark system
    b. shock parole
    c. parole supervision
    d. parole revocation
    e. ticket-of-leave

4. If a prisoner has been "flopped," what has happened to him?
   a. He has been convicted of a crime that makes him parole ineligible.
   b. While out on parole, he has been charged with a new felony offense.
   c. He has been denied parole.
   d. After he was approved for parole, the parole board moved back his release date.
   e. He has been changed from a good to a bad parole officer.

5. If you were sitting in a state prison cell serving a long term for armed robbery, which of the following would have the most practical application to your efforts to get out of prison?
   a. pardon
   b. amnesty
   c. commutation
   d. reprieve
   e. indictment

6. If the prisoner does not get parole but does get out early because of good-time credits, he is released on what is called:
   a. probation
   b. partial monitoring
   c. lax supervision
   d. conditional furlough
   e. mandatory release

7. In California, which has a very high rate of returns to prison for parole violations, the largest number of parolees are returned for:
   a. committing new felonies
   b. refusing to work
   c. drug use
   d. leaving the state without permission
   e. not keeping in contact with their parole officers

8. Which one of the following would be most likely to keep an offender out of Ohio's shock parole program?
   a. The offender is 20 years old.
   b. This is his first felony conviction.
   c. He has been convicted of burglary.
   d. He has serious mental problems.
   e. He was not living with his family.

9. The consolidated parole board of today is most commonly placed:
   a. under the authority of each prison warden
   b. in the department of corrections but independent of any institutions
   c. directly under the control of the governor
   d. in the health and human services department of state government
   e. in a private, non-profit corporation outside any governmental control

10. Shock incarceration is primarily different from shock parole in that shock incarceration:
   a. deals only with drug offenders
   b. deals only with older offenders
   c. has more of a military orientation
   d. is much more short term
   e. does not have any treatment programs

True or False

_____ 11. The executive clemency power was traditionally given to the judge who imposed the sentence on the offender.

_____ 12. As a legal term, parole was first used under Roman law to describe former slaves who had earned their freedom but could not have all their civil rights restored.

_____ 13. If you are a convict and the parole board declines to release you, you have to file a petition with the state attorney general's office to get that decision overturned.

_____ 14. Ohio's use of reintegration centers was directed primarily at parolees who were committing technical violations on parole.

_____ 15. The number of offenders on parole has declined sharply as the states move in the direction of phasing out parole.

_____ 16. With the idea of stricter supervision of parolees in mind, the average number of parole cases per officer has been reduced to about 25.

_____ 17. When a parolee is released from prison, he is still serving the sentence originally imposed on him.

_____ 18. Amnesty would usually be granted to a group or class of offenders who are all guilty of committing the same offense.

_____ 19. Studies show that the offender's participation in prison programs and his behavior in prison make no difference to the parole board considering his release.

_____ 20. In most states parole board members are appointed to office by the governor.

Fill In the Blanks

21. Parole supervision is said to be a combination of the two functions of _____ and _____.

22. The official with the most control over the makeup of parole boards in the states is the _____. _____.

23. Allen and Simonsen point out that the rate of successful terminations from parole is about _____ percent nationwide.

24. The theoretical justification for Ohio's shock parole program is _____.

25. New York's Shock Incarceration program was designed to keep offenders in prison for _____ months.

26. About _____ percent of prisoners are released to some form of community supervision when they leave prison.

27. If the governor granted you a(n) _____, your criminal guilt would be wiped out and all your civil rights restored.

28. If probation is under the control of the sentencing judge, then parole is under the control of the _____.

29. In 1817 New York became the first state to adopt the practice of _____, which was used to provide an incentive for good behavior in prison.

30. A parole violation that is not a criminal act is called a _____ violation.

Matching

_____ 31. The term for legislation that restricts parole and good-time release.

_____ 32. A recent trend that has altered the nature of parole hearings.

_____ 33. An old term meaning the inmate served every day of his prison sentence.

_____ 34. The idea of the paroled ex-convict as a menace to a crime-fearful society.

_____ 35. Sir Walter Crofton's plan for releasing offenders back into the community under supervision.

_____ 36. A synonym for the determinate sentencing model that limits parole usage.

_____ 37. The proper term for all forms of grace dispensed by the governor to wipe out criminal convictions, shorten sentences, and restore rights.

_____ 38. The proper term for boot camp programs leading to early parole.

_____ 39. The type of prison discharge based on the accumulation of good-time credits.

_____ 40. The term Alexander Maconochie applied to the conditional liberty granted those convicts who had earned enough marks to be set free from Norfolk Island.

a. released on parole
b. parole
c. truth in sentencing
d. "max out"
e. executive clemency
f. pardon
g. amnesty
h. reprieve
i. commutation
j. parole board
k. consolidated board
l. jamming time
m. good time
n. earned time
o. parole agreement
p. "flopped"
q. mandatory release
r. discretionary release

s. Alexander Maconochie
t. mark system
u. Walter Crofton
v. ticket-of-leave
w. Irish system
x. "convict bogey"
y. reintegration center
z. parole violation
aa. technical violation
bb. _Morrissey v. Brewer_ (1971)
cc. front end solutions
dd. shock parole
ee. shock incarceration
ff. shock probation
gg. boot camp
hh. "just deserts" model
ii. determinate sentencing
jj. victim participation

Discussion

41. Distinguish among the main forms of executive clemency.

42. From the convict's point of view, criticize the parole board.

43. Outline the regimen of a typical shock incarceration program.

44. What concepts important to Maconochie and Crofton laid the philosophical foundation of parole?

45. What should the parole board pay attention to, when deciding whom to release?

46. How has parole been affected by the truth in sentencing movement in recent years?

CHAPTER TWENTY-ONE

Community Corrections

CHAPTER OBJECTIVES

Far more offenders are under some form of community corrections supervision than are confined in institutions, and there is ample evidence that even more offenders now housed in secure settings could be safely transferred to non-secure community settings. Local community correctional centers could serve as the hub of the community-based correctional system of the future. After reading the material in this chapter, you should be familiar with:

1. the impact of the policy of selective incapacitation on prisons.
2. the operation of work release programs.
3. the role of the private sector in community corrections.
4. the different models of diversion programs.
5. the model of the community correctional center.
6. the integrated contract model of processing offenders.

KEY TERMS AND CONCEPTS

selective incapacitation
chronic offender
work release
Federal Prisoner Rehabilitation Act (1965)
partial incarceration
furlough
halfway house
community residential center (CRC)
prerelease guidance center
self-insured
diversion
community-based diversion
police-based diversion
court-based diversion

pretrial intervention programs
detoxification center
community corrections acts (CCAs)
statutory medium
change agents
risk-control tools
halfway-out
halfway-in
reintegration centers
community correctional center
integrated contract model
comprehensive reintegration plan
accountability
social justice model

CHAPTER SUMMARY

Prisons: At a Turning Point?

Although the American prison population has been on a steady upward climb for the past quarter-century, many corrections experts believe the time will come when the role of prisons narrows and an even greater number of offenders are kept close to home in community correctional centers. These experts suggest that the proper role of the prison is **selective incapacitation**--protecting the public not equally from all criminals but from those high-rate and violent criminals who pose the greatest threat to public safety. These **chronic offenders** will be confined in prison. Other offenders will be supervised under less severe sanctions in non-secure settings. There is some suggestion, in career criminal policies such as "three strikes and you're out," that the prison system is already moving in the direction of selective incapacitation. It is only that the chronic offenders are lost in the influx of offenders imprisoned for other reasons. If prison populations are ever to be brought under control, to level off, or even go into decline, the system of dealing with criminals outside of prison must be much more coordinated and highly developed. If the pendulum should swing back from increased incarceration, what will it swing toward?

Reentry into the Community from the Institution

One of the most direct applications of community corrections alternatives is to aid offenders in making the transition from prison to the community as they approach the end of their sentence. The **Federal Prisoner Rehabilitation Act**, passed by Congress in 1965, provided several options--work release, furloughs, and community treatment centers--to assist in reintegration. Many state laws today do the same, though many of the statutes may exclude more offenders than they include.

Work release was first authorized at the state level in a 1913 Wisconsin statute allowing misdemeanor offenders to work at outside jobs while they spent their nights in jail. Practically all states have some felons on work release today. Work release is not only good for the offender, by helping him or her get back in touch with society and make some money; it also benefits society through taxes, welfare savings, and offenders bearing the costs of their incarceration while living in work release facilities. Many authorities do not like to mix work release and non-work release inmates in the same secure facilities because of the problems of contraband being brought back in and conflict among inmates, but most correctional officials have no problem with work release inmates living in separate wings of secure prisons or living in the community in non-secure residential facilities.

The **halfway house**, which is now often called a **community residential center**, is probably used more today as a work release facility than for any other purpose. When halfway houses first gained popularity in the 1960s, they more often housed parolees and other discharged, homeless ex-offenders. Over time their purpose has changed to include more offenders still in custody--some in prerelease programming, some in educational release or taking vocational training, but mostly offenders in work release status. They live in the halfway house under varying degrees of restriction and work at full-time jobs they have been placed in.

Most halfway houses today are privately operated either for profit or more commonly by nonprofit organizations. Most offer residential facilities housing anywhere from a dozen to several dozen residents, often in an old residence in an urban neighborhood, though some halfway houses may use old apartment buildings or even former motels. Programs and services vary widely, but work is a constant, as is limited resources. Most halfway houses operate in a "break even" mode. Most contract with local, state, or federal correctional institutions to provide housing and certain specified services for a particular type of offender, usually the inmate who qualifies for work release at the end of his or her sentence. The small size of their operation is great for flexibility and making changes, but it makes the operation vulnerable to catastrophic events. The loss of one contract, for instance, can kill an otherwise viable halfway house. Likewise, because these small facilities must either carry expensive liability insurance as protection against lawsuits or go the **self-insured** route with their own usually meager cash reserves, one important legal action can virtually wipe out the operation financially or make it impossible for the organization to continue to get insurance coverage.

Many states and the federal government operate a different type of facility called a **prerelease guidance center**, or prerelease center, for inmates at the very end of their sentence. It is usually located in larger metropolitan areas, and inmates from those areas are sent home a few weeks early to get counseling, find a job, and establish contact with their family again.

Many states also use **furloughs**, another form of **partial incarceration**, as a way of helping selected inmates deal with family crises, get into particular programs, or reestablish family and community ties. Discretionary furloughs approved by the prison warden were once used much more extensively than they are today, when the risk of someone doing a crime while running around loose outweighs the potential reintegrative benefits.

Diversion: Keeping the Offender Out of the System

Programs to aid prerelease inmates or ex-offenders are at one end of the process. At the opposite end, before the offender acquires a record of criminal conviction, is another option called **diversion**. Diversion programs are said to be of three types: community-based, police-based, and court-based. **Community-based diversion**, which is more likely to be used with at-risk juveniles than with adults, sends the offender into an alternative treatment program prior to arrest and filing of charges. There may be some question of just what legal compulsion the offender is under in this arrangement, since diversion is based on the assumption that the offender can be returned to court for conventional processing if he or she fails to live up to the terms of the diversion contract.

Police-based diversion gives police officers the authority to send certain types of offenders, such as those involved in incidents of domestic violence, into counseling or treatment programs. A prime example of the impact of this type of diversion is the practice of taking common drunks to hospital **detoxification centers**. The prevalence of "detox" has resulted in a sharp decline in the number of drunks put in jail and processed as criminals. Police sometimes do not want this formal authority, to not put people in jail, which is based on the informal discretion that is already so much a part of routine police work.

Court-based diversion programs have become the most common. They are based on the concept that the judge has the authority to dismiss criminal charges if the offender completes a specified program of rehabilitation or self-improvement within a mandated time period. The offender signs a contract with the court to complete the program; if he or she fails to do so, the original charges are reinstated. Many jurisdictions operate **pretrial intervention programs**, under public or private authority, to get the offender to "take charge" of his or her life before the case comes to trial instead of waiting until after conviction to start corrective action. The big incentive to the offender is avoiding the stigma of a criminal conviction.

Some diversion programs feature treatment in substance abuse rehab facilities or other hospital environments. This is considered medical treatment, which requires the informed consent of the offender before participation, just as consent was required in the earlier period--from the 1930s into the 1970s--when prisoners took part in the pre-approval testing of new drugs. Probably the "hottest" form of court-based diversion going in the United States today is the drug court movement. These treatment and monitoring oriented courts, operating under the direction of judges who want to work with drug offenders as a special purpose clientele, are being established in local and state trial courts across the country.

Probation and Parole: A Changing Role in the Community

As more and more states pass **community corrections acts** to provide for a better organized network of intermediate sanctions and alternatives at the local level, more of a burden is placed on state and local probation and parole officers to monitor the performance of the local programs. Probation and parole are the longest established representatives of the corrections system in the community. Community corrections legislation--which Allen and Simonsen suggest is used as a **statutory medium** to bring together offenders, private alternative programs, victims' groups, employers, activist citizens, juvenile advocates, and public agencies--often gives probation and parole the task of coordinating this ambitious (and very undefined) undertaking. Most of us prefer simplicity; trying to put the many unconnected and sometimes seemingly contradictory people and programs together in a network is just the opposite--it is more complex than most of us would care to attempt. It makes the probation and parole officer's job much more complicated. Instead of just doing investigations, writing reports, field supervision, and going to court, the probation and parole officer becomes a **"change agent"** responsible for managing the offender's movement among a range of control levels. Instead of a simple yes/no determination, the community corrections program of the future might have a scale of ten different major options with lesser adjustments attached to each. Using his or her **risk-control tools**--residence, day reporting, curfew, community service, drug testing, electronic monitoring, and so on--the probation and parole officer would manage the offender individually, tightening or loosening controls over time in response to the offender's behavior. This is a much more sophisticated approach than the current practice of probation and parole, and not all probation and parole staff can be expected to move cheerfully into this problematical future.

Community Centers as Intermediate Alternatives

At the center of the movement toward community-based corrections, as Allen and Simonsen see it, is the **community correctional center**. This facility is an expanded or enhanced version of the current halfway house or community residential center, serving as the location for a wider variety of residential and non-residential programs for pretrial and sentenced offenders. You can almost envision it as a hotel with multiple floors: first floor, pretrial release; second floor, diversion; third floor, drug court; fourth floor, work release; fifth floor, day reporting; sixth floor, **"halfway-out"** prerelease inmates; seventh floor, **"halfway-in"** probationers in trouble; eighth floor, **reintegration centers** for closer monitoring of parolees in trouble for technical violations; ninth floor, electronic monitoring and house arrest.

Any number of programs and combinations of supervision--both residential and nonresidential--are possible within this unified structure. The advantages of this approach are several. It retains the general advantages of community corrections--lower cost (if sometimes only slightly lower) than institutional corrections, a recidivism rate no higher and in some instances several points lower than institutional programs, and a more normal, humane environment that places responsibility on the offender and requires him to be socially and economically productive while serving his sentence. The additional advantage of this combined facility is that different options can be interwoven to be applied to individual offenders, and offenders can be moved from one option to another as their behavior and needs change. The possibilities of the enhanced community correctional center seem exciting; the only problem is that it does not yet exist in the complete form the authors describe. The outlook for the future does look promising, however, as the traditionally diverse and uncoordinated community corrections "nonsystem" becomes better organized.

The Integrated Contract Model

Richard Seiter has proposed a model of offender management that would fit the community correctional center very nicely. Seiter's model, which Allen and Simonsen discuss at length, is called the **integrated contract model**. It would require the convicted felon to choose either punishment or reintegration. Some offenders would not get a choice. First-degree murderers, rapists, major drug dealers, third-time convicted felons, and firearms violators would go to prison to serve incapacitative sentences. If the offender chose reintegration, he or she would be placed in a **comprehensive reintegration plan** that described the services to be provided, victim restitution, the least restrictive environment, and the treatment and management of the offender. A binding contract between the legal system and the offender, providing for a range of options, levels, and controls, would be drawn up and signed by all parties. The offender would be obligated to work toward defined goals within the contractual time period. Fail to live up to the contract and you would go to prison after all.

The integrated contract model would keep out of prison a large number--certainly more than half--of all persons currently being admitted to prison each year. Like the enhanced community correctional center, it remains more a dream than reality. But as the costs of imprisonment continue to rise and concern over the impact of imprisonment on large numbers of marginal offenders grows, the integrated contract and the community correctional center have a better chance to be put into practice. The **social justice model**, which Allen and Simonsen discuss, suggests that community corrections is more just and fair to most offenders than imprisonment--and it is better for society in the long run. As expenditures for corrections continue to increase, drawing money away from other governmental services, the key word becomes **accountability**. If community corrections can control offenders more cheaply, with better results, with less trouble, and without compromising public safety, it can probably draw increased popular and political support in the future. Allen and Simonsen suggest that no more than 15 to 20 percent of convicted felons require imprisonment; the rest could be served by an expanded community corrections network. Several of the more progressive states are already moving in this direction.

SELF TEST

Multiple Choice

1. The offenders targeted by a policy of selective incapacitation would be:
    a. drug abusers
    b. white collar criminals
    c. minorities
    d. chronic offenders
    e. young, first-time offenders

2. The basic provisions of the Federal Prisoner Rehabilitation Act of 1965 concerned:
    a. secondary and higher education
    b. furloughs and work release
    c. parole and mandatory release
    d. psychological counseling and drug treatment
    e. halfway houses and the death penalty

3. Allen and Simonsen suggest that the more appropriate name for what used to be called the "halfway house" is the:
    a. "three-quarter house"
    b. "storefront center"
    c. "house of refuge"
    d. "flophouse"
    e. "community residential center"

4. Which one of these does NOT fit with the others?
    a. police-based diversion
    b. prison-based diversion
    c. community-based diversion
    d. court-based diversion

5. In 1913 the State of Wisconsin adopted the first state law authorizing:
    a. drug courts
    b. parole
    c. work release
    d. detoxification centers
    e. counseling of prison inmates before discharge

6. The most appealing step in recent years toward a community-based institution, according to Allen and Simonsen, is:
    a. the expanded use of the death penalty
    b. the community correctional center
    c. the closing down of old penitentiaries
    d. the spread of diversion programs
    e. the use of more restrictive forms of probation

7. Four of the following are commonly cited advantages of community corrections, in comparison to imprisonment; which one is NOT?
     a. the offender is more strictly controlled
     b. the costs are less than the costs of imprisonment
     c. the offender is made more responsible for himself
     d. the effect of prisonization is reduced
     e. community ties are better promoted

8. According to the integrated contract model, the convicted felon would choose either punishment or:
     a. freedom
     b. banishment
     c. community service
     d. state subsidy
     e. reintegration

9. Four of the following offenders would be excluded from consideration for the integrated contract model; which one would qualify for consideration?
     a. an offender who had a history of mental problems
     b. an offender who robbed a gas station with a gun
     c. an offender convicted of forcible rape
     d. an offender convicted of importing large quantities of cocaine
     e. an offender with four prior felony convictions

10. Allen and Simonsen suggest that about what percentage of convicted offenders requires imprisonment?
     a. no more than 2
     b. about 5 to 7
     c. about 15 to 20
     d. exactly 33
     e. about 60 to 70

True or False

_____ 11. The authors suggest that the public already interferes too much in prison operations; they recommend that people from the outside world be kept out of the prison as much as possible.

_____ 12. Most halfway houses are privately operated.

_____ 13. The crime rate has continued to increase at a rate roughly parallel to the growth of the prison population.

_____ 14. The Federal Bureau of Prisons no longer sends inmates to community correctional centers because of the lack of secure custody in these facilities.

_____ 15. Most government agencies are self-insured, meaning that they would rely on the government's financial resources to pay off liability claims.

_____ 16. The desirable outcome of a court-based diversion program is dismissal of charges against the defendant.

_____ 17. Allen and Simonsen suggest that custodial institutions work so well because of their access to community treatment programs, professional services, and public support.

_____ 18. The integrated contract model would be used primarily with older offenders who have been in prison a long time and need help readjusting to society.

199

_____ 19. In the past, home furloughs were used primarily as opportunities for sexual visits in those states that did not provide conjugal visiting within prisons.

_____ 20. Allen and Simonsen suggest that it is easier for private organizations, such as halfway houses, to expand and contract their operations as needs change than it is for public agencies to respond to the same changes.

Fill In the Blanks

21. The facilities the Bureau of Prisons operates in larger metropolitan areas to provide short-term programming for inmates about to released are called _____.

22. Criminologist Elmer Johnson suggests that the concept of community corrections is based on the role that _____ contribute to the offender's involvement in criminality.

23. Allen and Simonsen suggest that the shift toward alternatives to incarceration is also a shift away from the effects of the prison as a(n) _____.

24. The name Willie Horton is forever linked to the community corrections alternative called the _____.

25. Of court-based, police-based, and community-based diversion programs, the type that would be used the earliest would be _____.

26. In measuring the successful outcome of community-based correctional programs, Allen and Simonsen criticize the use of _____ as the primary indicator of recidivism.

27. The authors suggest that the states of _____ and _____ have the best implemented community corrections acts.

28. The obligations of the private halfway house that provides services, including room and board, to state prisoners is typically spelled out in a legal document called a(n) _____.

29. Under the integrated contract model, the objective of punishing the offender through imprisonment is _____.

30. The name of the federal statute from three decades ago that authorized more use of partial incarceration methods was the _____.

Matching

_____ 31. Any type of program, such as furloughs or work release, that allows prison inmates to be outside secure custody for part of the day.

_____ 32. A type of discretionary program that gives police authority to refer cases outside the legal system.

_____ 33. The model that seeks to eliminate (or reduce) crime by promoting an organically united community in which all persons are treated fairly and equally.

_____ 34. The idea that people operating a program are responsible for the results obtained with the resources expended.

_____ 35. A proposal to individualize the processing of criminal offenders through either punishment or reintegration programming.

_____ 36. The old generic term for a community-based facility that housed mostly parolees and ex-cons with no place to live.

_____ 37. The role that probation and parole officers would play in a more community-based correctional system.

_____ 38. The model of an expanded community-based facility of the future that would have a comprehensive range of sanctions, programs, and treatment alternatives under one roof.

_____ 39. The status of probationers who would be placed in a halfway house because they have not been complying with the conditions of probation.

_____ 40. The most common name for legislation that attempts to coordinate the different kinds of correctional alternatives available at the local level.

a. selective incapacitation
b. chronic offender
c. work release
d. Federal Prisoner Rehabilitation Act (1965)
e. partial incarceration
f. furlough
g. halfway house
h. community residential center (CRC)
i. prerelease guidance center
j. self-insured
k. diversion
l. community-based diversion
m. police-based diversion
n. court-based diversion

o. pretrial intervention programs
p. detoxification center
q. community corrections acts (CCAs)
r. statutory medium
s. change agents
t. risk-control tools
u. halfway-out
v. halfway-in
w. reintegration centers
x. community correctional center
y. integrated contract model
z. comprehensive reintegration plan
aa. accountability
bb. social justice model

Discussion

41. Describe how the enhanced community correctional center of the future should operate.

42. What are the good and bad points of halfway houses?

43. What are the three main models of diversion programs?

44. What choice does the integrated contract model offer offenders? What happens after offenders make this choice?

45. What are the advantages cited for work release programs?

46. A state legislator says, "All these community corrections programs accomplish is that they make it easier for criminals to victimize the innocent public. We need to put them all in prison where they belong." Briefly respond to his comment.

CHAPTER TWENTY-TWO

The Futures of Corrections

CHAPTER OBJECTIVES

This final chapter is different. It is an assessment and a prediction, a look at how we got to where we are now and a look ahead to where we may be going. Some of the major themes of this chapter that you should be familiar with after having read through this text include:

1. the place of the prison in American society.
2. the balance of imprisonment and community corrections.
3. problems in defining the mission of corrections.
4. how the corrections system might be improved in the future.

KEY TERMS AND CONCEPTS

supermax prisons
War on Drugs
quick fix
crime prevention
drug courts
transformative rationality
tourniquet sentencing
intermediate sanctions

"soft on crime"
law of unintended consequences
geriatric inmates
subsidy system
community corrections acts
accountability
chain gangs
boot camps

CHAPTER SUMMARY

The Role of the Prison in Society

The prison has become a dominant social institution in American society. Our jail and prison population has climbed to more than two million people, almost one percent of the population, and continues to increase steadily. The trend in imprisonment generally is to confine more prisoners under medium security and minimum security conditions, perhaps because it is cheaper; but we should not forget that the maximum security prison remains a total institution, with complete power over the prisoners confined within it. Maximum security prisons have become hardcore, volatile institutions. We are building more **supermax prisons** to hold the most dangerous and worst behaved inmates in permanent lockdown, and lots of people would like to see *all* prisoners confined in this manner. Americans do not seem to care much what happens inside prisons, as long as the prisoners do not escape. Mention the possibility of prison riots, using the examples of Attica and New Mexico, and the public response is, "Get tougher on prisoners. Take their privileges away." It is not, "Treat prisoners humanely. Try to make them better." We write off convicts as irredeemable losers, which widens the gap between prisoners and mainstream society.

The War on Drugs

For two decades we have pursued a policy of locking up as many drug offenders as we can process. Dealers, users, anyone involved with drugs is perceived as dirty and ought to go to prison, especially if the drug is crack cocaine. The result is that offenders in prison for drug crimes (not including crimes committed under the influence of drugs or alcohol or crimes committed to get money to buy drugs) make up a quarter of all state prison inmates and almost two-thirds of federal prison inmates. The increase in drug offenders is the principal reason our prisons are overcrowded today; remove the excess drug offenders and most prisons would be well within capacity. There is no compelling evidence that the "**War on Drugs**" has had any positive effect in reducing the use of drugs in America. **Drug courts**, applying a treatment approach within a legal framework, are beginning to make a dent in the number of drug offenders flowing into our correctional institutions, but drug offenders remain the largest single category of new admissions to prison in many states. Drug usage is part of the basic pathology of American society today; where social problems are the worst, drug usage is at its greatest. In an ironic twist, drug money is the only avenue for many poor Americans, especially minorities, to make a livable income. They would otherwise be locked into permanent poverty as members of the urban underclass. Take away the drug money and the whole infrastructure of the underclass would collapse.

The Politics of Crime Control

The politics of controlling crime today is full of slogans and sound bytes: "law and order," "get tough on crime," and "three strikes and you're out." The get-tough attitude seems even more evident today than it was ten or twenty years ago. And the problem with this attitude is that it gets incorporated into real laws and real corrections policies. Criminal laws really are more punitive. Judicial discretion has been limited by mandatory minimum sentencing laws and sentencing guidelines. Discretionary parole has been abolished in several states. Good time has been cut back. Far more people, including more of the "three strikes" habitual offenders, are given true natural life sentences. Institutional privileges have been restricted. We are much tougher on criminals, and we keep looking for new ways to be even more punitive. **Chain gangs** and prison stripes have come back into fashion. **Boot camps**, with their regimen of military discipline, are everywhere. They are used increasingly with at-risk juveniles; it may not be long until we see three- and four-year-olds out learning to march wearing their little fatigue uniforms. If we get tough on them while they're little, maybe we won't have to do it later. Crime control has become very political. Everyone wants to be tough on crime (and at the moment very tender to victims, who are becoming a major political force to contend with), and the ones who get the most attention are the ones who yell the loudest, wave their arms wildly, and make the most mean-spirited proposals. People want a "**quick fix**" on crime. It is difficult to get them to listen to longer-term **crime prevention** proposals or anything that appears to be treating offenders better. In this era it is the kiss of death to a politician to appear to be too nice to criminals. "**Soft on crime**" is as much a stigma to a politician as "ex-convict" is to an offender.

The Future of Imprisonment

We remain wholeheartedly committed to the abundant use of imprisonment as a social policy. It is very likely that our prison population will continue to increase for at least the next decade. Allen and Simonsen estimate that our jail and prison population will more than double, to more than four million in custody, by the year 2010. The face of the prisoner is changing. "He" is increasingly a "she"; the percentage of women inmates grows as more women are convicted of drug charges. Drug usage is also responsible for the growing number of prison inmates who are HIV positive. The housing and medical care of HIV and AIDS inmates present special problems and costs. The graying of prisons will continue into the foreseeable future as more middle-aged and older inmates come to prison and more long-term inmates grow old in prison. Our aging prisoner population is one example of the "**law of unintended consequences**;" we passed tougher laws to restrict the release of prisoners, and now these prisoners are growing old behind bars. Several state systems have already established "old age home" minimum security prisons for **geriatric inmates** who present no real danger but need to be removed from the prison's general population.

Many prison inmates suffer from disabilities; the effects of the modifications required by the Americans with Disabilities Act (ADA) are already being felt in many jails and prisons. The number of prison inmates who are substance abusers or mentally ill (or both) is substantial; indeed, if we could "cure" both substance abuse and mental illness, and remove the now-healthy, whole person from prison, our prison population would return to below the level of the 1960s, before the crime wave inundated America. This cure is highly unlikely to happen anytime soon.

Imprisonment is likely to stay much like it is at present. The role of private management firms should continue to grow. In the more progressive states, the walls between the prison and the community may begin to crack and open up again, at least for the minimum security facilities. Allen and Simonsen discuss **subsidy systems**, such as those California and Oregon have used, to get low-risk offenders out of prison and back at home under supervision. Many people who run prisons still believe in reintegration; they continue to search for the right way to make it politically and managerially feasible to get more inmates out into the community as early and as much as possible. Inmates at higher levels of security will just have to wait their turn and work their way down over time.

Community Corrections

It is not only prisons that have gotten tougher but also community corrections. The community corrections options, led by probation and parole, have become much more controlling and punitive in recent years. Community supervision is much more formal. Corrections officials use risk assessment as a tool to determine who should remain in the community and under what kind of controls. They use risk control measures to tighten or loosen restrictions on the offender while he or she is under supervision. Offenders in the community pay more victim compensation, they perform more community service work, and they pay more fees to provide for their own supervision than they ever have previously. More offenders are subject to electronic monitoring, which in time will surely mean that large numbers of people placed in community-based alternatives will be kept under computer surveillance. This will perhaps displace part of the need for some offenders to live in community residential centers. Under the **community corrections acts** already adopted in several states, the various community corrections options are better integrated and brought under state supervision, usually through the local probation and parole office. The whole direction is to make community corrections more structured, to provide a more comprehensive set of **intermediate sanctions**, and to keep better track of the offenders who are not in secure institutions. **Tourniquet sentencing**, with a scale of control options, is developing into a reality in many progressive jurisdictions. Net-widening undoubtedly occurs with this approach, but the likelihood that the offender will be provided with the services he or she needs to avoid criminal behavior is also greatly enhanced.

Juvenile Crime

The greatest social concern of corrections officials is that the juvenile crime problem is about to get out of hand again, unlike anything we have seen since the 1960s crime wave generated by the post-World War II baby boomers. What America is facing over the next decade or more is an "echo boom" in which the percentage of the population made up of adolescents, who are the most criminally active part of society, will increase sharply. Youth violence, which has declined of late, is predicted to increase again. Many behavioral scientists fear that the conditions of poverty, family disorganization, and social dysfunction prevailing in our cities at the end of the twentieth century will produce a strain of youthful criminals who are impervious to our efforts to change their behavior. They may not be "born criminals," but they are born to a life of crime, meaning that crime and deviance are seen as a perfectly normal alternative lifestyle. As more of these young people get into trouble as juveniles and later as adults, they will make the task of managing corrections even more difficult.

What Lies Ahead?

No one can predict with certainty what the long-term future or even the immediate future of corrections in America will look like. We do not expect to find a miraculous cure for crime, nor do we expect sudden spontaneous changes of direction, such as a decision to close down all maximum security prisons. For the short term, we should probably expect more of the same. Allen and Simonsen propose an approach they call **"transformative rationality,"** which involves adopting broad general policies that local and state governments can adapt to their own circumstances. But the present focus on **accountability**, on getting quick results from the expenditure of public funds, actually works against experimentation with new ideas. Corrections officials are often reluctant to try innovative approaches, for fear of failure.

Can the corrections system of the future be made better? Can it be made more humane, more effective, and more able to balance the interests of both society and criminal offenders? There is always room for hope, just as there is always room for doubt. What happens to individual offenders is as likely to be determined by the people working in corrections as it is by any dominant ideology driving the system one way or the other. Where does the future of corrections lie? It lies in the hands of young people in corrections classes in our colleges and training academies today who will make the countless decisions that shape the policies and determine the practices of the corrections system of tomorrow. Corrections is much more than an ideological bureaucracy; it is a human enterprise, with millions of people on one side working with millions of people on the other to control criminal behavior, and sometimes the lines between the sides get blurred. There are no givens, other than human nature under legal pressure. The future of corrections can move in any direction society and the legal system choose. It is the making of these choices and their consequences in the real world--their effects on human lives--that remain complex and uncertain.

SELF TEST

Multiple Choice

1. Between 1990 and 2000 the adult jail and prison population:
    a. fell by 50 percent
    b. almost doubled
    c. more than tripled
    d. quintupled
    e. remained exactly the same

2. Allen and Simonsen project that if current rates of increase continue, we could have _____ adults under some form of correctional supervision by the year 2010.
    a. about 1,000,000
    b. no more than 3,000,000
    c. just over 5,000,000
    d. more than 10,000,000
    e. almost 50,000,000

3. If we have been fighting a "War on Crime" for 30 years, in the last 15 years which one of the following has had the most impact on criminal justice?
    a. the "Attack on Terrorism"
    b. the "Battle against Abuse"
    c. the "War on Drugs"
    d. the "Struggle against Satanism"
    e. the "Campaign to Save the Family"

4. Four of the following can be identified as slogans of political punitiveness; which one is NOT?
    a. get tough
    b. chain gangs
    c. three strikes and you're out
    d. law and order
    e. restorative justice

5. Which option supervises the most offenders?
    a. jail
    b. parole
    c. probation
    d. prison

6. Allen and Simonsen see restorative justice as being closely linked to:
    a. community justice
    b. retribution
    c. treatment
    d. deterrence
    e. capital punishment

True or False

_____ 7. Allen and Simonsen suggest that community supervision strategies will increasingly be tied to the concept of tourniquet sentencing.

_____ 8. The percentage of blacks in the prison population is declining as we lock up more drug offenders.

_____ 9. The crime rate was declining steadily at the end of the twentieth century.

_____ 10. Georgia's use of tent prisons was primarily intended to reward good inmates with a more open environment.

_____ 11. The authors suggest that correctional administrators and corrections scholars are "natural adversaries."

_____ 12. Among the Western nations, only Russia has a higher rate of imprisonment than the United States.

Fill In the Blanks

13. By the year 2010, Allen and Simonsen project that about _____ percent of adults under correctional supervision will be in prison.

14. Harry Allen's opening remarks address the "debasing and humiliating" effects of _____.

15. The techniques used to tighten and loosen restrictions on offenders kept under community supervision are known as _____.

16. Allen and Simonsen suggest that corrections is changing (or needs to change) from being "offender-centered" to being "_____-centered."

17. To better supervise violent inmates, the authors propose that we consider the use of _____.

18. Allen and Simonsen's proposal for state governments to pay local governments to keep non-dangerous offenders in community programs is called a _____ system.

Matching

_____ 19. Legislation the provides for a more unified approach to providing community-based corrections.

_____ 20. The idea that correctional managers and political officials are responsible to the public for the expenditure of public funds in pursuit of increased public safety.

_____ 21. A currently popular form of punishment that combines hard work and public humiliation.

_____ 22. The idea that one simple, low-cost act will have great impact in improving our efforts to control crime.

_____ 23. Allen and Simonsen's term for adherence to broad policy principles that can be adapted to state and local efforts to make corrections work more effectively.

_____ 24. The phrase, like a curse, that would be death to a politician's future political aspirations.

a. supermax prisons
b. War on Drugs
c. quick fix
d. crime prevention
e. drug courts
f. transformative rationality
g. tourniquet sentencing
h. intermediate sanctions

i. "soft on crime"
j. law of unintended consequences
k. geriatric inmates
l. subsidy system
m. community corrections acts
n. accountability
o. chain gangs
p. boot camps

Discussion

25. Why does the prison population continue to increase if the crime rate has gone down?

26. What changes do you see happening in prison operations in the near future?

27. What are the most important changes in community corrections that have taken place in recent years?

28. Assess the impact of the "War on Drugs."

29. Outline your own predictions for the near future of corrections in America.

30. What should be the mission of corrections?

Answers to Chapter Self Tests

Chapter One

Multiple Choice	True or False	Fill In the Blanks	Matching
1. c (p. 6)	19. F (p. 7)	37. *lex talionis* (p. 8)	55. p (p. 11)
2. d (p. 7)	20. F (p. 8)	38. outlaw (p. 8)	56. i (p. 8)
3. e (p. 8)	21. T (p. 8)	39. blood feud (p. 7)	57. x (p. 14)
4. c (p. 9)	22. T (p. 9)	40. free will (p. 10)	58. a (p. 6)
5. b (p. 10)	23. F (p. 10)	41. the stocks/the pillory (p. 11)	59. z (p. 15)
6. d (p. 13)	24. F (p. 10)	42. the state (p. 9)	60. e (p. 7)
7. d (p. 14)	25. T (p. 10)	43. folkways (p. 6)	61. n (p. 9)
8. c (p. 15)	26. F (p. 11)	44. heretics (p. 10)	62. k (p. 7)
9. a (p. 16)	27. T (p. 14)	45. corporal punishment (p. 11)	63. h (p. 8)
10. d (p. 20)	28. F (p. 20)	46. Walnut Street Jail (p. 25)	64. rr (p. 24)
11. b (p. 20)	29. T (p. 25)	47. Classical School (p. 16)	65. vv (p. 26)
12. c (p. 21)	30. F (p. 27)	48. typhus (p. 20)	66. pp (p. 23)
13. c (p. 23)	31. F (p. 23)	49. America/Australia (p. 21)	67. mm (p. 21)
14. d (p. 25)	32. F (p. 16)	50. prevention (p. 16)	68. gg (p. 19)
15. c (p. 24)	33. F (p. 19)	51. Penitentiary Act (p. 19)	69. ee (p. 17)
16. a (p. 20)	34. F (p. 19)	52. Hospice of San Michele (p. 23)	70. oo (p. 21)
17. a (p. 19)	35. T (p. 21)	53. Pennsylvania (p. 27)	71. ww (p. 27)
18. e (p. 19)	36. T (p. 20)	54. Jeremy Bentham (p. 18)	72. aa (p. 15)

Chapter Two

Multiple Choice	True or False	Fill In the Blanks	Matching
1. d (p. 43)	19. F (p. 50)	37. silence (p. 39)	55. b (p. 34)
2. a (p. 34)	20. F (p. 50)	38. Pennsylvania (p. 39)	56. p (p. 43)
3. e (p. 49)	21. F (p. 43)	39. Auburn (p. 39)	57. gg (p. 54)
4. c (p. 47)	22. T (p. 34)	40. parole (p. 43)	58. cc (p. 50)
5. a (p. 43)	23. T (p. 35)	41. the Great Depression (p. 48)	59. t (p. 43)
6. c (p. 42)	24. F (p. 40)	42. idleness (p. 50)	60. v (p. 44)
7. d (p. 58)	25. T (p. 39)	43. reformatory (p. 43)	61. m (p. 42)
8. d (p. 48)	26. F (p. 41)	44. penitence (p. 61)	62. h (p. 39)
9. c (p. 35)	27. F (p. 52)	45. prison farms (p. 46)	63. d (p. 34)
10. c (p. 63)	28. F (p. 66)	46. War on Drugs (p. 67)	64. jj (p. 57)
11. b (p. 46)	29. F (p. 59)	47. hospital (p. 62)	65. bbb (p. 62)
12. d (p. 60)	30. T (p. 55)	48. pendulum (p. 63)	66. xx (p. 62)
13. b (p. 57)	31. F (p. 64)	49. selective incapacitation (p. 58)	67. oo (p. 58)
14. e (p. 57)	32. F (p. 57)	50. prediction (p. 60)	68. pp (p. 59)
15. c (p. 62)	33. T (p. 59)	51. the inmate's needs (p. 61)	69. kk (p. 57)
16. d (p. 62)	34. F (p. 67)	52. victim (p. 64)	70. vv (p. 61)
17. a (p. 61)	35. F (p. 60)	53. prevention (p. 62)	71. zz (p. 62)
18. d (p. 61)	36. T (p. 61)	54. stripes (p. 40)	72. ddd (p. 64)

Chapter Three

Multiple Choice	True or False	Fill In the Blanks	Matching
1. c (p. 82)	19. T (p. 80)	37. reported to police (p. 100)	55. t (p. 94)
2. b (p. 85)	20. T (p. 93)	38. felony (p. 80)	56. a (p. 80)
3. e (p. 91)	21. T (p. 82)	39. alcohol (p. 91)	57. q (p. 92)
4. c (p. 93)	22. T (p. 83)	40. the state (p. 80)	58. o (p. 89)
5. a (p. 81)	23. F (p. 87)	41. crimes against the person (p. 82)	59. c (p. 91)
6. d (p. 80)	24. T (p. 100)	42. detoxification center (p. 93)	60. i (p. 83)
7. d (p. 89)	25. T (p. 91)	43. domestic crime (p. 87)	61. h (p. 83)
8. e (p. 82)	26. F (p. 87)	44. misdemeanor (p. 91)	62. p (p. 91)
9. c (p. 88)	27. T (p. 80)	45. victims (p. 100)	63. d (p. 81)
10. d (p. 102)	28. F (p. 99)	46. plea bargaining (p. 102)	64. f (p. 100)
11. b (p. 101)	29. T (p. 100)	47. 22 (p. 100)	65. ee (p. 106)
12. e (p. 99)	30. T (p. 100)	48. correctional filter (p. 96)	66. y (p. 101)
13. c (p. 104)	31. F (p. 102)	49. UCR (p. 99)	67. e (p. 100)
14. c (p. 81)	32. T (p. 105)	50. prosecutor/defense lawyer (p. 103)	68. aa (p. 103)
15. b (p. 100)	33. F (p. 102)	51. shock probation (p. 104)	69. bb (p. 104)
16. a (p. 102)	34. F (p. 97)	52. charge/sentence (p. 100)	70. u (p. 95)
17. e (p. 103)	35. T (p. 106)	53. murder (p. 83)	71. x (p. 100)
18. c (p. 95)	36. F (p. 105)	54. dismissed (p. 101)	72. v (p. 99)

Chapter Four

Multiple Choice	True or False	Fill In the Blanks	Matching
1. e (p. 119)	19. T (p. 116)	37. good time (p. 127)	55. i (p. 117)
2. c (p. 118)	20. F (p. 118)	38. imprisonment (p. 125)	56. d (p. 118)
3. b (p. 117)	21. F (p. 116)	39. disparity (p. 117)	57. k (p. 126)
4. c (p. 126)	22. F (p. 119)	40. severity/inconsistency (p. 129)	58. p (p. 127)
5. d (p. 121)	23. F (p. 117)	41. justice model (p. 131)	59. r (p. 126)
6. a (p. 116)	24. T (p. 127)	42. rehabilitation (p. 116)	60. f (p. 118)
7. e (p. 129)	25. F (p. 122)	43. Texas (p. 117)	61. n (p. 121)
8. d (p. 121)	26. T (p. 124)	44. judges (p. 127)	62. q (p. 127)
9. d (p. 123)	27. F (p. 140)	45. aggravating (p. 121)	63. j (p. 121)
10. d (p. 132)	28. T (p. 142)	46. due process (p. 132)	64. xx (p. 142)
11. c (p. 122)	29. F (p. 136)	47. court order (p. 141)	65. x (p. 132)
12. c (p. 140)	30. T (p. 134)	48. court of appeal (p. 136)	66. pp (p. 132)
13. b (p. 136)	31. F (p. 140)	49. affirmation (p. 132)	67. ee (p. 134)
14. e (p. 137)	32. T (p. 143)	50. prisoners (p. 116)	68. qq (p. 136)
15. a (p. 132)	33. T (p. 123)	51. court master (p. 140)	69. v (p. 132)
16. b (p. 134)	34. F (p. 136)	52. state/federal (p. 133)	70. rr (p. 136)
17. d (p. 133)	35. F (p. 133)	53. judge (p. 134)	71. u (p. 116)
18. e (p. 129)	36. F (p. 144)	54. revolution (p. 139)	72. ii (p. 134)

Chapter Five

Multiple Choice	True or False	Fill In the Blanks	Matching
1. b (p. 168)	15. F (p. 156)	29. fees (p. 170)	43. j (p. 162)
2. a (p. 170)	16. F (p. 156)	30. prison (p. 167)	44. y (p. 171)
3. e (p. 170)	17. T (p. 162)	31. community service (p. 172)	45. b (p. 156)
4. b (p. 162)	18. F (p. 160)	32. direct supervision (p. 165)	46. v (p. 170)
5. e (p. 156)	19. T (p. 159)	33. hell (p. 168)	47. r (p. 167)
6. a (p. 166)	20. F (p. 171)	34. John Howard (p. 156)	48. e (p. 157)
7. c (p. 159)	21. T (p. 169)	35. county sheriff (p. 160)	49. c (p. 158)
8. e (p. 155)	22. F (p. 168)	36. weekender (p. 172)	50. w (p. 170)
9. a (p. 171)	23. F (p. 165)	37. detention (p. 160)	51. f (p. 162)
10. a (p. 162)	24. T (p. 161)	38. substance abuse (p. 174)	52. o (p. 166)
11. b (p. 160)	25. F (p. 157)	39. mental health (p. 176)	53. ff (p. 168)
12. c (p. 166)	26. T (p. 167)	40. presumed innocent (p. 157)	54. p (p. 167)
13. c (p. 176)	27. F (p. 158)	41. money (p. 167)	55. t (p. 168)
14. d (p. 158)	28. F (p. 167)	42. 11 (p. 153)	56. n (p. 159)

Chapter Six

Multiple Choice	True or False	Fill In the Blanks	Matching
1. e (p. 183)	11. T (p. 201)	21. supervision/conditions (p. 183)	31. n (p. 189)
2. d (p. 202)	12. T (p. 189)	22. John Augustus (p. 184)	32. e (p. 184)
3. e (p. 201)	13. F (p. 189)	23. Washington (p. 205)	33. f (p. 184)
4. a (p. 183)	14. f (p. 186)	24. benefit of clergy (p. 184)	34. a (p. 183)
5. e (p. 183)	15. T (p. 201)	25. homicide (p. 186)	35. j (p. 192)
6. d (p. 207)	16. F (p. 190)	26. co-morbidity (p. 194)	36. aa (p. 207)
7. e (p. 184)	17. F (p. 206)	27. probation revocation (p. 202)	37. i (p. 192)
8. a (p. 198)	18. T (p. 185)	28. presentence investigation (p. 190)	38. c (p. 183)
9. d (p. 190)	19. F (p. 205)	29. tourniquet sentencing (p. 198)	39. x (p. 194)
10. d (p. 198)	20. F (p. 202)	30. overcrowding or cost (p. 206)	40. p (p. 197)

Chapter Seven

Multiple Choice	True or False	Fill In the Blanks	Matching
1. d (p. 215)	11. F (p. 212)	21. overcrowding (p. 213)	31. g (p. 214)
2. e (p. 213)	12. T (p. 217)	22. control (punishment) (p. 217)	32. v (p. 222)
3. c (p. 214)	13. F (p. 213)	23. Georgia (p. 216)	33. a (p. 212)
4. a (p. 218)	14. F (p. 221)	24. Florida (p. 220)	34. z (p. 226)
5. c (p. 221)	15. F (p. 213)	25. residential center (p. 223)	35. i (p. 216)
6. c (p. 212)	16. T (p. 215)	26. probation (p. 221)	36. k (p. 216)
7. d (p. 224)	17. T (p. 218)	27. judge (p. 225)	37. t (p. 221)
8. e (p. 226)	18. F (p. 221)	28. discipline (p. 227)	38. l (p. 217)
9. c (p. 226)	19. T (p. 224)	29. surveillance (p. 218)	39. x (p. 225)
10. d (p. 212)	20. F (p. 226)	30. community service (p. 219)	40. r (p. 221)

Chapter Eight

Multiple Choice	True or False	Fill In the Blanks	Matching
1. e (p. 240)	11. T (p. 237)	21. War on Drugs (p. 239)	31. l (p. 249)
2. d (p. 242)	12. F (p. 239)	22. security/treatment (p. 243)	32. e (p. 243)
3. a (p. 256)	13. F (p. 241)	23. special housing unit (p. 258)	33. m (p. 249)
4. d (p. 242)	14. T (p. 243)	24. maximum (p. 245)	34. i (p. 246)
5. d (p. 242)	15. F (p. 243)	25. unwalled prison (p. 248)	35. g (p. 245)
6. c (p. 250)	16. T (p. 247)	26. actual time served (p. 245)	36. n (p. 250)
7. c (p. 247)	17. F (p. 248)	27. maximum (p. 248)	37. j (p. 248)
8. e (p. 248)	18. F (p. 250)	28. correctional officers (p. 260)	38. q (p. 259)
9. b (p. 261)	19. F (p. 261)	29. density (p. 243)	39. s (p. 260)
10. a (p. 261)	20. F (p. 247)	30. correction (or treatment) (p. 243)	40. f (p. 243)

Chapter Nine

Multiple Choice	True or False	Fill In the Blanks	Matching
1. a (p. 274)	11. T (p. 268)	21. California/Texas (p. 277)	31. b (p. 270)
2. c (p. 267)	12. F (p. 272)	22. accreditation (p. 290)	32. n (p. 274)
3. c (p. 272)	13. T (p. 288)	23. Philadelphia (p. 274)	33. y (p. 283)
4. a (p. 272)	14. T (p. 268)	24. 30 (p. 278)	34. m (p. 287)
5. e (p. 274)	15. T (p. 280)	25. glass top (p. 287)	35. i (p. 274)
6. b (p. 277)	16. F (p. 288)	26. reformation (p. 267)	36. bb (p. 288)
7. e (p. 285)	17. F (p. 281)	27. department of corrections (p. 273)	37. e (p. 272)
8. c (p. 280)	18. F (p. 284)	28. Eighth (p. 284)	38. g (p. 270)
9. d (p. 281)	19. T (p. 272)	29. classification (p. 288)	39. cc (p. 290)
10. b (p. 283)	20. F (p. 288)	30. maximum (p. 274)	40. f (p. 273)

Chapter Ten

Multiple Choice	True or False	Fill In the Blanks	Matching
1. c (p. 296)	11. F (p. 295)	21. 1930 (p. 298)	31. k (p. 299)
2. b (p. 296)	12. F (p. 303)	22. low/medium (p. 303)	32. q (p. 303)
3. a (p. 299)	13. F (p. 299)	23. high (p. 304)	33. h (p. 298)
4. c (p. 300)	14. F (p. 299)	24. 12th (p. 306)	34. u (p. 303)
5. e (p. 302)	15. F (p. 304)	25. women (p. 307)	35. w (p. 304)
6. b (p. 304)	16. T (p. 296)	26. Sentencing Commission (p. 308)	36. z (p. 308)
7. e (p. 307)	17. F (p. 303)	27. Mexico (p. 305)	37. y (p. 308)
8. d (p. 295)	18. T (p. 300)	28. military (p. 295/298)	38. f (p. 303)
9. b (p. 302)	19. T (p. 303)	29. Oakdale/Atlanta (p. 299)	39. l (p. 299)
10. e (p. 306)	20. F (p. 304)	30. four (p. 307)	40. x (p. 306)

Chapter Eleven

Multiple Choice	True or False	Fill In the Blanks	Matching
1. e (p. 314)	11. T (p. 313)	21. CRA (p. 313)	31. Q (p. 321)
2. d (p. 316)	12. F (p. 313)	22. work release (p. 319)	32. h (p. 315)
3. b (p. 317)	13. F (p. 313)	23. contract (p. 313)	33. V (p. 324)
4. a (p. 321)	14. F (p. 319)	24. correctional/industrial complex	34. o (p. 321)
5. a (p. 322)	15. F (p. 321)	(p. 321)	35. k (p. 318)
6. c (p. 324)	16. T (p. 322)	25. Texas (p. 327)	36. g (p. 315)
7. d (p. 322)	17. F (p. 328)	26. private prisons (p. 326)	37. i (p. 316)
8. a (p. 322)	18. F (p. 327)	27. maximum security (p. 315)	38. n (p. 320)
9. d (p. 331)	19. F (p. 323)	28. contractors (or providers) (p. 313)	39. l (p. 317)
10. a (p. 316)	20. T (p. 323)	29. competition (p. 331)	40. s (p. 322)
		30. Wackenhut (p. 323)	

Chapter Twelve

Multiple Choice	True or False	Fill In the Blanks	Matching
1. b (p. 342)	11. F (p. 340)	21. custody (p. 341)	31. dd (p. 356)
2. e (p. 356)	12. T (p. 341)	22. cost savings (p. 360)	32. q (p. 349)
3. c (p. 350)	13. T (p. 348)	23. the strongest inmate (p. 358)	33. j (p. 342)
4. c (p. 343)	14. F (p. 349)	24. thke warden (p. 364)	34. ee (p. 357)
5. a (p. 351)	15. F (p. 353)	25. treatment (p. 366)	35. t (p. 350)
6. d (p. 364)	16. F (p. 342)	26. blue flu (p. 348)	36. p (p. 348)
7. c (p. 348)	17. F (p. 366)	27. gangs/overcrowding (p. 349)	37. kk (p. 346)
8. d (p. 349)	18. T (p. 340)	28. Aryan Brotherhood (p. 350)	38. a (p. 340)
9. c (p. 359)	19. T (p. 344)	29. the count (p. 351)	39. h (p. 342)
10. d (p. 355)	20. F (p. 342)	30. minimum (p. 358)	40. i (p. 342)

Chapter Thirteen

Multiple Choice	True or False	Fill In the Blanks	Matching
1. b (p. 377)	15. F (p. 375)	29. federal (p. 373/380)	43. g (p. 379)
2. a (p. 380)	16. T (p. 380)	30. control (p. 379)	44. c (p. 373)
3. a (p. 374)	17. F (p. 381)	31. "model muddle" (p. 372)	45. a (p. 373)
4. b (p. 374)	18. F (p. 380)	32. aftercare (p. 379)	46. i (p. 380)
5. e (p. 386)	19. F (p. 381)	33. religion (p. 383)	47. l (p. 380)
6. a (p. 393)	20. F (p. 385)	34. prison managers ((p. 388)	48. cc (p. 395)
7. c (p. 384)	21. F (p. 387)	35. MDR (p. 384)	49. aa (p. 395)
8. e (p. 387)	22. F (p. 390)	36. television station (p. 383)	50. t (p. 393)
9. b (p. 384)	23. F (p. 387)	37. tuberculosis (p. 386)	51. p (p. 385)
10. d (p. 390)	24. T (p. 385)	38. the 1930s (p. 391)	52. hh (p. 389)
11. b (p. 390)	25. F (p. 387)	39. diagnosis (p. 394)	53. m (p. 382)
12. e (p. 393)	26. T (p. 389)	40. caseworker (p. 394)	54. o (p. 385)
13. d (p. 396)	27. F (p. 392)	41. mealtime (p. 397)	55. ss (p. 396)
14. c (p. 395)	28. F (p. 373)	42. the correctional officer (p. 398)	56. ff (p. 395)

Chapter Fourteen

Multiple Choice	True or False	Fill In the Blanks	Matching
1. d (p. 410)	11. f (p. 427)	21. drug (p. 416)	31. g (p. 414)
2. e (p. 411)	12. T (p. 409)	22. six (or seven) (p. 422)	32. n (p. 425)
3. e (p. 427)	13. F (p. 422)	23. co-correctional (p. 434)	33. k (p. 417)
4. b (p. 410)	14. T (p. 418)	24. prostitution (p. 410)	34. l (p. 418)
5. b (p. 428)	15. T (p. 421/424)	25. presidents of the ACA (p. 417)	35. q (p. 428)
6. c (p. 432)	16. F (p. 434)	26. crack cocaine (p. 418)	36. x (p. 414)
7. e (p. 434)	17. F (p. 425)	27. warden (p. 416)	37. a (p. 409)
8. c (p. 432)	18. T (p. 427)	28. Girl Scouts (p. 431)	38. p (p. 426)
9. b (p. 414)	19. F (p. 425)	29. homosexual (p. 432)	39. e (p. 412)
10. d (p. 410)	20. F (p. 416)	30. the community (p. 434)	40. d (p. 411)

Chapter Fifteen

Multiple Choice	True or False	Fill In the Blanks	Matching
1. e (p. 442)	11. T (p. 443)	21. robbery (p. 445)	31. l (p. 450)
2. a (p. 447)	12. T (p. 447)	22. 93 (p. 445)	32. v (p. 458)
3. c (p. 450)	13. F (p. 445)	23. pruno (p. 451)	33. k (p. 449)
4. d (p. 446)	14. T (p. 451)	24. guards (p. 451)	34. m (p. 450)
5. b (p. 442)	15. F (p. 453)	25. two (p. 454)	35. s (p. 455)
6. c (p. 456)	16. F (p. 448)	26. furloughs (p. 454)	36. h (p. 448)
7. a (p. 451)	17. F (p. 455)	27. designer drugs (p. 447)	37. j (p. 449)
8. d (p. 452)	18. F (p. 448)	28. drugs (p. 459)	38. d (p. 442)
9. c (p. 452)	19. F (p. 449)	29. political response (p. 459)	39. e (p. 442)
10. e (p. 450)	20. F (p. 455)	30. deprivation (p. 449)	40. a (p. 442)

Chapter Sixteen

Multiple Choice	True or False	Fill In the Blanks	Matching
1. c (p. 485)	11. F (p. 467)	21. chancery court (p. 468)	31. c (p. 468)
2. e (p. 468)	12. T (p. 471)	22. *Kent v. U.S.* (p. 489)	32. w (p. 484)
3. b (p. 489)	13. F (p. 482)	23. decriminalization (p. 491)	33. gg (p. 488)
4. c (p. 486)	14. F (p. 484)	24. status offenses (p. 491)	34. z (p. 496)
5. d (p. 479)	15. F (p. 489)	25. 17 (p. 480)	35. ii (p. 490)
6. c (p. 471)	16. F (p. 494)	26. a jury/a public trial (p. 485)	36. y (p. 482)
7. a (p. 492)	17. T (p. 478)	27. robbery (p. 472)	37. jj (p. 494)
8. d (p. 484)	18. T (p. 476)	28. 16 (p. 490)	38. f (p. 470)
9. a (p. 472)	19. F (p. 490)	29. counseling (p. 466)	39. p (p. 486)
10. c (p. 468)	20. F (p. 479)	30. JJDPA (p. 489)	40. g (p. 464)

Chapter Seventeen

Multiple Choice	True or False	Fill In the Blanks	Matching
1. c (p. 501)	11. F (p. 502)	21. invisible empire (p. 502)	31. b (p. 501)
2. c (p. 502)	12. F (p. 517)	22. mental hospital (p. 504)	32. o (p. 512)
3. b (p. 507)	13. F (p. 521)	23. four (p. 504)	33. z (p. 522)
4. b (p. 508)	14. F (p. 504)	24. injured (p. 509)	34. d (p. 502)
5. a (p. 513)	15. T (p. 507)	25. sex (p. 515)	35. g (p. 504)
6. e (p. 514)	16. T (p. 512)	26. assisted-living (p. 523)	36. l (p. 507)
7. c (p. 502)	17. F (p. 517)	27. hepatitis/tuberculosis (p. 519)	37. q (p. 510)
8. d (p. 505)	18. F (p. 521)	28. mentally disordered (p. 501)	38. x (p. 520)
9. a (p. 516)	19. F (p. 509)	29. child molester (p. 510)	39. i (p. 505)
10. e (p. 502)	20. F (p. 506)	30. AIDS (p. 520)	40. e (p. 502)

Chapter Eighteen

Multiple Choice	True or False	Fill In the Blanks	Matching
1. a (p. 549)	16. T (p. 539)	31. frequent filer (p. 541)	46. n (p. 545)
2. c (p. 543)	17. F (p. 539)	32. adequate (p. 548)	47. z (p. 549)
3. d (p. 539)	18. F (p. 539)	33. mediator (p. 548)	48. j (p. 543)
4. e (p. 541)	19. F (p. 544)	34. conjugal visiting (p. 541)	49. o (p. 545)
5. c (p. 543)	20. F (p. 545)	35. religious (p. 544)	50. e (p. 540)
6. d (p. 544)	21. F (p. 545)	36. contraband (p. 543)	51. c (p. 539)
7. d (p. 546)	22. T (p. 539)	37. six (p. 538)	52. k (p. 543)
8. b (p. 548)	23. T (p. 542)	38. possessing firearms (p. 553)	53. w (p. 549)
9. b (p. 551)	24. T (p. 564)	39. Constitution (p. 564)	54. ll (p. 560)
10. c (p. 552)	25. T (p. 551)	40. sex (p. 562)	55. oo (p. 563)
11. b (p. 559)	26. F (p. 563)	41. civil death (p. 539)	56. t (p. 563)
12. b (p. 555)	27. F (p. 561)	42. a job (p. 559)	57. gg (p. 552)
13. b (p. 561)	28. F (p. 565)	43. judge (p. 563)	58. v (p. 565)
14. d (p. 564)	29. F (p. 552)	44. ex-con (p. 550)	59. cc (p. 550)
15. a (p. 552)	30. T (p. 560)	45. civil rights (p. 549)	60. nn (p. 560)

Chapter Nineteen

Multiple Choice	True or False	Fill In the Blanks	Matching
1. e (p. 581)	11. T (p. 584)	21. public execution (p. 575)	31. e (p. 581)
2. c (p. 587)	12. F (p. 587)	22. the electric chair (p. 576)	32. l (p. 587)
3. d (p. 594)	13. F (p. 573)	23. 38 (p. 573)	33. n (p. 588)
4. d (p. 585)	14. T (p. 575)	24. Francis (p. 586)	34. q (p. 596)
5. c (p. 581)	15. T (p. 575)	25. Georgia (p. 587)	35. w (p. 601)
6. a (p. 581)	16. F (p. 573)	26. the Lindbergh baby kidnapping (p. 577)	36. r (p. 589)
7. c (p. 574)	17. F (p. 576)	27. the South (p. 581)	37. d (p. 592)
8. a (p. 590)	18. F (p. 591)	28. proportionality (similarity) (p. 588)	38. j (p. 585)
9. b (p. 588)	19. T (p. 589)	29. whites (p. 584)	39. f (p. 582)
10. e (p. 578)	20. F (p. 593)	30. one (or 1.3) (p. 598)	40. t (p. 590)

Chapter Twenty

Multiple Choice	True or False	Fill In the Blanks	Matching
1. a (p. 622)	11. F (p. 614)	21. surveillance/helping (p. 631)	31. c (p. 612)
2. b (p. 618)	12. F (p. 614)	22. governor (p. 630)	32. jj (p. 618)
3. b (p. 621)	13. F (p. 619)	23. 50 (p. 626)	33. l (p. 616)
4. c (p. 618)	14. T (p. 621)	24. specific deterrence (p. 624)	34. x (p. 620)
5. c (p. 614)	15. F (p. 612)	25. six (p. 625)	35. w (p. 620)
6. e (p. 620)	16. F (p. 626)	26. 70 (p. 629)	36. hh (p. 628)
7. c (p. 620)	17. T (p. 614)	27. pardon (p. 614)	37. e (p. 614)
8. d (p. 624)	18. T (p. 614)	28. parole board (p. 629)	38. ee (p. 624)
9. b (p. 616)	19. F (p. 617)	29. good time (p. 617)	39. q (p. 620)
10. c (p. 624)	20. T (p. 630)	30. technical (p. 622)	40. v (p. 621)

Chapter Twenty-One

Multiple Choice	True or False	Fill In the Blanks	Matching
1. d (p. 637)	11. F (p. 655)	21. prerelease guidance centers (p. 644)	31. e (p. 639)
2. b (p. 638)	12. T (p. 644)	22. community forces (p. 635)	32. m (p. 646)
3. e (p. 640)	13. F (p. 636)	23. total institution (p. 636)	33. bb (p. 654)
4. b (p. 645)	14. F (p. 644)	24. furlough (p. 645)	34. aa (p. 654)
5. c (p. 638)	15. T (p. 644)	25. community-based (p. 645)	35. y (p. 653)
6. b (p. 651)	16. T (p. 646)	26. re-arrest (p. 652)	36. g (p. 640)
7. a (p. 651)	17. F (p. 637)	27. Colorado/Florida (p. 647)	37. s (p. 648)
8. e (p. 653)	18. F (p. 654)	28. contract (p. 644)	38. x (p. 651)
9. a (p. 654)	19. F (p. 640)	29. incapacitation (p. 654)	39. v (p. 650)
10. c (p. 655)	20. T (p. 644)	30. Federal Prisoner Rehabilitation Act (p. 638)	40. q (p. 647)

Chapter Twenty- Two

Multiple Choice	True or False	Fill In the Blanks	Matching
1. b (p. 664)	7. T (p. 667)	13. 30 (p. 665)	19. m (p. 671)
2. d (p. 664)	8. F (p. 664)	14. chain gangs (p. 663)	20. n (p. 672)
3. c (p. 664)	9. T (p. 665)	15. tourniquet sentencing (p. 667)	21. o (p. 663)
4. e (p. 670)	10. F (p. 667)	16. community p. 670)	22. c (p. 665)
5. c (p. 664)	11. F (p. 668)	17. glass-topped cells (p. 669)	23. f (p. 666)
6. a (p. 670)	12. T (p. 664)	18. subsidy (p. 671)	24. i (p. 668)